CROSS-CULTURAL VISIONS IN AFRICAN AMERICAN MODERNISM

From Spatial Narrative to Jazz Haiku

YOSHINOBU HAKUTANI

The Ohio State University Press
Columbus

Library of Congress Cataloging-in-Publication Data

Hakutani, Yoshinobu, 1935–
Cross-cultural visions in African American modernism : from spatial narrative to jazz haiku / Yoshinobu Hakutani.
    p. cm.
Includes bibliographical references and index.
ISBN-13: 978-0-8142-1030-7 (alk. paper)
ISBN-13: 978-0-8142-9107-8 (cd-rom)
    1. American literature—African American authors—History and criticism. 2. American literature—Foreign influences. 3. Influence (Literary, artistic, etc.)—History—20th century. 4. African Americans—Intellectual life—20th century. 5. Modernism (Literature)—United States. I. Title.
    PS153.N5H223 2006
    810.9'896073—dc22
                    2006014116

Cover design by Dan O'Dair.
Type set in Adobe Garamond.
Printed by Thomson-Shore, Inc.

The paper used in this publication meets the minimum requirements of the American National Standard for Information Sciences—Permanence of Paper for Printed Library Materials. ANSI Z39.48–1992.
9 8 7 6 5 4 3 2 1

*For Michiko Hakutani
and my late parents*

Contents

Preface   vii

Acknowledgments   ix

Introduction   1

PART I: AMERICAN DIALOGUES

Chapter 1   The Chicago Renaissance, Theodore Dreiser, and Richard
             Wright's Spatial Narrative   19

Chapter 2   The Cross-Cultural Vision of Ralph Ellison's
             Invisible Man   44

Chapter 3   *No Name in the Street:* James Baldwin's Exploration of
             American Urban Culture   60

Chapter 4   *If Beale Street Could Talk:* Baldwin's Search for Love
             and Identity   72

Chapter 5   *Jazz* and Toni Morrison's Urban Imagination of Desire
             and Subjectivity   82

PART II: EUROPEAN AND AFRICAN CULTURAL VISIONS

Chapter 6   Wright's *The Outsider* and French Existentialism   101

Chapter 7   *Pagan Spain:* Wright's Discourse on Religion and Culture   120

Chapter 8   The African "Primal Outlook upon Life":
             Wright and Morrison   139

PART III: EASTERN AND AFRICAN AMERICAN CROSS-CULTURAL VISIONS

Chapter 9   The Poetics of Nature: Wright's Haiku, Zen, and Lacan   153

Chapter 10 Private Voice and Buddhist Enlightenment in
            Alice Walker's *The Color Purple*   170
Chapter 11 Cross-Cultural Poetics: Sonia Sanchez's
            Like the Singing Coming Off the Drums   180
Chapter 12 James Emanuel's Jazz Haiku and
            African American Individualism   195

            Notes   219
            Works Cited   235
            Index   243

Preface

This book was initially conceived when I was exploring the relationships between Japanese poetics and the modernism of W. B. Yeats and Ezra Pound. While Yeats's symbolism was influenced by his cross-cultural visions of *noh* theatre and Irish folklore, Pound's imagism had its origin in classic haiku. It was Margaret Walker, who intimately knew Richard Wright, who first stated that Wright was interested in Pound among other modernist poets. As Ralph Ellison emulated Yeats along with other Western modernists, Wright in his later career became acquainted with haiku and Zen philosophy in his associations with the Beat poets living in Paris in the mid 1950s. I found not only that Lacan's concept of human subjectivity is extremely helpful to understanding the aesthetic principles involved in haiku composition, but also that Lacanian psychoanalysis has a strong affinity to Zen philosophy.

The present study also developed from my attempts to show, in Part I, "American Dialogues," that Richard Wright and James Baldwin were inspired by Theodore Dreiser and Henry James, respectively, the two most influential modern American novelists, who were poles apart in their worldviews and techniques. From time to time Wright stated that Dreiser was the greatest writer American culture had produced, just as Dostoevsky was for Russian culture. Wright modeled *Black Boy* after *Jennie Gerhardt,* which he considered Dreiser's best novel. Small wonder that Baldwin first regarded Wright as his mentor but soon took issue with him in describing African American experience, just as James and Dreiser were diametrically opposed in their social and cultural visions. In gauging the narrative techniques of modern African American writers, I have found Bakhtin's dialogic imagination, as well as his concept of the subject, most useful.

Part II, "European and African Cultural Visions," examines what Wright called "universal humanism," what is common among all cultures. This ideology, as expressed by Wright, Ellison, and Baldwin alike, transcends race, class, and culture. Chapter 6 on Wright's *The Outsider* is intended to show how differently universal humanism is expressed by a European existentialist like Camus and by Wright, an African American counterpart. Part II also explores what Wright calls "the African's primal outlook upon life," the most distinct African cultural vision that appears in Wright's later work, as well as in Toni Morrison's novels. I suggest that Wright's exile in France and his travels to West Africa and Spain transformed his understanding of African American experience. And subsequent African American writers, often regarded as postmodernists and postcolonialists, produced their works under the strong influence of the cross-cultural visions Wright had acquired in Europe and Africa. Although modernism and postmodernism in African American literature from time to time bear marked differences in their perspectives and characteristics, the two movements, sharing the same cross-cultural visions, are contiguous and evolving.

Part III, "Eastern and African American Cross-Cultural Visions," investigates the impacts of Eastern philosophy and religion on modern and postmodern African American literature. Whereas Wright's earlier work is characterized by Marxism, his later work reflects Eastern cultural visions. Like Yeats and Pound, Wright was fascinated with Japanese poetics, as seen in his massive haiku. Along with Wright's haiku, I have discussed the haiku written by Sonia Sanchez and James Emanuel. Part III also discusses the influences of Buddhism and Zen philosophy, in particular, not only on African American haiku poets but also on Alice Walker.

I hasten to add that what I have tried to demonstrate in this book represents some preliminary markers for more detailed future studies. My attempts here are heuristic and my observations are not conclusive. There are also several omissions in reading contemporary African American writers whose works thrive on their cross-cultural visions, such as Amiri Baraka, Ishmael Reed, Charles Johnson, and haiku poet Lenard D. Moore.

Acknowledgments

I am indebted to many writers and sources, as acknowledged in the notes and works cited. I would like to thank, in particular, the late John Reilly, the late Philip Gerber, Robert Tener, Wilfred Samuels, Heather Lee Miller, and the anonymous readers for The Ohio State University Press, who have read part or whole of the manuscript and offered useful, constructive suggestions.

Over the years the Kent State University Research Council has provided several research leaves and travel grants, and I am grateful for their support.

I have used in modified form my previously published articles: "No Name in the Street: James Baldwin's Image of the American Sixties" in *Critical Essays on James Baldwin* (1988); "Richard Wright's *The Outsider* and Albert Camus's *The Stranger*," *Mississippi Quarterly* (1989); "Erza Pound, Yone Noguchi, and Imagism," *Modern Philology* (1990); "If the Street Could Talk: James Baldwin's Search for Love and Understanding" in *The City in African-American Literature* (1995); "Richard Wright, Toni Morrison, and the African 'Primal Outlook upon Life,'" *Southern Quarterly* (2001); "Private Voice and Buddhist Enlightenment in Alice Walker's *The Color Purple*" in *Postmodernity and Cross-Culturalism* (2002).

Introduction

The publication of Richard Wright's *Native Son* in 1940 marks an epoch in the development of African American literature in modern times. In discussing the historical importance of the book, Irving Howe wrote in 1963, "The day *Native Son* appeared, American culture was changed for ever." In the abolitionist era, African American writers often addressed themselves to audiences they expected would be largely European American. Before Wright, however, they primarily addressed African American audiences. If they had written for European American audiences, they would have been expected to present stereotyped pictures of African Americans. Exceptions like W. E. B. Du Bois and Charles W. Chesnutt were largely unheeded, for African Americans, as Wright observed, "possessed deep-seated resistance against the Negro problem being presented even verbally, in all its hideous dullness, in all the totality of its meaning." It was somewhat miraculous that both African and European Americans believed what they read in *Native Son,* in which Wright destroys the white myth of the patient, humorous, subservient black man.

One assumes Wright to be in the tradition of American naturalism. In *Black Boy* (1945), Wright states that he was inspired by Theodore Dreiser's *Jennie Gerhardt* (1911) and *Sister Carrie* (1900): "It would have been impossible for me to have told anyone what I derived from these novels, for it was nothing less than a sense of life itself. All my life had shaped me for the realism, the naturalism of the modern novel, and I could not read enough of them." Such testimony, however, merely tells Wright's youthful taste in books; it hardly proves that he became a doctrinaire naturalist. To what extent he is part of American naturalism has become an issue about Wright's work. In *Native Son* does Wright subscribe to the novel's implicit assumption that American racial conditions are directly responsible for the oppression of African Americans? Recent criticism has modified or refuted the naturalistic reading, suggesting that Wright and his fellow American writers went beyond naturalism.

The pessimistic determinism often associated with naturalism had shown African American writers, such as Wright, Ralph Ellison, and James Baldwin, the meaning of racial oppression. Victims of oppression themselves, these writers by necessity directed their energy toward rebellion. While they escaped the pessimistic outlook of naturalism, their respect for the philosophy of naturalism helped them develop their own versions of human subjectivity and endow their characters with self-determination. Self-pity and rage alone would not have impressed modern readers. As these writers moved beyond anger and protest, they developed a new concern for character and literary discipline, seeking a deeper involvement in the world of philosophy and discourse. Naturalism showed them how to determine the position of human beings in the world; existentialism showed them how to liberate their fellow human beings from the strictures imposed on them.

Naturalism meant that human behavior is solely under the control of heredity and social environment. Just as American realist writers like Mark Twain and Theodore Dreiser had taken issue with naturalistic determinism, African American writers were diametrically opposed to the concept of human subjectivity as demonstrated by a novelist like Emile Zola. In deterministic naturalism, the major character in a novel or an autobiography, falling victim to his or her heredity and social environment, those forces external to the person, fails to achieve his or her subjectivity. With *Native Son* and *Black Boy,* Wright proved to the literary public that not only do Bigger Thomas and the young Richard Wright overcome the forces, but they also succeed in achieving subjectivity.

As *Native Son, Black Boy,* and their predecessor *Uncle Tom's Children* (1938–39) were making a revolutionary impact on African American literary criticism, Wright was also producing their two subtexts, "Blueprint for Negro Writing" (1937) and *12 Million Black Voices: A Folk History of the Negro in the United States* (1941). These works, involving not only Wright, Ellison, and Baldwin but also liberal critics such as Irving Howe, turned out to be a beginning of the African American literary debate that was to shape the subsequent African American literature. Given a patriotic climate of the war years, *12 Million Black Voices* betrays the tensions between Wright's Marxism and his concept of American democracy. Wright tries to reconcile the modern, industrial working-class culture of African Americans and its subsequent class antagonism with the Popular Front emphasis on the progressive American democracy. "We black folk, our history and our present being," Wright declares, "are a mirror of all the manifold experiences of America. What we want, what we represent, what we endure is what America *is.*"

In "Blueprint," on the other hand, such tensions are absent. Rather than

viewing African American writing in the light of Marxism and class consciousness, Wright tries to define African American modernism in terms of
its own themes and points of view. As he theorizes in this manifesto, his own
earliest work serves as a model for the African American writer who "is being
called upon to do no less than create values by which his race is to struggle,
live and die." Such writing, Wright argues, is endowed with a consciousness
that draws on the fluid, historically influential "lore of a great people."
"Reduced to its simplest and most general terms," he asserts, "theme for
Negro writers will rise from understanding the meaning of their being trans-
planted from the 'savage' to a 'civilized' culture in all of its social, political,
economic, and emotional implications." By "savage culture," Wright means
the proud origin of black peoples in Africa, as well as the history of slavery in
the South.

Even the incipient stage in the development of African American modernism was buttressed by this cross-cultural vision. In "Blueprint," one of the
theoretical principles calls for the African American writer to explore universal humanism, what is common among all cultures. "Every iota of grain in
human thought and sensibility," Wright argues, "should be ready grist for his
mill, no matter how far-fetched they may seem in their immediate implications." Universal humanism, Wright observes, transcends race, class, and culture. The presentation of such cultural and cross-cultural visions "should be
simple, yes; but the complexity, the strangeness, the magic, the wonder of life
that plays like a bright sheen over the most sordid existence should be there.
To borrow a phrase from the Russians, it should have a *complex simplicity.*"

Like Wright, Ellison was deeply involved with the issues of race, but, as his
masterpiece *Invisible Man* (1952) exhibits, Ellison succeeded, with his skill
and imagination, in making what is racial and regional into what is humanistic and universal. At the outset of his career, following Wright's lead in
Marxism, as stated in "Blueprint," Ellison also argued that the rhetorical and
political devices of proletarian fiction were the means by which to advance a
radical black literature. His first publication, a review of Waters Edward
Turpin's *These Low Grounds,* appeared with "Blueprint" in *New Challenge* in
1937, closely reflecting Wright's views: the African American racial or nation-
alist expression by a Marxist writer entails an inherent class consciousness.

A series of book reviews Ellison published in *New Masses* in 1940 still
reflected a Marxist perspective as defined in "Blueprint." In "Stormy
Weather," a review of Langston Hughes's autobiography *The Big Sea* (1940),
Ellison tried to make Hughes the chief spokesperson of the literary move-
ment that distanced itself from the accommodationist aesthetics of the
Harlem Renaissance and leaned toward a revolutionary black literature.

Ellison assailed the New Negro writers as proponents of a black middle class which had become self-conscious through the economic alliances it had made in supporting World War I. The work of the New Negro writers was politically influenced by the black middle-class interests and failed to express the painful experiences of the black masses. Ellison realized that "white faddists" were perpetuating the image of the black American as "primitive and exotic," a deceptively racist perception that signifies the spiritual and moral decay of the postwar period. It looked as though the same white men were paying these African American writers to contain the working-class militancy prompted by the riots and lynchings during World War I by championing the passive black middle class.

Wright and Ellison were trying to lure Hughes, the leader in the Harlem Renaissance of the 1920s, to their camp under the banner of Marxist and proletarian writing. During the 1930s, as his well-known poems such as "The Negro Speaks of Rivers" (1921), "The Weary Blues" (1926), and "I, Too" (1932) powerfully expressed the deep-seated feelings of the African American masses, Hughes's voice resounded with those of Wright and Ellison. Of the three, Wright was the only one who was formally and actively involved in the activities of the Communist Party, attending the John Reed Club meetings. However, not only were all three comrades in action; they were also united in the cause of African American modernism.

By the time his *12 Million Black Voices* appeared in 1941, Wright was still interested in Marxist theory but became disenchanted with its practice by the American Communist Party. Similarly, Ellison's enthusiasm for Marxism began to decline. Instead of relying on Wright's Marxist views and democratic principles, expressed in *12 Million Black Voices,* Ellison's theory of the black folk focused on a transformation of African Americans from their Southern roots to the Northern industrial environment. As his reviews in the early 1940s indicate, Ellison ultimately disputed with Wright, who predicted in *12 Million Black Voices* that the folk in the city would decline and that a working-class and "modern" consciousness would rise. Ellison's writings also intimate his opposition to Gunnar Myrdal's sociological study, *An American Dilemma: The Negro Problem and American Democracy* (1944). Ellison questioned Myrdal's premise that "blackness" in American culture is the result of white oppression. Myrdal tried to demonstrate that this "blackness" is "a distorted development" and "a pathological condition" of American culture. Myrdal posits that while European Americans resolve the problems of race, African Americans will be assimilated into American culture.

Wright, on the other hand, revisiting his Chicago school of sociology, was drawn to Myrdal's study. By 1945, attempting to reinvent himself from a post-Marxist point of view, Wright agreed with Myrdal in rejecting a Marxist analysis of racial problems in America. As his introduction to St. Clair Drake's and Horace Cayton's *Black Metropolis* (1945) indicates, Wright supported Myrdal's observations of African American culture: a large African American population is defeated by its "crude and brutal" experience in the industrial North. By contrast, Ellison saw African Americans' ability and will to create cultural forms: folklore, art, music, and literature. For Ellison, African American cultural forms also subsume the critique of Myrdal's "higher" American culture and the rejection of "white patterns." Calling for deeper cultural forms than those sociologists and Marxists had found, Ellison found them in the emerging culture of the black working folk in the industrial North. He argued that the cultural forms of the black dance halls in the Northern cities—the blues, jazz, dance, and dress—were proof of modern African American culture: the traditional folk culture existing in the present, as Invisible Man declares that "a whole unrecorded history is spoken."

Despite their differences in perspective as evident in the early 1940s, by the mid 1940s Wright and Ellison had come to share the fundamental tenets of African American culture. The fruits of their labor were shown in their respective writings in the war years and the late 1940s, but modern African American literature reached its apogee with the appearance of Wright's *Black Boy* (1945). It is this book, subtitled *A Record of Childhood and Youth,* that not only Ellison and his fellow African American writers but a host of modern European American writers like Dreiser praised and regarded as a model of writing. Ellison disagreed with Wright in theory but agreed with him in practice.

Today *Black Boy* is acclaimed not only as the finest autobiography written by an African American but as one of the finest autobiographies written in America. In fact, many American autobiographies are ethnic and cross-cultural. As *Black Boy* discusses the experience of an African American youth who grew up in the South, Dreiser's *Dawn* (1931) treats the life struggle that the son of a German immigrant faced in the North. Benjamin Franklin's *Autobiography* (1771–90) is not ethnic in the usual sense of the word, but as an important cross-cultural document for the young nation, it directly concerns American and European cultures. Franklin's life exemplifies the American dream of a poor boy who made good in Pennsylvania, an English colony. What these autobiographies have in common is not only an eloquent portrayal of early life but a poignant expression of cross-cultural visions.

From another perspective, Wright's portrayals of Bigger Thomas in *Native Son* and the young self in *Black Boy* thrive on what Mikhail Bakhtin called "a dialogic imagination." As Wright explains in his introduction to *Native Son,*

"How 'Bigger' Was Born," the hero of the novel does not merely express his subjectivity; he is representative of all others like him. In *Black Boy,* Wright uses the young self as a mask: the attitudes and sentiments expressed by the young Wright are not totally his own but represent the responses of those he calls "the voiceless Negro boys" of the South. The liberal critics were all in agreement that the book's chief value lies in leading the nation on the road to emancipation. Of all the reviews, Lionel Trilling's "A Tragic Situation" was most thorough. Granted, *Black Boy* was a most accurate account of misery and oppression published to that date, but Trilling observed that the book does not let its readers make "the moral 'escape' that can be offered by accounts of suffering and justice." What underlies the power and effect of Wright's book is not his personal experience, but his moral and intellectual power, as derived from others by dialogic imagination. Trilling suggested that Wright "does not make himself that different kind of human being, a 'sufferer.' His is not an object, he is a subject; he is the same kind of person as his reader, as complex, as free." What Trilling meant by "a subject" is an individual free of the ego of the subject, an individual representative of all others. Paradoxically, Wright converts the concept of subjectivity to that of objectivity: what Bigger Thomas or the young Wright expresses as the subject is what anyone like him does. Bakhtin theorized and demonstrated, as did Lacan, that the subject is not unique, nor is it different from the other.

In the development of modern African American fiction, the early 1950s marks an important turning point. Ellison's *Invisible Man* thrives on a set of symbols with conscious allusions to American history and ideology. Ellison's vision, like Wright's, is not that of Invisible Man, the subject, but is representative of others. Like *Black Boy, Invisible Man* is deeply concerned with the development of an African American youth into maturity. Evoking the name of Ralph Waldo Emerson suggests Ellison's serious concern with W. E. B. Du Bois's sense of double-consciousness, what Ellison calls himself in an essay "a Negro and an American, a member of the family and yet an outsider." In search of identity in American society, however, Ellison's vision focuses not only on broader culture and history, but on deeper self-realization. Wright's less successful *The Outsider* (1953), on the other hand, is considered an existential novel, which was in vogue in Europe in the aftermath of World War II. In contrast to French existentialists like Sartre and Camus, Wright is as profoundly concerned in this novel with the dilemma of double consciousness as is Ellison in *Invisible Man.* But, portraying the highly educated, mature intellectuals, Cross Damon and Invisible Man, both novels express the goal of modern African American novelists whose efforts have been to make their characters representative of others and universalize their cultural visions.

A third major African American novel, appearing in the early 1950s, James Baldwin's *Go Tell It on the Mountain* (1953), portrays Baldwin's early life replete with personal, familial, racial, and social turmoil, a raw experience that is mute in *Invisible Man* and *The Outsider*. Although Baldwin held in the highest regard Wright's *Black Boy* and Ellison's *Invisible Man* among African American books, he emulated Dostoevsky for his dialectic technique and Henry James for his impressionism. Baldwin met Wright, who, reading part of the manuscript of *Go Tell It on the Mountain,* encouraged him. This novel, much like *Black Boy,* is an autobiographical portrait of John Grimes, an African American youth in search of identity in racist society. Distinct from *Black Boy,* however, *Go Tell It on the Mountain* creates, in particular, the protagonist's sexual identity and guilt, as well as his ambivalent relationships with his parents.

Baldwin's most influential social and literary criticisms are collected in *Notes of a Native Son* (1955). Focusing on the problems of race in American society, he discusses literature of anti-slavery from Stowe to Wright, as well as his own experiences in America and Europe. Earlier Baldwin regarded Wright as his mentor but soon rebelled against him. Calling Bigger Thomas a descendant of Uncle Tom, Baldwin argued that *Native Son* "suggested a revolution of racial conflict that was merely the liberal dream of good will in which blacks would obliterate their personalities and become as whites." Baldwin disagreed with Wright's use of violence, which he called "gratuitous and compulsive because the root of the violence is never explained." Baldwin applauded Wright's courageous representation of the African American "rage," but to him the novelist must analyze raw emotion and transform it into an identifiable human experience. Baldwin's second novel, *Giovanni's Room* (1956), like *Go Tell It on the Mountain,* is his major achievement. Although *Giovanni's Room* was not written in the tradition of literary naturalism, it represents the author's attempt to write a Zolaesque experimental novel. Baldwin focuses on real characters taken from life: David, a bisexual white American; his fiancée Hella, a white American; and Giovanni, David's male homosexual lover. The story closely represents Hella's painful discovery of a mystery of human sexuality. *Another Country* (1962), a controversial novel, is nonetheless his most ambitious work. Whereas his experiment in *Giovanni's Room* involves only white characters and society, *Another Country* conducts an experiment on a variety of interracial and sexual relationships. *Another Country* comprises the four narratives interrelated at certain points in the novel. Most of the events are perhaps too carefully arranged, but Rufus's tragic suicide and Vivaldo and Ida's reconciliation are depicted with great compassion and understanding. Like Wright's and Ellison's novels, Baldwin's also thrive on a dialogic imagination that derives from the clashing interactions between the subject and others.

Two of Baldwin's later novels, *Tell Me How Long the Train's Been Gone* (1968) and *If Beale Street Could Talk* (1974), both explore the life of an African American artist. *Tell Me* is autobiographical, like Wright's *Black Boy,* and is lacking in precipitous events and actions, but through flashbacks it subtly conveys harrowing experiences of a middle-aged actor. *Beale Street,* unlike Baldwin's other novels, explores heterosexuality. This novel celebrates the love relationship of an African American couple consciously aware of the primacy of love over any racial or social obstacles and able to revive their genuine relationship and attain their deliverance. The ultimate domain of love, as Baldwin has shown throughout his work, is governed by the individuality of two human beings' deepest emotions that transcends their sexual orientation. Baldwin showed with all his heart and soul, as his American predecessors had scarcely done, that homosexuality is just as normal as is heterosexuality: here lies his greatest contribution to modern American fiction.

In subject matter and form, African American modernism, represented by Hughes, Wright, Ellison, and Baldwin, has an affinity with Anglo-American modernism. In fact, both groups of writers sought traditions, myths, and legends. In *The Waste Land* (1922), T. S. Eliot adapts the symbolic framework of the medieval Grail legend and other older fertility rites in contrast to the sordidness and sterility of modern life in the West. In creating Yoknapatawpha County, William Faulkner ponders the rise and fall of the genteel culture of the old Civil War South. For their subjects, Hughes and Wright respectively enlightened their heritages in an ancient river like the Congo and an ancient kingdom like the Ashanti and their religiosity and cosmology. For their techniques and styles, Hughes and Ellison both emulated the spirit, lyricism, and individualism that characterize the evolution of African American music from spirituals and gospel through the blues to jazz. Modern jazz today is a cross-cultural hybrid of African American and Western music.

One of the striking differences between Anglo-American and African American modernists has much to do with their attitudes toward their crafts. Hughes, for instance, advocated an aesthetic of simplicity and, like Whitman, voices of democracy. All in all, African American modernists shunned an elitist attitude which Western modernists at times betrayed. George Orwell deplored Western modernists' indifference to content and their preoccupation with form. "Our eyes," he wrote, "are directed to Rome, to Byzantium, to Montparnasse, to Mexico, to the Etruscans, to the subconscious, to the solar plexus—to everywhere except the places where things are actually happening." This formalism in the 1920s was regarded by many as the logical aesthetic for modernist writing. Western modernists believed that their art offers a privileged insight into reality and at the same time, because art creates its own reality, it is not at all concerned with commonplace reality: art is an autonomous activity.

While Anglo-American modernists like Pound, Eliot, Hemingway, and Faulkner conveyed their personal, subjective visions with privileged sensibility, African American counterparts like Hughes, Wright, Ellison, and Baldwin, as well as later African American writers such as Alice Walker and Toni Morrison, were intent on conveying their universal visions, their worldviews informed of other cultures. Despite the sentiments of fragmentation and alienation that both groups of American writers generated, they tried to redeem themselves through the creation of art. Man acts, as Heidegger observed, "as though he were the shaper and master of language, while in fact, language remains the master of man. Perhaps it is above all else man's subversion of this relation of dominance that drives his nature into alienation." To overcome alienation, postmodernists have attempted to integrate themselves with the worlds of others, the phenomena taking place in other fields of knowledge and in other cultures and traditions. If modernism is characterized by shifting the burden of knowledge from the rational to the aesthetic, postmodernism is viewed as refining the rational in terms of the phenomenal. While modernism, especially Western modernism, smacks of elitism, postmodernism, as shown by the later Wright, Walker, and Morrison, is widely concerned not only with the mundane but also with other kinds of knowledge and other cultures. The postmodern characteristics attributable to late Wright, Walker, and Morrison, however, are radically different from those of the postmodern texts by such writers as Amiri Baraka and Ishmael Reed.

As most postmodernists try to situate themselves in the contemporary world, some modernists gauge their world in relation to past culture. To Eliot, present culture is an embodied experience of the present arising from the contiguous transformation of the past. Most modernists are opposed to absolute polarities in human experience. Victorians and some early modernists like Henry James and W. B. Yeats, by contrast, had a penchant for the dichotomy of masculine and feminine, object and subject, the higher and the lower, the earlier and the later, present and past, time and place. On the contrary, late modernists like James Joyce, and postmodernists in particular, explore the notion of integrating the opposites. They view the opposites as convenient ways of discussing present phenomena, which, upon closer observation, reveal themselves to be related to one another or to be functions of one another.

Postmodernists, moreover, tend to parody past art, refrain from all absolutes, and deconstruct established images and ideas. Unlike Pound, who in "Hugh Selwyn Mauberley" laments over a culture filled with "mendacities" and "the classics in paraphrase," a postmodernist is inclined to deal with copies more seriously than with originals. As a deconstructor, a postmodernist is fascinated not by the signified but by their "free signifiers." Postmodern writers, as in contemporary visual arts, refuse to acknowledge any limits to the world of imaginary representation, whether it is a psychologically autonomous entity or a physically constructed realm fully integrated with the world of historical experience. The predominant modes of postmodernism are not as controlled and disciplined as those of modernism: the postmodern modes of expression tend to be ironic, parodic, digressive, and complex.

The hermeneutic reading of the text, however, eventually manifests the fundamental difference between the two modes of writing. As most critics have noted, postmodernism is characterized by the decentered text. The postmodern text deals with oppositions, what Jacques Derrida calls *différance*. In each signifying text, internal conflicts develop independently of the author, the supposedly central informant. Consequently the text deconstructs itself because of the oppositional and conflictual nature of language. Because the *différance* is at work in the text, the author, let alone the reader, can scarcely claim absolute authority over a given text; hence there arises a structural impossibility of imposing a central idea, a summary, or a conclusion to the text. It is for this reason that many postmodern texts incorporate segments of mass culture and late capitalism and draw on parodic forms in order to minimize autonomy, self-referentiality, and centralized vision. Postmodern texts, then, are said to denote a fundamental loss of rational and ontological certainty.

The lack of center and the recognition of gaps and oppositions that characterize the postmodern text suggest that postmodernists are bent on abolishing marginality and extending referentiality in their text. As postmodern texts, such as Wright's *The Color Curtain* (1956) and Salman Rushdie's *The Satanic Verses* (1989), reveal, their visions and dialogues have come to include relations not only between East and West, Old and New, but between the First, Second, and Third Worlds within as well as across national cultures. The conflict between Rushdie's postmodern satirism and the ancient Muslim dogma, as fictionalized in *The Satanic Verses,* and the clash between left and right, race and religion, as depicted in *The Color Curtain,* are dramatic examples of postmodern cross-culturalism, just as are the recent international challenges to South African apartheid and ethnic cleansing in the Balkans. This cross-culturalism, however, finds its origin in a much earlier period. One of the idiosyncrasies of Victorian thought was Western chauvinism. As late as the middle of the twentieth century, as Wright argued in *Black Power: A Record of Reactions in a Land of Pathos* (1954), the West was perceived as an advanced culture while Africans were regarded as primitive. Victorian intellectuals respected Chinese and Indian societies, which represented ancient cultures, but they considered these societies decadent and backward. Rudyard Kipling deemed it the moral duty of the West to help the nonwhite races of the world.

More recently, postmodernist critics in the West, such as Roland Barthes and Derrida, have viewed Japanese culture as decentered. Because they define modernist writing as structural, systematic, and rational, they theorize that Japanese culture is essentially postmodern. Barthes argues and illustrates that Japan is a decentered culture in which the Buddhist state of *mu,* nothingness, represents the lack of a privileged *Signified* behind what he calls the "empire of signs." Modernism, as well as romanticism, suppressed a decentered culture and the very margins in a culture which have come to gain power in postmodernist writing. Such margins are converted to signs of power, and these signs are used to reshape the ostensibly fixed material world of history and produce new and more humane identities for human beings.

As a result, the power of language in postmodernism operates in contrast to the function of language in realism. Realistic language, which functions as a mirror, conveys a common view by suppressing contradictory voices; it reflects the commonly experienced world outside the text. That is, experience is prior to language. In postmodern writing, language, though often derived from experience, has its own power and development independent of experience. Walker's *The Color Purple* (1982), for example, shows that Celie's voice realistically echoes racist experience but simultaneously reflects what Wright calls in *Black Power* "a primal African attitude." Celie laments that cutting a young tree is like cutting her own arm. Walker's text is reminiscent of Wright's: Wright was fascinated by the African reverence for nonhuman beings, a primal African philosophy that corresponds to the Buddhist belief. Both *The Color Purple* and *Black Power* as postmodern texts poignantly express the cross-cultural vision that humankind is not at the center of the universe.

Another postmodern text conducive to a cross-cultural reading is Wright's *Pagan Spain* (1957). In this text, anomalies appear on the surface of the text: Spain looks like a Christian as well as a Pagan society. Wright's discourse conveys such a message on the surface, but on the same surface it contains anomalies, or "gaps," which, when taken into account, are found to conflict with and put into question what is signified. These gaps exist on the virtual margins of the text, but as the reader focuses on the gaps, the text begins to deconstruct itself. The gaps spread and immerse themselves throughout the text. For example, the Black Virgin at Montserrat, an established symbol of Catholicism, becomes a powerful signifier, a text that systematically deconstructs itself before the reader's expectant eyes. In sharp contrast to the male principle of life, for which Christianity stands, Spanish religiosity underscores the female principle of life the Virgin signifies.

Such a reading leads to the basic assumption of a feminist criticism that there are innate differences between men and women and, further, that women are inherently superior, as *Pagan Spain* reveals that Spanish women are the pillar of Spanish culture. Julia Kristeva, a contemporary champion of feminist writing and a follower of Lacanian psychoanalysis, was fascinated with medieval Chinese womanhood when she visited northern Chinese villages in the late 1980s, just as Wright admired Spanish womanhood when he traveled to Spain in the mid 1950s. A postmodern reading of *Pagan Spain,* then, is to restore the matriarchal power in an earlier culture, which merely existed in the margins of the premodern text. Not only has postmodern writing subverted the premodern text by shifting the margins to the center of the text, but the decentric mode of writing has also produced the effect of collapsing and destroying the time-honored oppositions: male and female, fact and fiction, civilized and indigenous, colonial and postcolonial, East and West, America and Europe.

The most influential East-West artistic, cultural, and literary exchange that has taken place in modern and postmodern times was reading and writing of haiku. Among others, Richard Wright distinguished himself as a haiku poet by writing over 4,000 haiku in his last eighteen months of his life while in exile in Paris. Between Wright's death in 1960 and the publication of *Haiku: This Other World* (1998), a collection of the 817 selected by Wright, only twenty-three of them had appeared in some journals and books, but the entire manuscripts of Wright's haiku have been available for study since 1990. Since 1998, in particular, Wright's haiku have made an impact on some of the contemporary American poets, most notably Robert Haas, Sonia Sanchez, and James Emanuel. Robert Haas, U.S. Poet Laureate 1995–97, wrote in *The Washington Post:* "Here's a surprise, a book of haiku written in his last years by the fierce and original American novelist Richard Wright. . . . What an outpouring!"

Back in 1955 Wright attended the Bandung Conference of the Third World; two years later he was a member of the First Congress of Negro Artists and Writers, which met in Paris in September. During that same period he liked to work in his garden on his Normandy farm, an activity that supplied many themes for his haiku. Of his experience in this period, Wright's travel to the newly independent Ghana in West Africa had a great impact on his writing of haiku. The African philosophy of life Wright witnessed among the Ashanti, "the African primal outlook upon life," as he called it, served as an inspiration for his poetic sensibility.

The decade of the 1950s was rich in possibilities for Wright. The Third World was coming into its own artistically, socially, and politically. But set against this positive cultural climate were the effects of his financial and personal problems. By the beginning of 1959 he was sick and confined to his bed. In the introduction to *Haiku: This Other World,* Wright's daughter Julia Wright, then an eighteen-year-old Sorbonne student of sociology, writes:

> But, the wound that went the deepest, the piece of news that hit him by far the hardest, was the death of his mother, Ella, in January 1959, the very same month a writer he highly admired, Albert Camus, was killed in an automobile accident. . . . The haiku enabled him to mourn a mother whose physical absence from his life had begun way before her death. . . . A form of poetry which links seasons of the soul with nature's cycle of moods enabled him to reach out to the black part of himself still stranded in a South that continued to live in his dreams. With the haiku, a self-nurturing could begin albeit so close to his own death.

Wright was approaching the end of the decade in an ambivalent mood ready for union with that which lies beyond the artist, a theme appropriate for haiku. Exhausted by his sickness and the polemic drain on his rational powers, he was mentally and emotionally receptive to the ideas, beauty, and form of haiku under the influence of R. H. Blyth and his Zen concepts, as well as of African philosophy.

Unlike the other sects of Buddhism, Zen teaches that every individual possesses Buddhahood and all he or she must do is to realize it. One must purge one's mind and heart of any materialistic thoughts or feelings and appreciate the wonder of the world here and now. Zen is a way of self-discipline and asceticism. Its emphasis on self-denial is derived from the prophetic admonishment Gautama Buddha is said to have given to his disciples: "Seek within, you are the Buddha." Zen's emphasis on self-enlightenment is analogous to Emersonian transcendentalism, in which an individual is taught to discipline the self and look within, for divinity resides not only in nature but in human beings.

In contrast to Zen, however, Emerson defines human enlightenment as the subject's consciousness of the over-soul. In "The Over-Soul," Emerson describes this state of mind as a boundless sphere in which "there is no screen or ceiling between our heads and the infinite heavens." No sooner does the consciousness of the subject disappear than the over-soul appears on the scene. As Emerson writes, "[M]an, the effect ceases, and God, the cause, begins." To Emerson, the over-soul is so pervasive "a light [that it] shines through us upon things and makes us aware that we are nothing, but the light is all." In his essay "Nature," this light is so powerful that one becomes "a transparent eyeball" which cannot see beyond one's state of mind. In Zen, one is taught to annihilate this eyeball before *satori* is attained: *satori* is the achievement of *mu,* nothingness. The state of nothingness is free of human subjectivity; it is so completely free of any thought or emotion that such a consciousness, or "the unconscious" in psychoanalytical terms, corresponds to the state of nature. Unlike a Zen master, Emerson seems to empower God to conquer human subjects while allowing them to cling to their subjectivity.

In Zen, if the enlightened person sees a tree, for instance, the person sees the tree through his or her enlightened eye. The tree is no longer an ordinary tree; it now exists with different meaning. In other words, the tree contains *satori* only when the viewer is enlightened. From a similar point of view, Wright saw in African life, as reported in *Black Power,* a closer relationship between human beings and nature than that between human beings and their social and political environment:

> Africa, with its high rain forest, with its stifling heat and lush vegetation, might well be mankind's queerest laboratory. Here instinct ruled and flowered without being concerned with the nature of the physical structure of the world; man lived without too much effort; there was nothing to distract him from concentrating upon the currents and countercurrents of his heart. He was thus free to project out of himself what he thought he was. Man has lived here in a waking dream, and, to some extent, he still lives here in that dream.

Africa evokes in one "a total attitude toward life, calling into question the basic assumptions of existence," just as Zen teaches one a way of life completely independent of what one has been socially and politically conditioned to lead. As if echoing the enlightenment in Zen, Wright says: "Africa is the world of man; if you are wild, Africa's wild; if you are empty, so's Africa."

Wright's analysis of the African concept of life is also suggestive of Zen's emphasis on transcending the dualism of life and death. Zen master Dogen (1200–1254), whose treatise *Shobogenzo* is known in Japan for his practical application rather than his theory of Zen doctrine, observed that since life and death are beyond human control, there is no need to avoid them. Dogen's teaching is a refutation of the assumption that life and death are entirely separate entities as are seasons or day and night. To Freud, the unconscious includes a death instinct, an instinct in opposition to libido—an instinct to turn into elements in opposition to reproduction of organisms. To Lacan, the death instinct is not "an admission of impotence, it isn't coming to a halt before an irreducible, an ineffable last thing, it is a concept." Lacan takes issue with Freud, for Freud defines death as the opposite of life: the pleasure principle underlying life is opposed to the death wish, which "tends to reduce all animate things to the inanimate." Lacan, on the other hand, defines this change from life to death as "human experience, human interchanges, intersubjectivity." Lacan's concept of death, then, has a strong resemblance to Dogen's.

The funeral service Wright saw in an Ashanti community, reported in *Black Power,* showed him that "the 'dead' live side by side with the living; they eat, breathe, laugh, hate, love, and continue doing in the world of ghostly shadows exactly what they had been doing in the world of flesh and blood," a portrayal of life and death reminiscent of Philip Freneau's "The Indian Burying Ground" and, more recently, Toni Morrison's *Beloved.* In Freneau's poem, the Native Americans bury their dead in a sitting posture. Like the dead Ashanti, the buried man continues to be involved in his life activities after death: "His imaged bird, and painted bowl, / And venison, for a journey dressed, / Bespeak the nature of the soul, / Activity, that knows no rest." Freneau's images, like haiku images, function as representations of intersubjectivity instead of subjectivity. The dead man's "imaged birds, and painted bowl" do not convey Freneau's ideas, although these images are what Freneau as a subject sees. Because the images express the Indian's ideas, the images constitute the reflections of another subject.

Wright was, moreover, fascinated by the African reverence for the nonhuman living, a primal African attitude which corresponds to the Buddhist belief. He observed in *Black Power* that the pre-Christian African, like a Buddhist, was impressed with the littleness of a human being. The concept of unity, continuity, and infinity underlying that of life and death is what the Akan religion and Buddhism share. Wright's reading of the African mind conforms to both religions in their common belief that not only are human beings unable to occupy the center of the universe; they are merely an infinitesimal fraction of time and space. The Akan religion and Buddhism both de-emphasize human subjectivity. It is this revelatory and emulating relationship which nature holds for human beings that makes the African primal outlook upon life akin to Zen Buddhism.

With the advent of postmodern writing, American culture with its economic and political influences across the shores is bent on Americanizing the world but at the same time is trying to globalize it. Perhaps the most positive lesson of the cross-cultural visions, as strongly reflected in African American literature, is that seeing human existence can be achieved in ways which do not necessarily assert the self by excluding the other: truth is often a revelation from the other. However historically different their ideas and representations may have been, both African American modernists and postmodernists have mediated upon the possibility of multiple worlds for human subjectivity.

Part I

American Dialogues

The Chicago Renaissance, Theodore Dreiser, and Richard Wright's Spatial Narrative

1.

As African Americans found the rural South a living hell and dreamed of escaping racial prejudice and exclusion and of living in northern cities, African American writers were at the pains of conveying the sufferings and hopes of the African American people. The mode of their writing was diametrically opposed to that of nineteenth-century American novelists who often described the mood of pastoral idyll inspired by a longing for a simpler agrarian society. This type of fiction was written largely as a reaction to the disharmony and friction that occurred among rugged individualists, strong-willed white men living in urban society. The new kind of white man was not only able to live in harmony with nature; he would also find a bosom friend in the stranger, a dark-skinned man from whom he learned the values of life he had not known. Natty Bumppo in James Fenimore Cooper's leather-stocking novels strikes up friendship with Chingachgook and Hard-Heart, noble savages of the wilderness. Ishmael in *Moby-Dick* is ritualistically wedded to Queequeg, a pagan from the South Seas. Huck Finn discovers a father figure in Jim, a runaway slave.

In twentieth-century American literature, however, a substantial reversal of the anti-urban sentiment is found in both European American and African American writings, a new literary tradition often critical of the values expressed in earlier American literature. In *Jennie Gerhardt*, for example, Dreiser described the city as a site of freedom and individualism. A realistic modernist like Dreiser, who intimately knew the squalor and corruption brought on by city life, used the urban environment as a space in which to dramatize individual liberty and pursuit of happiness. For both men and women, the city was envisioned as a site of confluence between the individual and society, a space that was fluid and wide enough to enable citizens and workers to interact with an industrialized culture.

Much of the important African American literature that has emerged since the Depression has also been largely urban in character. Although never hesitant to criticize the negative aspects of city life, it has only rarely suggested that pastoral alternatives to the city exist for African Americans. This large and significant body of literature, moreover, contains some surprising celebrations of city life. One way to explain this positive image of the city is to examine the historical experience of African Americans. From the very onset, African Americans were denied imaginative access to a pre-urban homeland in Africa because the institution of slavery did everything possible to stamp out the memory of that world.[1] And the actual experience of slaves in America did not permit them the luxury of romantically imagining the nonurban settings which are so mythically prominent in nineteenth-century American fiction by such writers as Cooper, Melville, and Twain. As Huck Finn and Jim sadly discovered, the territories ahead could be truly liberating only for European Americans. In the era following the literal end of slavery, new strategies for re-enslavement were devised in the South where codes of segregation and the practice of sharecropping made it impossible for African Americans to establish a positive image of rural life which could serve as a counterbalance to the pull of urban life.

For Richard Wright, Chicago was split between wonder and terror, but it was always preferable to the southern environment he had so categorically rejected. What is remarkable about his impression of Chicago was its dichotomous vision:

> Then there was the fabulous city in which Bigger lived, an indescribable city, huge, roaring, dirty, noisy, raw, stark, brutal; a city of extremes: torrid summers and sub-zero winters, white people and black people, the English language and strange tongues, foreign born and native born, scabby poverty and gaudy luxury, high idealism and hard cynicism! A city so young that, in thinking of its short history, one's mind, as it travels backward in time, is stopped abruptly by the barren stretches of windswept prairie! But a city old enough to have caught within the homes of its long, straight streets the symbols and images of man's age-old destiny, of truths as old as the mountains and seas, of dramas as abiding as the soul of man itself! ("How 'Bigger' Was Born" xxvi)

Not only did Chicago in the 1930s and 1940s present itself as the center of a powerful, industrialized economy, but it was also a striking representation of a modern civilization buttressed by multiculturalism. It is no small wonder, then, that Chicago produced—besides Wright—Margaret Walker, Gwendolyn Brooks, and a host of American writers whose cultural legacies were other than Anglo-Saxon and mostly ethnic, such as Dreiser, James T. Farrell, Nelson Algren, and Saul Bellow.[2]

Farrell was one of the earliest American writers who championed Wright's narrative as an unusual intermixture of realism and lyricism. He wrote in *Partisan Review* that *Uncle Tom's Children* served as an exemplary refutation for those who wished to write "such fancy nonsense about fables and allegories." In response to such reviewers as Granville Hicks and Alan Calmer, who wanted Wright to pace more steadily in his narrative and delve more deeply into his material, Farrell argued that Wright effectively used simple dialogue "as a means of carrying on his narrative, as a medium for poetic and lyrical effects, and as an instrument of characterization" ("Lynch Patterns" 57). By contrast, as if in return for Wright's unfavorable review of her novel *Their Eyes Were Watching God,* Zora Neale Hurston categorized *Uncle Tom's Children* as a chronicle of hatred with no act of understanding and sympathy. As did some other critics, she opposed Wright's politics, arguing that his stories failed to touch the fundamental truths of African American life ("Stories of Conflict" 32).

For Wright, however, what enabled his narrative to convey the truth about African American experience was not an application of literary naturalism but a creation of perspective. Almost a decade earlier than James Baldwin's review of *Native Son,* Wright had posited a theory of African American narrative in "Blueprint for Negro Writing," published in *New Challenge.* This narrative, whether in fiction or in nonfiction, he argued, must be based on fact and history and cannot be motivated by politics or idealism. African American writing, then, does not assume the role of protest: "even if Negro writers found themselves through some 'ism,'" he asks, "how would that influence their writing? Are they being called upon to 'preach'? To be 'salesmen'? To 'prostitute' their writing? Must they 'sully' themselves? Must they write 'propaganda'?" The inquiry is "a question of awareness, of consciousness; it is, above all, a question of perspective." This perspective, Wright defines, is "that part of a poem, novel, or play which a writer never puts directly upon paper. It is that fixed point in intellectual space where a writer stands to view the struggles, hopes, and sufferings of his people."[3]

Substantiating perspective with "intellectual space," Wright further posits that perspective must not be allied with "world movements" and must be established by the self. Because perspective is "something which he wins through his living," it is "the most difficult of achievement" ("Blueprint" 45–46). This intellectual space comprises, on the one hand, a writer's complex consciousness deeply involved in African American experience and, on the other, the writer's detachment from that experience. To Wright, detachment means a reflection accomplished in isolation, in a space where neither those afflicted nor those sympathetic to their plight, such as Marxists, are allowed to enter. "The conditions under which I had to work," Wright recalls in *American Hunger,* "were what baffled them [members of the Communist party in Chicago]. Writing had to be done in loneliness" (123).

His attempt to establish perspective and provide it with intellectual space accounts for his lifelong commitment to a narrative by which he was able to convey the truths of African American life from an impersonal, objective point of view. His entire work has shown that he was a remarkably resilient thinker and writer. At the outset of his career his writing was deeply influenced by Marxism, but later, as he came to establish his own point of view, he used only the doctrine of Marxist theory on class struggle, which made sense to African American life, while rejecting much of Marxist practice, which suppressed freedom and individualism.

Although some critics have regarded Wright's work as a product influenced by the earlier American and European literary movements, he never considered himself as belonging to any of them. In 1941 he told Edwin Seaver: "Dreiser could get his sociology from a Spencer and get his notion of realism from a Zola, but Negro writers can't go to those sources for background. . . . In fact, I think in many cases it is good for a Negro writer to get out on his own and get his stuff first hand rather than get it through the regular educational channels" (*Conversations* 46).

Whatever philosophy Wright had come across earlier in his life, he adamantly continued to adhere to his own theory of narrative. Whether he was interested in Marxism, Zolaesque naturalism, or French existentialism, none of them taught him how to attain his perspective and intellectual space. The Marxist doctrines of class struggle against capitalism proved less relevant to African American life than they did to American life in general. Literary naturalism, based on the concepts of heredity and social environment, would not have applied to African American narrative, for such concepts had less to do with African Americans than they did with European Americans. Racism alone, ever present in American society, made the social environment of African Americans vastly different from that of European Americans. By the same token, existentialism, as originally conceived for European society, would not have provided Wright's narrative with the perspective and intellectual space it required.

Not only did "Blueprint for Negro Writing," published in 1935, give a clear definition, but it also provided a remarkable illustration for his theory. Perspective, Wright wrote,

> means that a Negro writer must learn to view the life of a Negro living in New York's Harlem or Chicago's South Side with the consciousness that one-sixth of the earth surface belongs to the working class. It means that a Negro writer must create in his readers' minds a relationship between a Negro woman hoeing cotton in the South and the men who loll in swivel chairs in Wall Street and take the fruits of her toil. ("Blueprint" 46)

Focusing on the relationship between African American women workers in the South and European American businessmen in the North, Wright sounded as though he were giving a demonstration of American racial problems. But the perspective he urged the African American writer to achieve does not merely apply to African Americans; it signifies "the hopes and struggles of minority peoples everywhere that the cold facts have begun to tell them something" ("Blueprint" 46).

2.

Conversations with Richard Wright confirms that in his reading during the Chicago period, Wright paid utmost attention to such influential American novelists in the twentieth century as Dreiser, Faulkner, and Hemingway.[4] Of the three, Wright was least inspired by Hemingway. In a radio discussion of the New York Federal Writers' Project broadcast in 1938, he said: "I like the work of Hemingway, of course. Who does not? But the two writers whose work I like most today are André Malraux and William Faulkner. I think both of them in their respective fields are saying important things" (*Conversations* 10). Despite Hemingway's reputation, established by such novels as *The Sun Also Rises,* Wright realized that a Hemingway novel makes a great impression on the reader's mind not for establishing perspective but for creating style. Wright also realized that a Hemingway novel thrives on action, a technique lacking in French novelists like Sartre and Camus.[5] In the 1930s, Wright felt that he belonged to the latest literary generation, which included both Hemingway and Faulkner. He paid a greater tribute to Faulkner because he thought Faulkner's fiction conveyed a judicious point of view. In particular, he recognized Faulkner's importance in developing the

American novel, in which the "unhappiness" of the American people was realistically described (*Conversations* 109).

Among all the writers in English, Dreiser had the strongest influence on Wright's mode of understanding American history and culture. "The first great American novelist I came across," Wright said in retrospect shortly before his death, "was Theodore Dreiser. Thanks to him, I discovered a very different world in America" (*Conversations* 214). As early as 1941, Wright said, "I never could get into Dickens . . . He reeks with sentimentality. Theodore Dreiser . . . is the greatest writer this country has ever produced. His *Jennie Gerhardt* is the greatest novel" (*Conversations* 38). Toward the end of *Black Boy* he wrote:[6]

> I read Dreiser's *Jennie Gerhardt* and *Sister Carrie* and they revived in me a vivid sense of my mother's suffering; I was overwhelmed. I grew silent, wondering about the life around me. It would have been impossible for me to have told anyone what I derived from these novels, for it was nothing less than a sense of life itself. All my life had shaped me for the realism, the naturalism of the modern novel, and I could not read enough of them. (274)

Wright's affinity with Dreiser has conventionally been understood in terms of naturalism, but Wright never considered himself a naturalist.[7] That Wright made no distinction between realism and naturalism in reading Dreiser's novels suggests a predilection for the fiction that mirrors social reality, the writing that not only expresses the sentiments of the socially oppressed but also deals with the unalloyed feelings of individuals representative of the feelings of others. This objectivity on the part of the writer, which Wright deemed the most difficult to achieve, constitutes what he called "perspective" and "intellectual space," the twin elements indispensable to his narrative.

One of the chief reasons why *Jennie Gerhardt* had a strong affinity for Wright is that Dreiser's novel is not a naturalistic novel as is, for example, Stephen Crane's *Maggie: A Girl of the Streets*. As an American realist, Dreiser took pains to deal with young women's search for happiness in the city. Just as the young Wright, finding the rural South a living hell, escaped to Chicago, as so poignantly portrayed in *Black Boy,* Jennie, suffering social ostracism in small Ohio communities, moved to a happier life in Chicago, where she faced less prejudice of class and gender. Unlike Maggie in Crane's novel, to whom the "shutters of the tall buildings were closed like grim lips . . . the lights of the avenues glittered as if from an impossible distance,"[8] Jennie finally finds in Chicago not only privacy and individualism but also the gay, energetic spirit of life that frees her from oppressive social conventions. Given a slum section of the city and a self-centered family situation, on the contrary, Crane's portrayal of Maggie's life becomes utterly predictable. Growing up in such a family, Maggie has little desire to leave the slum life or to better herself. Although she is described as "blossomed in a mud puddle" and "a most rare and wonderful production of a tenement district, a pretty girl" (Crane 141), she is deprived of any sense of autonomy and vision.

In *Jennie Gerhardt* Dreiser achieves what Wright calls *perspective* by gauging the relationship between Jennie and Lester Kane, two individuals placed poles apart in society just as Wright urged his fellow novelists to envision the distance between a black woman cotton picker in the South and a white businessman in Wall Street. Even though Lester is heir to a millionaire business tycoon, he is attracted with great compassion to Jennie, a daughter of poor immigrants, who helps her mother scrub hotel floors in Columbus. Far from a victim of social environment, Lester is described as "a naturally observing mind, Rabelaisian in its strength and tendencies." From Jennie's vantage point, "the multiplicity of evidences of things, the vastness of the panorama of life," which Lester is aware of, makes her quest for liberation from class oppression less painful (125). As she moves from Cleveland to Chicago, the multiple and panoramic vision of urban life intensifies. "Yes, Chicago was best," Dreiser declares. "The very largeness and hustle of it" made the concealment of Lester's liaison with Jennie "easy" (173).

Unlike Maggie and her family, who forever remain victims of the big city slum environment, Jennie and her family are endowed with abilities to circumvent the situation and create space for themselves. While Maggie is trapped and her movement is circular at best, Jennie, like the narrator of *Black Boy,* who went from Natchez, Mississippi, to Memphis and then to Chicago, moves from smaller cites to larger ones, from Columbus to Cleveland and then to Chicago. And just like the mature Wright, who later went to New York to broaden his horizon, Jennie is also able to visit the metropolis. Unlike Maggie's brother Jimmie, who cares only about his own life, Jennie's brother Bass—although early on caring very little for his family—not only becomes concerned about the family's welfare but also develops a great sympathy for his sister. In an immigrant family, the oldest son, being young and most acculturated to the American way of life, served as the catalyst for the success of his family.

Of the literary influences Wright had, he was inspired by Dreiser's spatial narrative, through which the city in Jennie's ordeal becomes her savior. In Dreiser's narrative, living in a city not only separates her from the restrictive past dominated by class and gender prejudices but also gives her the fluid, indeterminate space in which to gain her individualism. Furthermore, the spirit of freedom that the city inspires in Jennie is also shared with Lester. Whether she succeeds in her search for liberation has a corollary in what happens to his life in Chicago. In *Maggie,* on the contrary, the Bowery life, which is extremely confined, does not allow for the residents' mobility, let alone their travels.

In *Jennie Gerhardt,* the idea and excitement of travel is expressed throughout the novel. As the Gerhardt children walk to the railroad tracks to steal coal, they watch luxurious trains pass by. "Jennie, alone, kept silent," Dreiser remarks, "but the suggestion of travel and comfort was the most appealing to her of all" (28). After his father's death Lester decides to leave the wagon factory owned by his family and departs on a European tour with Jennie, as Wright, while living in exile in Paris, extended his travels to Pagan Spain, West Africa, and Southeast Asia. Jennie, Dreiser writes, "was transported by what she saw and learned":

> It is curious the effect of travel on a thinking mind. At Luxor and Karnak—places Jennie had never dreamed existed—she learned of an older civilization, powerful, complex, complete. . . . Now from this point of view—of decayed Greece, fallen Rome, forgotten Egypt, and from the notable differences of the newer civilization, she gained an idea of how pointless are our minor difficulties after all—our minor beliefs. (*Jennie Gerhardt* 307)

Although Lester is portrayed initially as an animalistic man, he turns out to be "a product of a combination of elements—religious, commercial, social— modified by the overruling, circumambient atmosphere of liberty in our national life which is productive of almost uncounted freedoms of thought and action" (126). Despite her lack of education and experience, Jennie is also inspired by the same spirit of freedom that Lester attains.

In contrast to Crane's deterministic portrayal of Maggie, the fluid, spatial narrative that informs Jennie's liberation had profound influence on Wright's mode of understanding American history. Dreiser's heroine is a victim of gender prejudice and social and economic oppression. At the outset of his career in Chicago, Wright himself attempted to acquire his own perspective and intellectual space through the John Reed Club. As he told Edward Aswell, he had a strong affinity for Marxism at that time: "I was a member of the Communist Party for twelve years ONLY because I was a Negro. Indeed the Communist Party had been the only road out of the Black Belt of Chicago for me. Hence Communism had not simply been a fad, a hobby; it had a deeply functional meaning for my life" (qtd. in Fabre, *Quest* 542). As Wright also wrote for the *Daily Worker* in 1937, the aim of Marxist African American writers like him was "to render the life of their race in social and realistic terms. For the first time in Negro history, problems such as nationalism in *literary perspective,* the relation of the Negro writers to politics and social movements were formulated and discussed" (qtd. in Fabre, *Quest* 129; emphasis added).

At the very inception of his Chicago period, Wright was indeed intent upon subverting the traditional, hierarchical discourse in American writing, a hegemonic, racist mode of expression. Such a mode of understanding American history was rigid and antithetical to the spirits of freedom and democracy, the twin ideals of American culture. In place of the traditional narrative, Wright wanted to create a spatial model of amelioration. While he lived in Chicago, Marxist writing indeed served his initial purpose: his early writing, and *Uncle Tom's Children* in particular, vividly demonstrated Marxist conceptions of history as the forums through which power relations are understood.

3.

"Big Boy Leaves Home," the first story in the 1938 and 1940 editions of *Uncle Tom's Children,* features a young black boy's escape from his violent southern community.⁹ Four innocent, happy-go-lucky black boys are discovered naked by a white woman while they are swimming in a pond and later drying their bodies on a white man's premises. When she screams, her male companion without warning begins shooting and kills two of the boys. Big Boy manages to overcome the white man and accidentally kills him. Now the two surviving boys must take flight. Bobo gets captured, but Big Boy reaches home and is told by black church leaders to hide in a kiln until dawn, when a truck will come by to take him to Chicago. While hiding, he watches Bobo lynched and burned. Witnessing such an event gives Big Boy not only a feeling of isolation, terror, and hatred but also a sense of self-awareness and maturity.

Not only is "Big Boy Leaves Home" based upon Wright's personal experience, but the sexual taboo that precipitated this tragedy originates from a fact which both black and white people in the South knew so well and which is revealed as the story unfolds: white women are closely guarded and protected by the white world. "In that world," as Blyden Jackson has noted, "at least when 'Big Boy Leaves Home' was written, all Negro males, even young and with their clothes on, were potential rapists. And so this woman screams, and screams again, for someone named Jim, and Jim himself, a white man from her world, comes apace, with a rifle in his hands."[10]

Instead of a comparison between what happens in "Big Boy Leaves Home" and the facts of racism in America, the story has been compared to an ancient myth.[11] In Ovid's *Metamorphoses,* the myth of Actaeon and Diana is told this way:

> Actaeon and his companions are out hunting at midday when Actaeon calls an end to the chase since "Our nets and spears / Dip with the blood of our successful hunting." Nearby, in a grotto pool nestled in a valley, the goddess Diana, herself tired from hunting, disrobed and disarmed, bathes with her maidens. Quite by accident, Actaeon, now alone, comes upon the idyllic scene. Finding no weapon nearby, Diana flings a handful of the pond's water on the hapless hunter, taunting, "Tell people you have seen me, / Diana, naked! Tell them if you can!" He flees from the scene, by stages transformed into a stag, a metamorphosis he does not comprehend (though he marvels at his own speed) until he pauses to drink. Then he "finally sees, reflected, / his features in a quiet pool 'Alas!' / He tries to say, but has no words." Stunned he hears his hounds approach. "The whole pack, with the lust of blood upon them / Come baying . . . Actaeon, once pursuer / Over this very ground, is now pursued . . . He would cry / 'I am Actaeon . . .' / But the words fail." The hounds set upon him "And all together nip and slash and fasten? Till there is no more room for wounds." Meanwhile, his companions arrive, call for him, and rue that he is missing the good show. "And so he died, and so Diana's anger / Was satisfied at last." (Atkinson 251–52)

The parallels between Wright's story and this classical myth are indeed striking. Both tales begin with idyllic scenes before the plot focuses on an initial encounter between the opposite sexes. Big Boy, the leader of the group, and three friends, who are supposed to be at school, walk through the woods, laughing, beating vines and bushes as if they are hunting anything that interests them. As Big Boy, accompanied by his sidekicks, is pursuing his avocation in a most enjoyable environment, Actaeon, too, with his companions, is hunting in good weather. Before the unexpected appearance of a woman, both Actaeon and Big Boy are at rest, Actaeon tired from hunting and Big Boy warming his body after swimming in the cold pond. Another similarity is the hero's fleeing the scene. Before seeing Diana, Actaeon is alone now that his companions have retired from hunting; upon seeing her, he flees the scene. Similarly, Big Boy flees the scene alone since two of his friends have been killed, and Bobo takes a separate route and is eventually captured. Finally, both protagonists sustain serious wounds during their flight. It is, furthermore, significant that the wounding of the hero occurs in two stages. Actaeon suffers what Michael Atkinson calls "the transformative sprinkling with pondwater, which removes his humanity, and the obliterative tearing by the dogs' teeth, which destroys the last form and vestige of life" (257). In Wright's tale, Big Boy first suffers the loss of Buck and Lester, whose blood is sprinkled over him, and second he suffers from watching Bobo's body being mutilated.

But the points of difference between the tales are equally striking and significant. While in the Roman myth the male protagonist alone encounters a goddess, in Wright's story a group of young boys see an adult woman. However accidental it might be, it is Actaeon who comes upon the scene where Diana is bathing with her maidens in a secluded pond. The circumstances under which Wright's story begins are reversed: it is the lady who comes upon the scene where Big Boy is swimming with his friends. The initial setting Wright constructs in "Big Boy Leaves Home" poses a serious question: should underage boys be judged morally wrong when they are seen naked, while swimming, by an adult woman? In the Actaeon myth, given the tradition of privacy behind it, Actaeon is deemed clearly guilty of watching a naked goddess surrounded by her maids. If Big Boy were Actaeon, he would be arrested as a Peeping Tom in any society. Even if Big Boy were Actaeon, his punishment would be only blindness, as legend tells that Peeping Tom looked at Lady Godiva riding naked through Coventry and was struck blind. But blindness, the price Peeping Tom paid for his offense, is a far cry from the psychological wounds Big Boy and all other black boys in America indeed suffered: the shooting death of Buck and Lester by an Army officer on leave and the lynching of Bobo by a white mob.

It is also significant that unlike Actaeon, none of the black boys in Wright's story is alone when a member of the opposite sex appears on the scene. The woman in question, moreover, is fully protected by an adult male companion with a shotgun which could be legally used should she be molested and raped by the unarmed black boys. In the myth, however, the goddess is protected neither by those who can overcome a potential seducer nor by any kind of weapon save for her flinging of a few drops of magical pondwater. In terms of crime and punishment, those who are guilty in Wright's story, the lynch mob and the woman who screams, go unpunished, whereas those who are innocent, the four black boys, are physically or psychologically destroyed. In the myth, Actaeon, the only one who is guilty, meets his death while all the innocent—Diana, her maids, and Actaeon's companions—survive the ordeal. If the Actaeon myth and the legend of Peeping Tom tell us anything significant about an ancient system of justice which meted out punishment for humankind, then the system of justice that Wright condemns in "Big Boy Leaves Home" is not only unjust but fundamentally corrupt.

While "Big Boy Leaves Home" and the classical myth of Actaeon and Diana are thematically different, Wright's treatment of the sexual theme in this story has a closer resemblance to Dreiser's "Nigger Jeff."[12] It is quite likely that before writing "Big Boy Leaves Home," Wright read "Nigger Jeff." Dreiser's story, in which a white mob lynches a black youth, deals with the same problems of race and miscegenation in America as does Wright's. In "Nigger Jeff," a white cub reporter named Elmer Davies is sent out by the city editor to cover the lynching of an alleged black rapist, Jeff Ingalls. Jeff is first captured by a sheriff to await trial, but he is later taken away by a mob of white men led by the brother and father of a white woman, the supposed rape victim, and is finally hanged from a bridge over a stream. After learning the circumstances of the rape, Jeff's behavior, his family's grief, and above all the transcending beauty and serenity of nature against the brutality and criminality of the mob, Davies realizes that his sympathies have shifted.

At the outset of each story, the author stresses the peace and tranquility of the setting where people, black and white, are meant to enjoy their lives in harmony with nature. In Wright's story, the four innocent, happy black youths, as mentioned earlier, roam about the woods and pasture, laughing, chanting, smelling sweet flowers. "A quartet of voices," Wright describes, "blending in harmony, floated high above the tree tops" (*Uncle Tom's Children* 17). In Dreiser's story, a young, impressionable man comes upon the setting on a lovely spring day in the beautiful countryside of Pleasant Valley. As Big Boy and his friends are happy not only with themselves but with the world, Davies, as Dreiser describes, "was dressed in a new spring suit, a new hat and new shoes. In the lapel of his coat was a small bunch of violets . . . he was feeling exceedingly well and good-natured—quite fit, indeed. The world was going unusually well with him. It seemed worth singing about" (76). Under such circumstances no one would expect violence to intrude and destroy peace and harmony.

Both stories are told through the protagonist's point of view. In the beginning both Big Boy and Elmer Davies are young and naive, but the violence and injustice they witness make them grow up overnight. In the end, Big Boy, though stunned and speechless, is determined to tell the world what he has learned. As *Black Boy* suggests, Big Boy was modeled after the young Richard Wright himself growing up in the 1920s. Dreiser's *A Book about Myself,* one

of the finest autobiographies in American literature—as is *Black Boy*—also
suggests that Elmer Davies was indeed the young Dreiser himself when the
future novelist was a newspaper reporter in St. Louis in the early 1890s. Just
as Wright fled the South for Chicago to write his early short stories, so also
Dreiser left the Midwest for New York to write his.

In both stories, the plot, which does not hinge upon a conflict of social
forces, is based on a progression of vision. Each story opens with pastoral
idylls, moves through the visions of violence and injustice, and reaches the
hero's losing his relative state of innocence. Both writers take pains to show
that the point-of-view character, the protagonist, rather than society, the
antagonist, is capable of vision. The climactic scene in Wright's story, where
the victim is hanged and mutilated, is presented with bright firelight. The
mob is situated so close to the scene of violence that they cannot see what is
transpiring. By hiding in the dark in a kiln, creating space, and establishing
perspective, Big Boy can see it far better than can the mob. "Big Boy," Wright
says, "shrank when he saw the first flame light the hillside. Would they see
him here? Then he remembered you could not see into the dark if you were
standing in the light" (48). From his own perspective Dreiser, too, presents
the climax for Elmer Davies rather than the mob to see, as Dreiser describes
the scene: "The silent company, an articulated, mechanical and therefore terrible thing, moved on. . . . He was breathing heavily and groaning. . . . His
eyes were fixed and staring, his face and hands bleeding as they had been
scratched or trampled upon. . . . But Davies could stand it no longer now.
He fell back, sick at heart, content to see no more. It seemed a ghastly, murderous thing to do" (*Free* 103–4). Witnessing a horrific murder makes Davies
feel as though he has himself become a murderer and seems to retard the progression of the story, but the pace and the space of the revelation increase as
Dreiser describes the scene.

In Wright's story, too, Big Boy remains in the kiln through the night after
the mob departs and becomes the victim's sole companion. Just as morning
comes for a truck to deliver Big Boy to Chicago, dawn breaks for Davies to
return to his office. After the crowd departs, Davies thinks of hurrying back
to a nearby post office to file a partial report. But he decides against it since
he is the only reporter present, just as Big Boy is, and because "he could write
a fuller, sadder, more colorful story on the morrow" (*Free* 105), just as Big
Boy could have when he left for Chicago in the morning. By creating time
and space, this momentary delay in Davies's action gives his revelation perspective, as well as a heightened effect.

Moreover, Dreiser's description of dawn in "Nigger Jeff," as that of the
opening scene, is tinged with a transcendental vision: "As he still sat there the

light of morning broke, a tender lavender and gray in the east. Then came the roseate hues of dawn, all the wondrous coloring of celestial halls, to which the waters of the stream responded." During the lynching, Davies sees the signs of evil on the struggling body, the black mass, and black body hanging limp. Images of the dark are intermingled in his mind with those of the light that suggest hope: "the weak moonlight," "the pale light," "the glimmering water," "the light of morning," "a tender lavender and gray in the east," "the roseate hues of dawn," "the white pebbles [shining] pinkily at the bottom" (*Free* 105–6). As the story ends, signifiers of hope increasingly dominate those of despair.

The same pattern of imagery is also created toward the end of Wright's story. During the night, Big Boy has to protect himself from cold wind and rain as well as a persistent dog. Even though morning arrives with the warm sunlight and brightened air, he is still reminded of "a puddle of rain water" and "the stiff body" of the dog lying nearby. "His knees," Wright describes, "were stiff and a thousand needlelike pains shot from the bottom of his feet to the calves of his legs. . . . Through brackish *light* he saw *Will's truck* standing some twenty-five yards away, *the engine running*. . . . On hands and knees he looked around in the *semi-darkness*. . . . Through *two long cracks* fell *thin blades of daylight*. . . . Once he heard *the crow of a rooster*. It made him think of *home,* of *ma* and *pa*" (*Uncle Tom's Children* 51–52; emphasis added). At the final scene the nightmare that has tormented Big Boy throughout the night is now chased out of his mind and destroyed by the blades of the sun: "The truck swerved. He blinked his eyes. The blades of daylight had turned brightly golden. The sun had risen. The truck sped over the asphalt miles, sped northward, jolting him, shaking out of his bosom the crumbs of corn bread, making them dance with the splinters and sawdust in the golden blades of sunshine. He turned on his side and slept" (53).

In the ending of "Nigger Jeff" as well, Dreiser still makes the hero's consciousness move back and forth between hope and despair as if the images of light and dark were at war. When Davies visits the room where the body is laid and sees the victim's sister sobbing over it, he becomes painfully aware that all "corners of the room were quite dark. Only its middle was brightened by splotches of silvery light." For Davies, another climactic scene of his experience takes place when he dares to lift the shirt covering the body. He can now see exactly where the rope tightened around the neck. The delineation of the light against the dark is, once more, focused on the dead body: "A bar of cool moonlight lay just across the face and breast" (*Free* 109–10). Such deliberate contrasts between the light and the dark, good and evil, suggest that human beings have failed to see "transcending beauty" and "unity of nature," which are merely illusions to them, and that they have imitated only the cruel and the indifferent which nature appears to signify.

At the end of the story, like Big Boy, Davies is overwhelmed not only by the remorse he feels for the victim but also by his compassion for the victim's bereft mother he finds in the dark corner of the room:

> Davies began to understand. . . . The night, the tragedy, the grief, he saw it all. But also with the cruel instinct of the budding artist that he already was, he was beginning to meditate on the character of story it would make—the color, the pathos. The knowledge now that it was not always exact justice that was meted out to all and that it was not so much the business of the writer to indict as to interpret was borne in on him with distinctness by the cruel sorrow of the mother, whose blame, if any, was infinitesimal. (*Free* 110–11)

The importance of such fiction is not the process of the young man's becoming an artist—as Big Boy or the young Richard Wright is surely not trying to become merely an artist. It is the sense of urgency with which the protagonist living in American society is compelled to act as a reformer. In such a narrative, Dreiser and Wright are both able to create their space and perspective. With his final proclamation, "I'll get it all in" (*Free* 111), Davies's revelation culminates in a feeling of triumph. Although, to Dreiser as well as to Wright, human beings appear necessarily limited by their natural environment and by their racial prejudice, both writers in their respective stories are asserting that human beings are still capable of reforming society.

Protest fiction, the term critics have assigned to "Big Boy Leaves Home," becomes successful literature only if it is endowed with a universal sense of justice, and "Big Boy Leaves Home" and "Nigger Jeff" are exemplars of such literature. Such a narrative must address an actual and pressing social issue, whether it is a lynching that a European American writer witnessed in a border state in the 1890s or a problem of race and miscegenation that an African American writer encountered in the Deep South of the 1920s. As both stories show, great social fiction can be created not so much with the artistry the writer can put into it—much of which is taken for granted in these stories— as with the writer's moral space and perspective required by the subject matter. In "Big Boy Leaves Home," this urgency does not come from Big Boy's will—to borrow psychoanalytic terms, the ego of the subject. Nor does it have much to do with the collective will of African Americans, the concept of intersubjectivity. Rather, it comes from the conscience of humanity, the conscious or unconscious truth of human existence. It is a revelation given to Big Boy, as it is given to Elmer Davies. And through the protagonist and with the skills of a gifted writer, it is disseminated to the modern world.

4.

Except for the obvious issues of race, Wright and Dreiser shared remarkably similar experiences before they became novelists. Since their boyhood, both had been economically hard-pressed; they were always ashamed that they had grown up on the wrong side of the tracks. As boys they witnessed struggling and suffering and felt excluded from society. They grew up hating the fanatic and stifling religion practiced at home. In each of their lives, the family suffered because of the father's inadequacies as a breadwinner; the son inevitably rebelled against the father, and the family was somehow held together by the suffering mother. Under these circumstances, their dream of success was merely survival; they tried to hang on to one menial job after another. As a result, both had nurtured a brooding sensibility. At twelve, Wright held "a notion as to what life meant that no education could ever alter, a conviction that the meaning of living came only when one was struggling to wring a meaning out of meaningless suffering" (*Black Boy* 112), a statement which also echoes in *Dawn,* Dreiser's autobiography of youth.

It would seem that both authors, being literary realists, used authentic court records in writing *An American Tragedy* and *Native Son.* Dreiser drew on the Gillette murder case in upstate New York; Wright on the Leopold and Loeb kidnap-murder as well as the Robert Nixon murder trial and conviction in Chicago. Both works strongly imply that Clyde and Bigger are the products of American culture and that society, not the individuals involved in the crimes, is to blame. But doesn't such a narrative *always* create tensions in the life of the hero, growing out of an environment over which he has no control and about which he understands very little and by which he is *always* victimized. If so, *Native Son* does not exactly fit into this genre. While Dreiser and Wright share the perspective of a disadvantaged individual, the characterization of the individual in his or her respective society differs considerably.

It is true that both novels employ crime as a thematic device. In *Native Son,* the murder of Bessie is the inevitable consequence of Mary Dalton's accidental death; in *An American Tragedy,* Clyde's fleeing the scene of the accident which kills a child leads to his plotting of murder later in the story. Without the presence of crime in the plot, neither author would have been able to make significant points about his protagonist. But the focus of the author's idea differs in the two books. Wright's center of interest, unlike Dreiser's, is not crime but its consequences—its psychological effect on his hero. Before committing his crime, Bigger is presented as an uneducated, uninformed youth; indeed he is portrayed as a victim of white society who grew up in the worst black ghetto of the nation. Readers are surprised to see him gain identity after the murder. The crime gives him some awareness of himself and of the world—an awareness he had never been capable of before. Readers are surprised to learn that after the murder Bigger is well versed in world affairs. "He liked to hear," Wright tells us, "of how Japan was conquering China; of how Hitler was running the Jews to the ground; of how Mussolini was invading Spain" (*Native Son* 110). By this time he has learned to think for himself. He is even proud of Japanese, Germans, and Italians, because they "could rule others, for in actions such as these he felt that there was a way to escape from this tight morass of fear and shame that sapped at the base of his life" (109–10).

Despite a death sentence handed down by his white rulers, Bigger now proclaims his own existence. Even Max, who has taken a sympathetic attitude toward the racially oppressed, is bewildered by Bigger's deep urges for freedom and independence. "I didn't want to kill," Bigger tells Max. "But what I killed for, I *am!*" (*Native Son* 391–92). Having overcome white oppression, Bigger now stands as a heroic exemplar for the members of his race. His brother Buddy, he realized, "was blind . . . went round and round in a groove and did not see things." Bigger sees in Buddy "a certain stillness, an isolation, meaninglessness" (103). And he finds his sister and mother to be equally weak individuals. "Bigger," says Wright, "was paralyzed with shame; he felt violated" (*Native Son* 280).

In both *Native Son* and *An American Tragedy* a preacher appears before the trial to console the accused. But in *Native Son* the black preacher is described in derogatory terms. Bigger immediately senses that the Reverend Hammond possesses only a whitewashed soul and functions merely as an advocate of white supremacy. Wright offers this explanation: "The preacher's face was black and sad and earnest. . . . He had killed within himself the preacher's haunting picture of life even before he had killed Mary; that had been his first murder. And now the preacher made it walk before his eyes like a ghost in the night, creating within him a sense of exclusion that was as cold as a block of ice" (*Native Son* 264).

During his act of liberation, Bigger is also consciously aware of his own undoing and creation. To survive, Bigger is forced to rebel, unlike Clyde, who remains a victim of the tensions between individual will and social determinism. In rebelling, Bigger moves from determinism to freedom. He knows how to escape the confines of his environment and to gain an identity. Even before he acts, he knows exactly how Mary, and Bessie later, has forced him into a vulnerable position. No wonder he convinces himself not only that he has killed to protect himself but also that he has attacked the entire civilization. In *An American Tragedy,* Dreiser molds the tragedy of Clyde Griffiths by generating pity and sympathy for the underprivileged in American society. In *Native Son,* Wright departs from the principles of pity and sympathy which white people have for black citizens. In "How 'Bigger' Was Born," Wright admits that his earlier *Uncle Tom's Children* was "a book which even bankers' daughters could read and weep over and feel good about" (xxvii). In *Native Son,* Wright would not allow for such complacency. He warns readers that the book "would be so hard and deep that they would have to face it without the consolation of tears" (xxvii).

The meaning of *Native Son* derives not from crime itself but from its result. Dreiser's interest in *An American Tragedy* lies not in the result of crime but in its cause. While Bigger at the end of his violent and bloody life can claim his victory, Clyde at the end of his life remains a failure. *Native Son* ends on an optimistic note; *An American Tragedy* as a whole stems from and ends on the dark side of American capitalism. F. O. Matthiessen is correct in maintaining that the reason for Dreiser's use of the word *American* in his title "was the overwhelming lure of money-values in our society, more nakedly apparent than in older and more complex social structures" (Matthiessen 203). Helen Dreiser, Dreiser's second wife, seems to confirm Dreiser's argument in the book that materialism is the culprit of Clyde's tragedy. Commenting on Dreiser's choice of the Chester Gillette murder case for fictionalization, Helen Dreiser writes:

> This problem had been forced on his mind not only by the extreme American enthusiasm for wealth as contrasted with American poverty, but the determination of so many young Americans, boys and girls alike, to obtain wealth quickly by marriage. When he realized the nature of the American literature of that period and what was being offered and consumed by publishers and public, he also became aware of the fact that the most interesting American story of the day concerned not only the boy getting the girl, but more emphatically, the poor boy getting the rich girl. Also, he came to know that it was a natural outgrowth of the crude pioneering conditions of American life up to that time, based on the glorification of wealth which started with the early days of slavery and persisted throughout our history. (71–72)

Dreiser's fascination with this subject resulted in his treatment of Clyde as a victim of the American dream. Bigger, too, a product of the same culture, cherishes a dream of his own. Like anyone else, he reads the newspapers and magazines, goes to the movies, strolls the crowded streets. Bigger is intensely aware of his dreams: "to merge himself with others . . . even though he was black" (*Native Son* 226). Unlike Dreiser, Wright must have clearly recognized his hero's sense of alienation from the rest of the world. It is an alienation that Wright himself, not Dreiser, often experienced as a boy and as a man. But it never occurs to Bigger that he can pursue such a dream. Indeed, throughout the text Wright amply documents the prevailing social mores, economic facts, and public sentiments to prove that Bigger's actions, attitudes, and feelings have already been determined by his place in American life. It is understandable for James Baldwin to say of *Native Son* that every black person has "his private Bigger Thomas living in the skull."[13] Given such a determined state of mind, Bigger would not be tempted to pursue his dreams. Ironically, the racial oppression and injustice in fact enhance his manhood. To Clyde Griffiths, the flame of temptation is brighter and more compelling. He is easily caught, and he thrashes about in a hopeless effort to escape the trap. Under these circumstances, "with his enormous urges and his pathetic equipment" (qtd. in Matthiessen 189), as Dreiser once characterized the plight of such an individual in America, there is no way out for Clyde but to plot murder.

The central meaning of *An American Tragedy* comes from the economic and social forces that overpower Clyde and finally negate his aspirations. Where a Bigger Thomas before liberation must always remain an uninformed, immature youth, a Clyde Griffiths is one whose mind is already ingrained with that glorious pattern of success: one must climb the social ladder from lower to middle to upper class. Money is necessarily the barometer of that success. At the beginning of the story Dreiser creates social space and perspective by directly showing how the family's mission work, in which Clyde is compelled to take part, appears contrary to his dreams. Dreiser at once comments that "his parents looked foolish and less than normal— 'cheap' was the word. . . . His life should not be like this. Other boys did not have to do as he did" (*American Tragedy* 12). A basically sensitive and romantic boy, he cannot help noticing the "handsome automobiles that sped by, the loitering pedestrians moving off to what interests and comforts he could only surmise; the gay pairs of young people, laughing and jesting and the 'kids' staring, all troubled him with a sense of something different, better, more beautiful than his, or rather their life" (10). This scene functions in the story as a great contrast to a similar scene in *Native Son*. Near the beginning Bigger goes to the movies and sees double features. *The Gay Woman,* portraying love and intrigue in upper-class white society, quickly loses his attention, and *Trader Horn,* in which black men and women are dancing in a wild jungle, shows him only life in a remote world. Bigger is placed in no-man's-land; he is only vaguely aware that he is excluded from both worlds. Unlike Wright, however, Dreiser places his hero in *An American Tragedy* at the threshold of success and achievement.

The two novelists' divergent attitudes toward the problem of guilt are reflected in the style and structure of their books. *Native Son,* swift in pace and dramatic in tone, displays considerable subjectivity, involving the reader in experiences of emotional intensity. The 1930s were hard times for both white and black people, and it was impossible to take a calm and objective view of the situation. Wright himself was a victim of the hard times, and he could speak from his heart. Wright makes Bigger Thomas a composite portrait of numerous black individuals Wright knew in his life. As shown in "How 'Bigger' Was Born," all of them defied the Jim Crow order, and all of them suffered for their insurgency (xii). As in the novel, Wright lived in a cramped and dirty flat. He visited many such dwellings as an insurance agent ("Man Who Went to Chicago" 210–50). In Chicago, while working at the South Side Boys' Club, he saw other prototypes of Bigger Thomas—fearful, frustrated, and violent youths who struggled for survival in the worst slum conditions (Kinnamon 120).

The 1920s, the background of Dreiser's novel, had not of course erupted into the kind of social strife witnessed a decade later. Unlike the hostile racial conflicts dramatized in *Native Son,* what is portrayed in *An American Tragedy* is Clyde Griffiths's mind, which is deeply affected by the hopes and failures of the American dream. A later reviewer of *An American Tragedy* accused Dreiser of scanting, "as all the naturalists do, the element of moral conflict without which no great fiction can be written, for he fobbed the whole wretched business off on that scapegoat of our time, society" (Adams 2). But the depiction of such a conflict was not Dreiser's intention for the novel in the first place. Rather, the poignancy of Clyde's tragedy comes from his helpless attraction and attachment to the dream that society had created. Dreiser defines this essential American psyche in an essay:

> Our most outstanding phases, of course, are youth, optimism and illusion. These run through everything we do, affect our judgments and passions, our theories of life. As children we should all have had our fill of these, and yet even at this late date and after the late war, which should have taught us much, it is difficult for any of us to overcome them. Still,

no one can refuse to admire the youth and optimism of America, however much they may resent its illusion. There is always something so
naïve about its method of procedure, so human and tolerant at times; so
loutish, stubborn and ignorantly insistent at others, as when carpetbag
government was forced on the South after the Civil War and Jefferson
Davis detained in prison for years after the war was over. ("Our National
Character" 24)

In contrast to Bigger's violent life, Clyde's state of mind can be conveyed only
by a leisurely pace and undramatic tone. Dreiser's approach is basically psychological, allowing us to sympathize with the character whose principal
weaknesses are ignorance and naiveté. Consequently we become deeply
involved with Clyde's fate. Above all, the relative calmness and objectivity in
which Clyde's experience is traced stem from a mature vision of the tribula-
tions shared by any of us who have ever dreamed.

The lack of dramatic tone in *An American Tragedy* is also due to change of
setting. Dreiser's restless protagonist begins his journey in Kansas City, flees
to Chicago, and finally reaches his destination in upstate New York. In contrast, Wright achieves greater dramatic intensity by observing a strict unity of
setting. All of the action in *Native Son* takes place in Chicago, a frightening
symbol of disparity and oppression in American life. Wright begins to height-
en the conflict and sharpen the division between Chicago's two worlds early
in the novel. In the beginning, the Thomases' apartment is described as the
most abject place imaginable, while the Dalton mansion suggests the white
power structure that ravages black people and destroys their heritage. The
conflict is obvious throughout, and the descriptions of the two households
present ironic contrasts. Whereas everything at the Thomases' is loud and
turbulent, at the Daltons' it is quiet and subdued. But the true nature of the
racial oppressor is later revealed: Mr. Dalton, a real estate broker and philan-
thropist, tries to keep African American residents locked in the ghetto by
refusing to lower their rent. During the trial, the prosecutor, the press, and
the public equally betray the most vocal racial prejudice and hatred. The central action of Book III is for the defense to confront and demolish this wall
of injustice before Bigger's life can be spared.

The narrative pattern in *An American Tragedy* is entirely different.
Although the novel is divided into three parts as is *Native Son,* Dreiser's division is based upon change of time, space, and characters. Each part has its
own complete narrative, and one part follows another with the same character dominating the central scene. Each unit is joined to the other not only by
the principal character but also by the turn of events that underlies the theme

of the novel. Book I begins with Clyde's dreams of success but ends in an accident that forebodes a disaster. This narrative pattern is repeated in Book II, beginning with a portrayal of the luxurious home of Samuel Griffiths in Lycurgus and ending with the murder. Book III opens with a depiction of Cataraqui County, where Clyde is to be tried and executed. Clyde's defense, resting upon the most sympathetic interpretation of his character as a moral and mental coward, clearly indicates the possibility of hope but nonetheless ends on a note of despair. The death of a child caused by an automobile accident at the end of Book I does not make Clyde legally guilty, but his fleeing the scene of the accident makes him morally culpable. This pattern is also repeated at the end of Book II, where he willfully ignores Roberta's screams for help, an act of transgression for which he is tried and punished. Such a narrative pattern is not given to the death of Mary and Bessie in *Native Son,* since one murder is necessarily caused by the other. Despite the fact that Bessie's death is caused by a premeditated murder, Bigger's crime does not raise the same moral issue as does Clyde's.

In *An American Tragedy* the author's voice is relatively absent. In contrast, *Sister Carrie* is noted for a lengthy philosophical commentary inserted at every significant turn of event, as well as for a strong tendency to identify with the characters, especially the heroine. But in *An American Tragedy* Dreiser's comments are not only few but short. Despite Clyde's resolution to work hard and steadily once he has reached the luxurious world of the Green-Davidson, Dreiser's comment is devastatingly swift: "The truth was that in this crisis he was as interesting an illustration of the enormous handicaps imposed by ignorance, youth, poverty and fear as one could have found" (*American Tragedy* 384).

In contrast to *Native Son,* Dreiser in *An American Tragedy* also reduces the author's omniscience by relying upon the method of indirect discourse. When Clyde is helplessly trapped between his loyalty to Roberta and his desire for Sondra, the insoluble dilemma is rendered through his dreams involving a savage black dog, snakes, and reptiles. About the possibility of Roberta's accidental murder, Dreiser depicts how Clyde is trying to dismiss the evil thought but at the same time is being enticed to it. Clyde's actual plot to murder, suggested by the newspaper article, now thrusts itself forward, as the narrator says, "psychologically, born of his own turbulent, eager and disappointed seeking." This crucial point in Clyde's life is explained in terms of a well-known myth: "there had now suddenly appeared, as the genie at the accidental rubbing of Aladdin's lamp—as the efrit emerging as smoke from the mystic jar in the net of the fishermen" (*American Tragedy* 463). The immediate effect of such a passage is that the reader feels compassion for the character whose mind is torn between the two forces with which the character is incapable of coping. Given Clyde's weaknesses, then, the reader is more likely to sympathize with than despise such a soul.

On the contrary, Bigger's manhood—which is as crucial a point in his life as Clyde's dilemma in his—is rendered through direct discourse. It is not the narrator's voice but the character's that expresses his inner life—the newly won freedom. His murder of a white girl makes him bold, ridding him of the fear that has hitherto imprisoned him. In the midst of describing Bigger's intoxication over his personal power and pleasure, Wright shifts the tone of the narrative to let Bigger provide a lofty voice of his own. While preparing a ransom note, Bigger utters: "Now, about the money. How much? Yes; make it ten thousand. *Get ten thousand in 5 and 10 bills and put it in a shoe box.* . . . That's good. . . . He wrote: *Blink your headlights some. When you see a light in a window blink three times throw the box in the snow and drive off. Do what this letter say*" (*Native Son* 167). Even more remarkable is Bigger's final statement to Max:

> "What I killed for must've been good!" Bigger's voice was full of frenzied anguish. "It must have been good! When a man kills, it's for something. . . . I didn't know I was really alive in this world until I felt things hard enough to kill for 'em. . . . It's the truth, Mr. Max. I can say it now, 'cause I'm going to die. I know what I'm saying real good and I know how it sounds. But I'm all right. I feel all right when I look at it that way. . . ." (*Native Son* 392)

Bigger's utterance, in fact, startles the condescending lawyer. At this climactic moment Max, awestricken, "groped for his hat like a blind man" (*Native Son* 392). Unlike Wright's portrayal of Bigger, Dreiser's presentation of Clyde in the same predicament is given through indirect discourse:

> He walked along the silent street—only to be compelled to pause and lean against a tree—leafless in the winter—so bare and bleak. Clyde's eyes! That look as he sank limply into that terrible chair, his eyes fixed nervously and, as he thought, appealingly and dazedly upon him and the group surrounding him.
>
> Had he done right? Had his decision before Governor Waltham been truly sound, fair or merciful? Should he have said to him—that perhaps—perhaps—there had been those other influences playing upon him? . . . Was he never to have mental peace again, perhaps? (*American Tragedy* 811)

In contrast to this characterization of Clyde, who is largely unaware of his guilt and his manhood, the final scene of *Native Son* gives the ending its dramatic impact. Despite his crimes and their judgment by white society, Bigger's final utterance elicits from readers nothing but understanding and respect for the emerging hero.

The sense of ambiguity created by Dreiser's use of portraits, dreams, and ironies in *An American Tragedy* is suited to the muddled mind of Clyde Griffiths. But Bigger can hardly be explained in ambivalent terms, for he has opted for the identity of a murderer. Clyde is presented as a victim of the forces over which he has no control, and Dreiser carefully shows that Roberta's murder—the climax of the book—has inevitably resulted from these forces. The principal interest of the novel, centering on this crime, lies in Clyde's life before the murder and the effect of the murder on him. In Book III, Clyde is depicted not merely as a victim of society but more importantly as a victim of his own illusions about life. In the end he still remains an unregenerate character as Dreiser has predicted earlier in the story.

5.

Like Clyde, Bigger in *Native Son* is presented in the beginning as an equally naive character, and his life is largely controlled by fear and hatred. He kills Mary Dalton because he fears his own kindness will be misunderstood. He hates in turn what he fears, and his violence is an expression of this hatred. But unlike Clyde, he has learned through his murders how to exercise his will and determination. Each of the three sections of *Native Son* is built on its own climax, and Book III, "Fate," is structured to draw together all the noble achievements of Bigger's life. Each of the changes in Bigger's development is also measured by his own language. The difference in characterization between the two Americans is reflected in the style and structure of the novels. Granted, both novelists deal with similar material, but their treatments of a young man's crime and guilt in American society differ in ideology and in discourse.

In some respects, earlier American writers provided Wright with models for conveying his painful vision of American society and culture. Hawthorne and James, who dealt with women's search for freedom and individualism, represented by such figures as Hester Prynne and Isabel Archer, focused on an older, more rigid society. But such materials were far removed from what appealed to Wright's endeavor. Twain, who dramatized the relation of European and African Americans in *Huck Finn* and *Pudd'nhead Wilson,* satirized racist society. But his assailing of American life might have sounded quite benign, as Van Wyck

Brooks thought that Twain's seriousness about American society was "arrested" by his humor.[14] Despite his high regard for Twain's skills as a humorist, Dreiser, too, was critical of Twain's fictional discourse. As Dreiser noted, Twain's mode of writing diverts its author "almost completely from a serious, realistic, and . . . Dostoevskian presentation of the anachronisms, the cruelties, as well as the sufferings, of the individual and the world which, at bottom, seem most genuinely to have concerned him" (Dreiser, "Mark Double Twain" 621).

By "a serious, realistic, and . . . Dostoevskian presentation," Dreiser meant, as did Mikhail Bakhtin, not only that the novel conveys the individual's voice but that it must represent all the social and ideological voices of the world. Bakhtin's dialogic narrative has a strong resemblance to Dreiser's spatial narrative, for both techniques are based on the twin principles of space and perspective. From Dreiser, Wright acquired a narrative technique—the technique of merging all these voices into what Bakhtin called "a microcosm of heteroglossia" (411). The hero or heroine of the novel is not an already complete person but must be a changing, evolving, and developing one. The protagonist's character thrives on the novelist's dialogic imagination as it is derived from the clashing interactions between the person and the others who inhabit society. To Wright, Dreiser is the posited author who creates a worldview against the expected literary horizon. This new worldview belongs to the posited author: it is productive because it shows the object of representation in a new light to illuminate new sides and dimensions while it, in turn, reveals in a new way the conventional worldview.

The models that appealed most to Wright's understanding of American life were Dreiser's *Jennie Gerhardt* and "Nigger Jeff." It is not surprising that Wright considered Dreiser the greatest writer whom American culture had produced. It is, indeed, Chicago that provided the young Richard Wright, as it did Jennie Gerhardt, with ample space in which to move about freely, interact openly with others, cherish dreams, and fulfill desires. Having recovered from the first economic depression the nation experienced, Chicago in the 1910s to Dreiser was a throbbing city with space and energy. Wright's Chicago two decades later was similarly a volatile, fluid city, what Wright called "the fabulous city" ("How 'Bigger' Was Born" xxvi). And it is also not surprising that the nexus of Wright and Dreiser was characterized by mutual admiration. Only recently has it come to light that Dreiser shortly before his death regarded *Black Boy* as a model of writing, "an honest forth right book."[15] American literary history will record that *Black Boy* is not only one of the greatest autobiographies ever written by an American author but also the greatest achievement of the Chicago Renaissance, a literary movement which would not have flourished without Dreiser's precedence and influence.

CHAPTER 2

The Cross-Cultural Vision of Ralph Ellison's *Invisible Man*

Among the well-known twentieth-century African American novels, *Invisible Man* (1952) has distinguished itself as unique racial discourse. As a novel of racial prejudice, Richard Wright's *Native Son* awoke the conscience of the nation in a way that its predecessors had failed to do. Toni Morrison's celebrated novel *Beloved* (1987) is perhaps one of the most poignant re-creations of the legacy of slavery. For the expression of an African American woman's love and suffering, Alice Walker's *The Color Purple* (1982) excels in its use of a vernacular, as does *Adventures of Huckleberry Finn,* told by an innocent, uneducated youth. Such novelists as Wright, Morrison, and Walker have succeeded in recording the ineffable agonies and rage of the racial victims because the authors' works are solidly based on fact and history. None of these novels, however, concerns the mindset of an individual more subtly than does *Invisible Man.* And this novel, unlike other African American novels, features the complexity of the protagonist's mind thoroughly foregrounded with a cross-cultural heritage.

The different styles of writing notwithstanding, *Invisible Man* and *Native Son* both capture the plight of an African American trapped in a racist society at mid-century. While the social and economic backgrounds of the two novels are similar, Ellison's technique is more modernistic than Wright's, which is more realistic. As a result, Ellison's protagonist is by far more articulate and subtle than Wright's. To defend the racial victim, Wright as a literary realist, as mentioned earlier, can rely on authentic court records like those of the Robert Nixon murder trial and conviction in Chicago in the late 1930s. Ellison, on the other hand, as a psychological and highly imaginative realist, vividly recalls his personal experiences with an evocation of the social realities and cultural myths.

When such experiences, facts, and memories are presented in the novel, they become metaphoric rather than realistic. *Invisible Man* reads like a cross-cultural rather than a social discourse. It is little wonder, then, that when Ellison's protagonist-narrator revisits these historical and cultural sites and moments in the novel, he becomes invisible in particular to those who have excluded the existence of African Americans from their lives.

1.

In "The World and the Jug," Ellison writes: "More important, perhaps, being a Negro American involves a *willed* (who wills to be a Negro? *I* do!) affirmation of self as against all outside pressures—an identification with the group as extended through the individual self which rejects all possibilities of escape that do not involve a basic resuscitation of the original American ideals of social and political justice" (*Shadow* 132). Throughout *Invisible Man,* as Ellison reminds white Americans of their blindness to the true identity of their fellow citizens, he also proves how invisible an African American is to white American society at mid-century. To help white Americans better understand black life, Ellison is urging black Americans to re-create themselves instead of accommodating white Americans' superiority complex and allowing their condescension. To Ellison, then, making African Americans' invisibility visible means "a *willed* affirmation of self," the ultimate achievement of freedom and equality guaranteed in the Constitution.

Ellison's argument for the invisibility of the African American identity also suggests that black life in America constitutes not only the lives of African Americans but those of all Americans. Ellison's observation bears a strong resemblance to Wright's, as shown in *12 Million Black Voices,* published in 1941.[1] This well-documented work demonstrates that the principal motive African Americans had for their exodus from the rural South to the industrial North was their quest for freedom and equality. Wright, himself a victim of racial prejudice and hatred, also fled to Chicago in search of the kind of freedom and dialogue he had never experienced in the South. "For the first time in our lives," he wrote, "we feel human bodies, strangers whose lives and thoughts are unknown to us, pressing always close about us." In stark contrast to the situation in the South, where African Americans were not allowed to communicate freely with white citizens, the crowded and noisy apartments in the northern cities became hubs of interracial mingling and communication, places where the migrant African Americans came in close contact with "the brisk, clipped men of the North, the Bosses of the Buildings." Unlike the southern landlords, the city businessmen, Wright discovered, were not "at all *indifferent.* They are deeply concerned about us, but in a new way" (*12 Million* 100).

In the industrial city, as Wright observed, an African American functioned as part of a "machine." Unlike his or her life in the rural South, which depended upon "the soil, the sun, the rain, or the wind," life in the North was controlled by what Wright called "the grace of jobs and the brutal logic of jobs" (*12 Million* 100). Living and working ever so closely with the white bourgeoisie, the minority workers in the city strove to learn their techniques. Consequently, Wright noted, African American workers "display a greater freedom and initiative in pushing their claims upon civilization than even do the petty bourgeoisie" ("Blueprint" 38). The harsh conditions under which African American workers had to produce and compete with white workers became an incentive to achieve a higher social and economic status. The interaction, dialogue, and competition involved in their activities created the African Americans workers' initial consciousness of self-reliance. In short, the African Americans of the industrial North were given a chance to shape their own lives. Economically an individual was a machine, and his or her production was measured not by his or her race but by his or her merit.

White citizens who worked in close contact with African Americans in turn viewed them with respect and friendliness. When white workers realized that they shared with African Americans the same working conditions and worldview, they became curious about African Americans' cultural legacy and, in particular, their musical heritage. In *12 Million Black Voices* Wright traces the cross-racial and cross-cultural dialogue that took place in the industrial North:

> Alone together with our black folk in the towering tenements, we play our guitars, trumpets, and pianos, beating out rough and infectious rhythms that create an instant appeal among all classes of people. Why is our music so contagious? On the plantations our songs carried a strain of other-worldly yearning which people called "spiritual"; but now our blues, jazz, swing, and boogie-woogie are our "spirituals" of the city pavements, our longing for freedom and opportunity, an expression of our bewilderment and despair in a world whose meaning eludes us. (*12 Million* 127–28)

To Wright, and to Ellison as well, the contribution of African American music to American life and culture served as a catalyst to developing affinities between African and European Americans. To Americans today, jazz and the blues have become national music as much as they remain an African

American legacy. More recently Toni Morrison has also observed that the presence of African Americans has enriched American life and culture: what she calls *Africanism* was the yoke of American culture. "Black slavery," she argues in *Playing in the Dark,* "enriched the country's creative possibilities" (38).

While Ellison shows in *Invisible Man* that African Americans' freedom and identity can be achieved through genuinely autonomous cultural voices such as jazz and the blues, he also evokes Yeats, Joyce, and O'Casey because the contribution of these writers to British culture is similar to the influences of African American music on American culture.[2] To envision the latent consciousness of the invisible man, Ellison relies on the techniques of French writers like André Malraux and Paul Valéry. Among the European existential works, Malraux's *Man's Fate* had an influence on Ellison's characterization of the invisible man.[3] In commenting on the psychological makeup of Wright's *Black Boy,* Ellison points out that "all men possess the tendency to dream and the compulsion to make their dreams reality . . . and that all men are the victims and the beneficiaries of the goading, tormenting, commanding and informing activity of that imperious process known as the Mind—the Mind, as Valéry describes it, 'armed with its inexhaustible questions'" (*Shadow* 81). Ellison considers *Black Boy* and *Invisible Man* not merely accurate representations of African American life but typical twentieth-century works that poignantly reflect humanity's quest to find meaning in existence.

As Ellison amply acknowledges in his essays, collected in *Shadow and Act* and *Going to the Territory,* he was also influenced by American writers, including Melville, Twain, Stephen Crane, Henry James, T. S. Eliot, Hemingway, and Faulkner. Although Ellison was hesitant to express his closer ties with his African American predecessors such as Hughes and Wright than he was aware, he frequently discussed their works in the light of his own ideas and techniques underlying *Invisible Man.* All in all, what makes *Invisible Man* a unique modernist novel is the various cultural strands that have gone into its composition.[4]

2.

Many of Ellison's essays indicate that he underplayed the concept of self-creation, a major ideology inherited from national character, whether the ideology was ingrained in the African American or the European American tradition. The treatment of this theme in *Invisible Man,* however, strongly suggests that Ellison was highly conscious of the theories and practices of self-creation advocated by his American predecessors, such as Wright and Emerson who both taught Ellison that it is essential for African Americans to create themselves rather than be given identity by society. Wright's and Emerson's writings alike provided Ellison with the admonition that if a writer does not find needed extant theories, techniques, and representations, the writer must invent them.

Wright's conception of self-creation is shown in *Black Boy,* the book Ellison admired the most among Wright's works. In that autobiography Wright enabled the narrator to convey the truth about African American experience, as did Ellison in *Invisible Man.* What distinguishes *Black Boy* from Wright's other narratives is not an application of literary naturalism but a creation of perspective as shown in *Black Boy.* This concept of perspective, which Wright finds it most difficult to represent in a narrative, has an affinity with Ellison's concept of invisibility in his novel. Wright theorizes that intellectual space comprises, on the one hand, an African American writer's complex consciousness deeply involved in his or her experience and, on the other, a detachment from it. By *detachment* Wright means a reflection accomplished in isolation, in a space like the underground hideout in *Invisible Man,* where neither those afflicted, such as Trueblood, Wheatstraw, and Mary, nor those sympathetic to their plight, such as Jack, Ras, and Sybil, are allowed to enter. Writing, though foregrounded in the clashing dialogue between the protagonist and others in society, as Wright argued in *American Hunger,* "had to be done in loneliness" (123).

Wright's attempt to establish perspective and provide it with intellectual space, as noted earlier, accounts for his lifelong commitment to a narrative by which he was able to express his own vision of life. Wright's determination to bring home such a narrative is similar to Ellison's dedication to writing *Invisible Man.* Wright's entire work has shown that he, like Ellison, was a remarkably resilient thinker and writer. At the outset of his career his writing was deeply influenced by Marxism, as were those of some other American writers, including Ellison. But later, as Wright became independent of the Marxist manifesto, he not only considered the theory of class struggle valid and applicable to African American life, as pointed earlier, but rejected, as did Ellison's invisible man, much of the Marxist practice, which suppressed freedom and individualism.

Whether Ellison attempted to draw an analogy between his concept of self-creation and Emerson's or wished to subvert Emerson's political ideology,[5] the reader is reminded of Ellison's creation of a fictional character named Emerson in *Invisible Man.* In his essay "The Negro and the Second World War," a 1943 editorial in *Negro Quarterly,* Ellison declared: "As long as

Negroes fail to centralize their power they will always play the role of a sacrificial goat, they will always be 'expendable.' Freedom, after all, cannot be imported or acquired through an act of philanthropy, it must be won" ("The Negro" 238). Ellison's admonition for African Americans' self-creation and autonomy in this editorial echoes Ralph Waldo Emerson's, stated in an 1844 journal entry:

> When at last in a race a new principle appears an idea, that conserves it. Ideas only save races. If the black man is feeble & not important to the existing races, not on a par with the best race, the black man must serve & be sold & exterminated. But if the black man carries in his bosom an indispensable element of a new and coming civilization, for the sake of that element no wrong nor strength nor circumstance can hurt him, he will survive & play his part. . . . The intellect, that is miraculous, who has it has the talisman, his skin & bones are transparent, he is a statue of the living God, him I must love & serve & perpetually seek & desire & dream on: and who has it not is superfluous. . . . I esteem the occasion of this jubilee to be that proud discovery that the black race can begin to contend with the white. . . . The negro has saved himself, and the white man very patronizingly says, I have saved you. If the negro is a fool all the white men in the world cannot save him though they should die. (*Selected Writings* 123–24)

Although Emerson's statement on the anti-slavery issue betrays his condescension to African Americans, his argument for self-help and self-creation concerns humanity as a whole. Emerson, moreover, bases his argument on transcendentalism, his own observation that intellect—individualism—is a divine gift. "Days," Emerson's favorite poem, written six years after the journal entry above, reads:

Daughters of Time, the hypocritic Days,
Muffled and dumb like barefoot dervishes,
And marching single in an endless file,
Bring diadems and fagots in their hands.
To each they offer gifts after his will,
Bread, kingdoms, stars, and sky that holds them all.
I, in my pleached garden, watched the pomp,
Forgot my morning wishes, hastily
Took a few herbs and apples, and the Day
Turned and departed silent. I, too late,

Under her solemn fillet saw the scorn.
(*Selected Writings* 481)

This poem expresses Emerson's condescension to himself as a mere human being, just as does his earlier journal entry to African American slaves. Emerson, however, places greater emphasis on human beings' tendency to be remiss in heeding God and rely on others than he does on the issues of race and gender.

In *Invisible Man,* self-reliance and self-creation function as Ellison's central theme. As Ellison's protagonist begins to doubt the import of Marxism in achieving African American individualism and independence, he reminisces about his college professor, who once discussed James Joyce's hero. "Stephen's problem, like ours," the invisible man heard his professor say, "was not actually one of creating the uncreated conscience of his race, but of creating the *uncreated features of his face.* Our task is that of making ourselves individuals" (354). To Ellison, Stephen's achievement is not the Irishman's success in transcending the oppression of the Irish by the English but his creation of an individual capable of seeing himself not as a member of a race, class, and gender but as a member of the human race. "[If] you have man," Emerson asserts, "black or white is insignificance. . . . I say to you, you must save yourself, black or white, man or woman. Other help is none" (*Selected Writings* 123).

Not only do Ellison and Emerson agree on the principles of self-help and individualism, but both also share the vision that the achievement of African American individualism leads to the creation of a culture worthy of universal respect and admiration. Emerson projected in the journal entry quoted earlier that "if the black man carries in his bosom an indispensable element of a new & coming civilization . . . he will survive & play his part" (*Selected Writings* 123). In the same journal entry Emerson recognized that African Americans were on the verge of creating a culture worthy of his respect. In *Invisible Man,* on the other hand, Ellison draws an analogy between the creation of Irish culture conceived by Joyce's hero Stephen and the creation of African American culture seen by the invisible man. For Ellison, creating a culture for African Americans means creating "something far more important" than a race. "For the first time, lying there in the dark," the invisible man says, "I could glimpse the possibility of being more than a member of a race" (*Invisible Man* 354–55).

Throughout the novel the Emersonian concept of self-reliance underlies the development of the invisible man's character. Even at the outset of his search for identity, Ellison's hero suspects that fighting a battle royal might lure him away from finding himself. "In those pre-invisible days," he ponders, "I visualized myself as a potential Booker T. Washington" (18). In his subsequent search and ordeal, various personages he encounters serve as a catalyst to making him less invisible to himself and others. Mr. Emerson's secretary gives the invisible man advice: "But I want to help you do what is best. . . . What's *best*, mind you. Do you wish to do what's best for yourself?" (188). "Oh, God!" the secretary finally utters, "Don't you see that it's best that you do *not* see him?" (189).

Later in the novel, other figures likewise play the role of a catalyst for the invisible man's self-realization. The veteran the invisible man meets urges him to be self-reliant and independent.[6] Wheatstraw serves as a model of the ideal African American—independent, self-reliant, and compassionate. As he comes in contact with his Marxist comrades like Brother Jack and Extortionist Ras, he slowly realizes his own identity: "For one thing," he says, "they seldom know where their personalities end and yours begins; they usually think in terms of 'we' while I have always tended to think in terms of 'me'—and that has caused some friction, even with my own family" (316). It is this concept that Ellison finds lacking and hence invisible in American life.

3.

Commenting on the essays collected in *Shadow and Act,* Ellison writes:

> The very least I can say about their value is that they performed the grateful function of making it unnecessary to clutter up my fiction with half-formed or outrageously wrong-headed ideas. At best they are an embodiment of a conscious attempt to confront, to peer into, the shadow of my past and to remind myself of the complex resources for imaginative creation which are my heritage. (xxii–xxiii)

Ellison sounds modest in calling some of his ideas "half-formed or outrageously wrong-headed." But when he calls these essays "an attempt to transform some of the themes, the problems, the enigmas, the contradictions of character and culture native to my predicament, into what André Malraux has described as 'conscious thought'" (xix), Ellison is acknowledging the import of existentialism, an ideology that underlies *Invisible Man* equally as other philosophies of life do.

Ellison also remarks in the same introduction:

When I began writing in earnest I was forced, thus, to relate myself consciously and imaginatively to my mixed background as American, as
Negro American, and as a Negro from what in its own belated way was
a pioneer background. More important and inseparable from this particular effort, was the necessity of determining my true relationship to that
body of American literature to which I was most attracted and through
which, aided my what I could learn from the literatures of Europe, I
would find my own voice, and to which I was challenged, by way of
achieving myself, to make some small contribution, and to whose composite picture of reality I was obligated to offer some necessary modifica-
tions. (xix)

Indeed, *Invisible Man* reverberates various voices heard in some of the well-
known existential works of fiction by Ellison's contemporaries in America as
well as in Europe. But what is interesting about and significant to Ellison's
novel as a representation of modern African American culture is that the protagonist's existential outlook is subtly tempered and modified by other related and yet different kinds of experience and thought Ellison cherished as an
African American.

One of the existential works of fiction to which *Invisible Man* bears a striking resemblance is Wright's novella "The Man Who Lived Underground"
(1945). In both stories the protagonist's identity is withheld throughout: the
invisible man is anonymous, as is Wright's protagonist, whose name is never
mentioned. Wright's underground man once spells his name on a typewriter
in lower keys as "freddaniels" (55). Alienation from society, a dominant
theme in existential writing, is also characteristic of both works: initially the
invisible man is convinced as is Daniels that his being an African American
is responsible for his alienation from society at large. The two men, who try
to be good, law-abiding citizens, both suffer from the oppression that stems
from what they consider a lawless, amoral, corrupt, and chaotic world with
little human value and little hope for renewal.

Despite their anonymity, both protagonists are portrayed as highly realistic characters. Throughout the story, Fred Daniels is not an African American
man in name only. Not only is his plight real, but all the major incidents and
characters he is involved with, which at times appear to be clumsily constructed representations, nevertheless reflect the racial struggle and oppression that an African American like him suffers. Ellison's novel, on the other
hand, is replete with such realistic personages as Dr. Bledsoe, Norton,
Wheatstraw, the veteran, Mary, Sybil, Ras, and Jack. Once confined in the
sewers, Daniels is completely isolated from the white world, and the only

group of people he encounters is an African American congregation in a basement church. Even though they are African Americans, he feels completely alienated from them. "After a long time," the narrator says, "he grew numb and dropped to the dirt. Pain throbbed in his legs and a deeper pain, induced by the sight of those black people groveling and begging for something they could never get, churned in him" (*Eight Men* 33).

Similarly, once the invisible man settles down in his Harlem underground, he loses interest in returning to "Mary's, or to the campus, or to the Brotherhood, or home" (*Invisible Man* 571). The invisible man, finding the members of the Brotherhood a group of deluded Marxists, becomes disenchanted with their activities just as Daniels, seeing the black congregation, a group of fanatic Christians, comes to despise them. Such scenes in both stories are not inserted as symbols but serve as graphic details of the futility and oppression of modern life. Such episodes not only make for depth but also are subtle representations of existential ideology and protest.

Despite such similarities, however, there remain considerable differences in outlook between the two works. Wright's vision of society is far more deterministic than Ellison's: unlike a typical antihero of the modernist novel who the invisible man is, Daniels, a racial victim, has no choice but to flee to the underground world. He has no choice as well but to confess to a crime he did not commit. The narrator at once intimates that Daniels "was tired of running and dodging" (*Eight Men* 27)—his life was a case history of oppression and persecution. The reader learns later that Daniels has been falsely accused of the murder of one Mrs. Peabody. Her identity as a white woman is not suggested until the midpoint of the story. Immediately after the episode in the grocery, as Daniels steps into the world above, the narrator says, "A few shy stars trembled about him. The look of things was beautiful, yet he felt a lurking threat." Walking toward a deserted newsstand, Daniels sees "a headline: HUNT NEGRO FOR MURDER" (49). At the end of the story the racial theme is once again intensified. Unable to comprehend Daniels's vision of the underworld, Lawson, one of the policemen, shoots him down, insisting, "You've got to shoot his kind. They'd wreck things" (92). Unlike Daniels's motive for living underground, the invisible man's is to hibernate and, by doing so, to re-create himself. "Here, at least," the invisible man says, "I could try to think things out in peace, or, if not in peace, in quiet. I would take up residence underground. The end was in the beginning" (*Invisible Man* 571).

In contrast to Ellison's existential view of African American life, Wright's idea of the universal human condition is expressed in terms of a dialectic. Daniels, now settled in the underground cave, argues: "Maybe *any*thing's right, he mumbled. Yes, if the world as men had made it was right, then anything else was right, any act a man took to satisfy himself, murder, theft, torture" (*Eight Men* 64). What Daniels calls "the world as men had made it" is precisely the fact of human history, not a utopia, philosophy, or religion. For him, of course, it constitutes a world of racism and oppression. If such a world were deemed right, then, it would follow that any one person's offense—"murder, theft, torture"—would be right. What Daniels is saying rings true because one person's offense, however serious it may be, can scarcely compare with even a fraction of the past, not to mention the future, injustices in American society.

The ambiguity in Daniels's judgment of human behavior and the conflict between the personal and societal judgments lead to a nihilistic spirit which Wright, unlike Ellison, attempted to express in this story. For Daniels, at least, a human action, whether it is well intended or not, has no meaning. For a person to find value in his or her act or in a society that has victimized the person is sheer futility. If such value should exist, Daniels asserts, it should be annihilated.

On the contrary, the invisible man's worldview is not nihilistic. A series of epiphanies given underground provide the invisible man with an uplifting, congenial expression for human existence. He now realizes that he should be able to emulate an African American like Trueblood, an existential hero, who has created himself and now has his own life and destiny under control. Upon severing his lingering ties with the Brotherhood, the invisible man now begins to conceive a more compassionate worldview with a concept of brotherhood quite different from what Marxists and Communists believe in. He now wonders:

> If only I could turn around and drop my arms and say, "Look, men, give me a break, we're all black folks together . . . Nobody cares." Though now I knew *we* cared, they at last cared enough to act—so I thought. If only I could say, "Look, they've played a trick on us, the same old trick with new variations—let's stop running and respect and love one another. . . ." (*Invisible Man* 560)

The attitude he now takes toward his fellow African Americans is in singular contrast to the one he had at the beginning of the novel. Living under the tutelage of Dr. Bledsoe, he was pretentious and condescending to his peers, just as was Norton to Dr. Bledsoe and to him.

The invisible man's compassion for others is reminiscent of the vision that Cross Damon in Wright's existential novel has as he lies dying on a New York street. Wright presents Damon's worldview with some contradiction. Early in the novel Damon considers himself a nihilist, but at the end of his life he becomes a man of compassion. In *The Outsider,* Wright seems to have taken the risk of contradicting himself not only because of the realistic accumulation of detail but also because of his insistence that Damon judges life inherently meaningful, as does Ellison's invisible man. What is common between the two African American intellectuals is their constant compulsion to take action in search for the meaning of their lives. Unlike Daniels, they are endowed with what Emerson called "[the] intellect, that is miraculous" and god-given (*Selected Writings* 123), as well as with the spirit of freedom to create an essence. Their actions result in something, whether it is love or hatred, happiness or tragedy. In the end, they create their existence and achieve their identity.

4.

Some of the modernist novelists in Europe and America who produced existential works were also interested in Eastern thoughts and religions and in Zen Buddhism in particular. Camus's *The Stranger,* for example, presents Meursault as an antihero who finds no meaning in life. Using crime as a thematic device, Camus focuses on the psychological effect of Meursault's crime on his vision of existence. After Meursault is sentenced to death, however, he realizes for the first time that his life has been enveloped in the elusive beauty of the world. "To feel it so like myself, indeed, so brotherly," he says, "made me realize that I'd been happy, and that I was happy still" (154). Despite his death sentence, he remains calm, and happy, for he has cleansed his mind of materialistic desire and fear. The prisoner, though alone and trapped by a society without human values, is freed from within. Meursault's state of mind at the end of his life is akin to Zen enlightenment.

Like Meursault, Daniels in Wright's story is also liberated from desire, greed, and hatred. In fact, Daniels is free of self-centered thought. His state of mind at the end of his life recalls that of Wright himself who wrote numerous haiku shortly before his death, one of which reads:

> It is September,
> The month in which I was born;
> And I have no thoughts.
> (*Haiku* 127)

It is difficult to determine whether Wright had Zen philosophy in mind when he wrote "The Man Who Lived Underground." But there is much evidence to indicate that at least toward the end of his life Wright was interested in Zen philosophy and aesthetics, especially in haiku, as noted in the introduction and discussed later in chapter 9.[7]

The visions of human life Meursault and Daniels have at the end of their lives also resemble the outlook upon life Ellison's invisible man gains underground. Early in the novel the invisible man, coming in contact with Trueblood, has a revelation about African American life and identity. The invisible man learns that Trueblood, encountering the hardship of his life, "looks up and sees the stars and I starts singin'." "I don't mean to," Trueblood says, "I didn't think 'bout it, just start singin'. I don't know what it was, some kinda church song, I guess. All I know is I *ends up* singin' the blues" (*Invisible Man* 66).

Like Wright's haiku "It Is September," Trueblood's observation of human life is based not on thought but upon his spontaneous response to natural spirituality. In Zen-inspired art, nature is the mirror of humanity. Zen practice calls for self-effacement; one should not allow oneself to control action. "Drink tea when you are thirsty," writes Yone Noguchi, "eat food in your hunger. Rise with dawn, and sleep when the sun sets. But your trouble will begin when you let desire act freely; you have to soar above all personal desire" (Noguchi, *Story* 242). This tenet of Zen, which teaches the followers to emulate nature, was one of the Taoist influences on Zen. Lao Zse said: "Man takes his law from the earth; the Earth its law from Heaven; Heaven its law from *Tao;* but the law of Tao in its own spontaneity" (Noguchi, *Spirit* 43). The twin deeds—naturalness and spontaneity—are in Zen the means by which human beings can be connected with the absolute, the achievement of *satori.* From a Zen point of view, such a vision of life as Trueblood attains is devoid of much thought and emotion. Trueblood thus enlightens himself by looking up and seeing stars and expresses his *satori* by singing the blues. For him, natural spirituality and the blues are the means by which he attains his enlightenment.

At the outset of the novel the invisible man is also aware of various means by which he may be able to achieve his enlightenment. "Perhaps," he says, "I like Louis Armstrong because he's made poetry out of being invisible" (*Invisible Man* 8). To make his invisibility visible, Ellison's protagonist literally and figuratively uses the electricity stolen from Monopolated Light & Power. "And I love light," he says. "Perhaps you'll think it strange that an invisible man should need light, desire light, love light. But maybe it is exactly because I *am* invisible. Light confirms any reality, gives birth to my form."

The invisible man's form, then, is analogous to the state of nothingness in Zen. The hole in his Harlem underground has nothing in it and is dark, but now it is lit up like Broadway and the Empire State Building, the two brightest spots, which, he satirically remarks, "are among the darkest of our whole civilization—pardon me, our whole *culture* (an important distinction, I've heard)." Ellison is treating this hole as a trope, for the invisible man says, "the point is now that I found a home—or a hole in the ground, as you will. Now don't jump to the conclusion that because I call my home a 'hole' it is damp and cold like a grave; there are cold holes and warm holes. Mine is a warm hole" (6).

Trueblood is also conscious of this state of mind when he sings the blues: "I sings me some blues that night ain't never been sang before, and while I'm singin' them blues I makes up my mind that I ain't nobody but myself and ain't *nothin'* I can do but let whatever is gonna happen, happen" (66; emphasis added). Not only is Trueblood's state of mind devoid of desire, egotism, and untruth; it is also capable of destroying any false social or political convention, tradition, and belief. Like Trueblood, a Zen Buddhist must purge his or her mind and heart of any materialistic thoughts and feelings and appreciate the wonder of the world here and now.

As does Trueblood, the invisible man gradually realizes that he has followed false conventions and beliefs. When the invisible man is handed yams and is called "one of these old-fashioned yam eaters," he nonchalantly responds, "They're my birthmark. . . . I yam what I am" (266). But at the same time it occurs to him: "What and how much had I lost by trying to do only what was expected of me instead of what I myself had wished to do? . . . I had accepted the accepted attitudes and it had made life seem simple . . ." (266–67). Once he has settled down in his Harlem underground, however, he redeems himself. He finally realizes that, unlike Robert Frost as portrayed in his poem "The Road Not Taken," the invisible man has been a conformist all his life. "So after years of trying to adopt the opinions of others," he declared, "I finally rebelled. I am an *invisible* man. Thus I have come a long way and returned and boomeranged a long way from the point in society toward which I originally aspired" (573).

While the invisible man's rebellion against convention leads to his embrace of Emersonian self-reliance and individualism, his resolution at the end of the novel suggests that he is not entirely satisfied with his view of himself. The difference in the concept of individualism between Emersonian transcendentalism and Zen philosophy lies in one's view of self. Emerson defines enlightenment as self's consciousness of the over-soul, God, while Zen calls it self's achievement of relating self to the spirit of nature, a state of nothingness, where neither the ego of an individual nor the over-soul of God exists.

In contrast to Emerson, Zen, as suggested in the introduction, is strikingly similar to Lacan.[8] In particular, the primacy of natural spirituality over human subjectivity which Zen stresses has a closer resemblance to Lacan's critique of subjectivity which posits the human subject's inability to attain the real of natural experience. In *The Seminar of Jacques Lacan: Book I,* Lacan as a Zen master challenges his students to undermine their subjectivity. Because the emergence of the unconscious for Lacan constitutes reaching "the real Other," the conscious self—subjectivity—which is corrupted by male-oriented language and society must be undermined.[9] For Emerson, on the other hand, the conscious self identifies its individuality with God, the over-soul; but this subjectivity is still emphasized in terms of the self.

Ellison's concept of individualism, represented by the invisible man, seems more closely allied with the concept of human subjectivity in Zen and Lacan than it is with Emerson. In fact, *Invisible Man* has few references in which the word of God or the over-soul is heeded. Earlier in the novel, the invisible man describes Dr. Bledsoe: "He stood before us relaxed, his white collar gleaming like a band between his black face and his dark garments, dividing his head from his body; his short arms crossed before his barrel, like a black little Buddha's" (118). The invisible man, seeking an interview with Mr. Emerson, sees in his office, which looks like a museum, "an ugly ebony African god that seemed to sneer (presented to the school by some traveling millionaire)" (181). It appears, however, that while Emerson wishes to rely on the self as much as on God, Ellison and Lacan refuse to rely on Him. Zen's doctrine of self calls for the follower to annihilate self in reaching the state of nothingness so as to liberate self from the habitual way of life. In Zen, one must destroy, just as must the invisible man and Lacan, not only the self contaminated by society, but also God, Buddha, Christ, any prophet, or any idol because it is only the true self, the self without the ego, that can deliver the person enlightenment.

It is this state of mind, a state of nothingness, that Ellison's protagonist is trying to achieve. At the end of the novel he calls the Zen-like state of mind "the *mind*": "So I took to the cellar; I hibernated. I got away from it all. But that wasn't enough. I couldn't be still even in hibernation. Because, damn it, there's the mind, the *mind*" (573). Later in the epilogue Ellison again intensifies his fascination with this state of mind (580). The invisible man's definition of "the *mind*" is neither his mind in the past nor the Emersonian conception of self. It is remindful of the Zen conception of the "here and now," as well as of Lacan's notion of the real. "It [*the mind*] wouldn't let me rest," the invisible man says. "Gin, jazz and dreams were not enough. Books were not enough. My belated appreciation of the crude joke that had kept me running, was not enough" (573). Dismissing from his mind his past endeavors, he wonders: "But what do *I* really want, I've asked myself. Certainly not the freedom of a Rinehart or the power of a Jack, nor simply the freedom not to run. No, but the next step I couldn't make, so I've remained in the hole" (575).

What the invisible man means by "the next step" is the real step, which is neither imaginary nor guided by anyone. In Zen Buddhism, life is endowed with spontaneity and natural spirituality. "Life is to be lived," he says, "not controlled" (577). In the tradition of Zen instruction the attainment of *satori* is as practical as is actual human life. The young Bassui, who later became a celebrated Zen priest in Japan in the fourteenth century, asked his master, "What's the highway to self elevation?" The master replied, "It's *never stop.*" Failing to understand, Bassui persisted: "Is there some higher place to go on to?" The master finally answered, "It's just underneath your standpoint" (Ando 164).[10]

At the end of the novel the invisible man, without a Zen master, meditates underground, awaiting the answer to his own question. Later in the epilogue, Ellison intensifies the invisible man's preoccupation with this answer:

> In going underground, I whipped it all except the mind, the *mind.* And the mind that has conceived a plan of living must never lose sight of the chaos against which that pattern was conceived. That goes for societies as well as for individuals. Thus, having tried to give pattern to the chaos which lives within the pattern of your certainties, I must come out, I must emerge. (580–81)

This vision of life offers "infinite possibilities," one of which he says he has now taken. "What a phrase—still it's a good phrase," he says, "and a good view of life, and a man shouldn't accept any other; that much I've learned underground" (576). While his view of life looks like Melville's symbolization of the whiteness of the whale, in which the universe appears indefinite, void, and invisible,[11] his outlook upon his own life also has an affinity with the principle of the "here and now" in Zen.

CHAPTER 3

No Name in the Street:
James Baldwin's Exploration of
American Urban Culture

1.

Whether or not one agrees with his views on race, one may be persuaded that James Baldwin is one of the most gifted essayists America has produced. As an essayist writing about racial problems in American society, he has no equal. The incisiveness of his writing seems to derive not so much from his eloquence, which is beyond dispute, as from his depth of feeling. As an auto-biographical writer, he has an unquestionably authentic vision. In expressing the suffering, perseverance, and aspiration of a minority, Baldwin's essays brought out the truth about himself just as Theodore Dreiser's *Dawn* (1931) and Richard Wright's *Black Boy* (1945) had done earlier, in slightly different contexts, for their authors.

Still, many readers are more impressed with Baldwin's eloquence than with his arguments. One critic, recognizing that Baldwin's talent is for the essay, finds a Jamesian eloquence in *Notes of a Native Son* (1955) and "a style of flaming declamation" in *The Fire Next Time* (Howe, "Baldwin" 92, 95–100). Although elegance and declamation undoubtedly characterize Baldwin's writing, it is doubtful that his expression can generate such power without substance. What underlies his language is a desire to be "an honest man and a good writer," as he said at the beginning of his career (Baldwin, *Notes* 9). And yet later readers, even after *No Name in the Street* (1972) had appeared, were more impressed by his manner than his matter.

Nobody Knows My Name (1961), concerned with the "love" between black and white Americans, reflects the attitude of the liberals of the time. Similarly, *The Fire Next Time* (1963), Baldwin's revision of that concept of love,[1] reflects public sentiment on the subject at the time. Of *No Name in the Street,* Benjamin DeMott went so far as to say: "Baldwin speaks of killing because the advent of a new militancy, together with disillusionment about prospects for reform, dictates still further change" (156). DeMott's argument is that Baldwin's essay is less the product of his personal philosophy than the reflection of the times in which he lived. At times, however, one is hard-pressed to distinguish between a writer's personal feelings and the feelings generated by the events of society. Witness one instance in *No Name in the Street* in which Baldwin recounts a white juror's attitude toward the American system of justice:

> "As I said before, that I feel, and it is my opinion that racism, bigotry, and segregation is [*sic*] something that we have to wipe out of our hearts and minds, and not on the street. I have had an opinion that—and been taught never to resist a police officer, that we have courts of law in which to settle . . . that I could get justice in the courts"—And, in response to Garry's [the defense attorney's] question, "Assuming the police officer pulled a gun and shot you, what would you do about it?" the prospective juror, at length, replied, "Let me say this. I do not believe a police officer will do that." (159–60)

The juror's reply not only provides a "vivid and accurate example of the American piety at work" (160), as Baldwin observes, but also demonstrates the very honesty in Baldwin that makes his feeling credible to the reader.

To reveal this kind of malady in society as Baldwin attempts to do in *No Name in the Street* requires an artist's skills. The juror's response is reminiscent of Aunt Sally's response to Huck Finn, who reports that a steamboat has just blown out a cylinder head down the river:

> "Good gracious! anybody hurt?"
> "No'm. Killed a nigger."
> "Well, it's lucky; because sometimes people do get hurt. . . ." (175)

What Twain and Baldwin share is the genuine feeling of an intense individualist: both writers feel their own great powers and yet recognize the hopelessness of trying to change the world.

No Name in the Street is a departure from Baldwin's earlier books of essays in expressing his theory of identity and love. Baldwin does not sound like an integrationist in this book; he sounds as if he is advocating the ideals of a militant separatist who has no qualms about killing a white enemy. Whatever position he finally holds in the book, he is dealing with the issue more deliberately and quietly than one would think. As a result, far more than his previous works, *No Name in the Street* is a sustained examination of the falsehood to which Americans try to cling in their urban living. Underlying the harshness of his vision is a sense of calmness and perhaps of resignation. In espousing the concept of the human race as being damned, his voice in this book has an affinity with Twain's, and even with that of Swift toward the end of *Gulliver's Travels*. In short, *No Name in the Street* is a successful satire against humankind.

On the American scene the implications of Baldwin's satire are vast and prophetic. He had earlier argued that racism at home is closely related to racism abroad and to the power politics of the world in particular. Once again in 1972 he reminded the reader that America had sided with wrong regimes abroad to perpetuate white supremacy at home:

> And, of course, any real commitment to black freedom in this country would have the effect of reordering all our priorities, and altering all our commitments, so that, for horrendous example, we would be supporting black freedom fighters in South Africa and Angola, and would not be allied with Portugal, would be closer to Cuba than we are to Spain, would be supporting the Arab nations instead of Israel, and would never have felt compelled to follow the French into Southeast Asia. But such a course would forever wipe the smile from the face of that friend we all rejoice to have at Chase Manhattan. (178)

His vision of mid-century American urban culture is not only authentic but also prophetic, for, as he insists, "The course we *are* following is bound to have the same effect, and with dreadful repercussions" (178). In *Nobody Knows My Name* he chided Richard Wright, as he did in *Notes of a Native Son,* and said: "It is no longer important to be white—thank heaven—the white face is no longer invested with the power of this world" (Baldwin, *Nobody* 170). Wright and Ellison both tried to go beyond protest by defining the true meaning of African American individualism. Baldwin, on the other hand, by challenging Wright's and Ellison's philosophical argument, seemed to assail what he envisioned in the 1960s and 1970s, the imperialistic and capitalistic culture, as utterly inhuman and doomed.

2.

No Name in the Street employs its title as a thematic device. The title is taken from the speech by Bildad the Shuhite in the book of Job which denounces the wicked of his generation:

Yea, the light of the wicked shall be put out,
And the spark of his fire shall not shine.
His remembrance shall perish form the earth,
And he shall have no name in the street.
He shall be driven from light into darkness,
And chased out of the world.

(Fullington 77)

Baldwin sees in Bildad's curse a warning for Americans: without a name worthy of its constitution, America will perish as a nation. "A civilized country," Baldwin ironically observes, "is, by definition, a country dominated by whites, in which the blacks clearly know their place" (177). Baldwin warns Americans to remake their country into what the Declaration of Independence *says* the founders wanted it to be. America without equality and freedom will not survive; a country without a morality, in Baldwin's definition, is not a viable civilization and hence it is doomed. He foresees that unless such a warning is heeded now, a future generation of humankind, "running through the catacombs . . . and digging the grave . . . of the mighty Roman empire" (178), will also discover the ruins of another civilization called the United States.

The responsibility for Americans to rebuild their country, Baldwin hastens to point out, falls upon African Americans as heavily as upon European Americans. This point echoes what he has said before, but it is stated here with a more somber and deliberate tone. It sounds comfortable indeed to hear Baldwin say in *Notes of a Native Son* that "blackness and whiteness did not matter" (95). He thought then that only through love and understanding could white and black people transcend their differences in color to achieve their identity as a people and as a nation. In *No Name in the Street,* such euphoria has largely evaporated; the book instead alludes to the fact that African Americans are descendants of European Americans. "The blacks," Baldwin insists, "are the despised and slaughtered children of the great Western house—*nameless* and *unnameable* bastards" (185; emphasis added). A black man in this country has no true name: calling himself black and a citizen of the United States is merely giving himself a label without a name worthy of his history and existence. To Baldwin, then, the race problem is not a race problem as such; it is fundamentally a problem of how African Americans perceive their own identity.[2]

No Name in the Street also deals with the cultural heritage of African Americans. He admonishes them that the term *Afro-American* does not simply mean the liberation of African Americans in this country. The word, as it says, means the heritage of Africa and America. African Americans, he argues, should be proud of this heritage. He demands that they must at once discard the misguided notion that they are descendants of slaves brought from Africa—an inferiority complex deeply rooted in the American psyche. An Afro-American, in Baldwin's metaphysics, is considered a descendant of the two civilizations, Africa and America, both of which were "discovered" not by Americans but by European settlers.

Moreover, Baldwin's prophecy is rendered in epic proportion. "On both continents," he says, "the white and the dark gods met in combat, and it is on the outcome of this combat that the future of both continents depends" (194). The true identity of an Afro-American, the very name that Baldwin finds the most elusive of all names, is given a historical light. To be granted this name, as he writes toward the end of the book, "is to be in the situation, intolerably exaggerated, of all those who have ever found themselves part of a civilization which they could in no wise honorably defend—which they were compelled, indeed, endlessly to attack and condemn—and who yet spoke out of the most passionate love, hoping to make the kingdom new, to make it honorable and worthy of life" (194). Historically Baldwin is demonstrating his old contention that both African and European Americans on this continent are compelled to live together and determine their own destiny.

No Name in the Street ends on a dark note, as some critics have suggested,[3] precisely because Baldwin had not yet discovered the true name for Americans. The most painful episode in the book that influenced his outlook on the racial question in 1972 was his journey into the Deep South. There he discovered not only a sense of alienation between black and white people, who had lived together over the generations, but an alienation within a white man himself. While a southerner was conceived in Baldwin's mind as a man of honor and of human feeling like a northern liberal, he struck Baldwin as a man necessarily wanting in "any viable, organic connection between his public stance and his private life" (53–54). Baldwin felt, in fact, that southern white Americans always loved their black friends, but they never admitted it. This is why Baldwin characterizes the South as "a riddle which could be read only in the light, or the darkness, of the unbelievable disasters which had overtaken the private life" (55).

In these pages Baldwin's search for a national identity in the name of brotherhood and love does not seem to end; he returns to the North. In the eyes of middle-aged Baldwin, the potential for a truly American identity emerges in the urban culture of the North in the black and white coalition with the radical students and even in the confrontations between blacks and whites in cities and labor unions. Such an interaction is a rallying cry for

African Americans who have seized the opportunity to make the once-pejorative term *black* into what Baldwin calls "a badge of honor" (189). Though this confrontation may entail hostile and dangerous reactions, Baldwin clearly implies that it is a necessary crucible for them to go through in order to achieve their identity in modern times. In the context of the late 1960s, this is exactly what he meant by the experience that a person, black or white, must face and use so that the person might acquire his or her identity. Baldwin hoped that the alienation he saw in the South could not repeat itself in the North.

Baldwin's most romantic quest in this book involves the "flower children" he saw walking up and down the Haight-Ashbury section of San Francisco in the late 1960s. While he observed that African Americans then were putting their trust not in flowers but in guns, he believed that the scene brought the true identity to the threshold of its maturity. The flower children, in his view, repudiated their fathers for failing to realize that African Americans were the descendants of white fathers; the flower children, as if in defiance of their elders, treated the black children as their denied brothers. "They were in the streets," he says in reference to the title of the book, "in the hope of becoming whole" (187). To him, the flower children were relying on African Americans so that they could rid themselves of the myth of white supremacy. Baldwin, however, was undeniably a realist. He did not rely on the African Americans who were putting their trust in guns, nor did he trust the flower children. In this episode he is quick to warn African American listeners: "This troubled white person might suddenly decide not to be in trouble and go home—and when he went home, he would be the enemy" (188). In Baldwin's judgment, the flower children of the late 1960s and the early 1970s became neither true rebels nor true lovers, either of whom would be worthy of their name in their search for a national identity. In either case, he argues, perhaps to chide himself, "to mistake a fever for a passion can destroy one's life" (189).

The spectacle of the flower children figures as one of the saddest signs in *No Name in the Street*. Whereas the vision of the young Baldwin was immersed in love and brotherhood, the sensibility of the older Baldwin smacks of shrewdness and prudence. Idealism is replaced by pragmatism, and honesty and sincerity clearly mark the essential attitude with which he approaches the problem of identity in America. Baldwin's skeptical admiration for the flower children casts a sad note because they symbolized the closest point to which African and European Americans had ever come together in their search for understanding.

But at heart Baldwin was not a pessimist and would never be one. These pages, filled with love and tenderness, vividly express his feeling that, through these children, African Americans had learned the truth about themselves. And this conviction, however ephemeral it may have been, contributes to his wishfulness and optimism of the early 1970s. He had come to know the truth, stated before:[4] that African Americans can free themselves as they learn more about European Americans and that "the truth which frees black people will also free white people" (129).

3.

Although *No Name in the Street* is divided into two parts, "Take Me to the Water" and "To Be Baptized," it is not a collection of individual essays. Clearly the respective titles reflect the unity of thoughts that underlies the theme of the quest for a national identity. The epigraph to the first part of the book, taken from a slave song, suggests a rationale for the author's command, "Take Me to the Water": "Great God, then, if I had-a-my way / If I had-a-my way, little children, / I'd tear this building down." Similarly, the second part of the book, "To Be Baptized," has an epigraph quoted from "Traditional": "I told Jesus it would be all right / If He changed my name." The title of the entire book, however, signifies that this search for a viable identity for all Americans ended in failure and, despite their efforts, their true name is as elusive as ever.

Baldwin's attitude toward the failure is also reflected in the style and method of the book. Throughout the book he persists in his belief that the failure to achieve identity was caused by the deep-seated fear Americans had in facing reality. In defending themselves against this fear, both African and European Americans deluded themselves and created fantasies and myths about each other. Whereas his earlier books of essays, particularly *The Fire Next Time,* have demonstrated this fear and predicted its dire consequences, *No Name in the Street* focuses on how it manifests itself in contemporary American life. His voice here is less declamatory; he does not suggest the same burning mission as a spokesman for black people as in his previous works. Rather, he goes about it quietly with the use of impressionism and imagery. He has employed such techniques before, but here he uses them with greater frequency and with a larger canvas at his disposal.

He begins *No Name in the Street* with an anecdote about the rift between him and his stepfather, a well-known event in Baldwin's early life. "I am apparently in my mother's arms," he recalls, "for I am staring at my father [stepfather] over my mother's shoulder . . . and my father smiles." The narrative is abruptly interrupted with an interpolation to indicate that this is not only "a memory" but more significantly "a fantasy." Leaping in time and space, Baldwin then reveals the truth about his father, stated in the past tense: "One of the very last times I saw my father on his feet, I was staring at him over my mother's shoulder—she had come rushing into the room to separate us—and my father was not smiling and neither was I" (4). This is perhaps the strongest impression of the elder Baldwin that was ingrained in Baldwin's childhood memory. By pointing out the tendency of a mere child to delude himself, Baldwin is also directing the reader's attention to the adult world where delusion is a way of life. Such an incident accounts for Baldwin's basic argument for the achievement of identity. He demands that Americans, both white and black, see themselves directly, not through the racial myths that have hampered their vision in the past.

Another childhood incident Baldwin remembers is conveyed as an impression he made of his paternal grandmother, who loved him and tried to protect him from his father's tyranny. Immediately before her death Baldwin was called to her bed and was presented with a gift, an old metal box with a floral design. "*She* thought it was full of candy," he remembers, "and *I* thought it was full of candy, but it wasn't" (4). After her death he discovered that it contained needles and thread, something that any child would least desire. This anecdote vividly portrays not only the child's grief over the passing away of his grandmother, but his painful apprehension of reality—the reality of her death as well as of the gift.

The impressions that derive from his personal experience function as effective motifs in this book. Kinship figures as a foil against the alienation that exists between members of a race as well as between races in America. This is why Baldwin says of Richard Wright that his characterization of Bigger Thomas in *Native Son* is marred by a paucity of feeling the hero has for his fellow human beings.[5] The strongest sense of kinship Baldwin felt as a young boy came from a terrifying experience he had off the Coney Island shore:

> I still remember the slimy sea water and the blinding green—it was not green; it was all the world's snot and vomit; it entered into me; when my head was abruptly lifted out of the water, when I felt my brother's [step-brother's] arms and saw his worried face—his eyes looking steadily into mine with the intense and yet impersonal anxiety of a surgeon, the sky above me not yet in focus, my lungs failing to deliver the mighty scream I had nearly burst with in the depths, my four or five or six-year-old legs kicking—and my brother slung me over his shoulder like a piece of meat, or a much beloved child, and stroke up out of the sea with me, with me! (8)

"I learned," Baldwin tells us, "something about the terror and loneliness and the depth and the height of love" (8).

Well into the middle of "Take Me to the Water," Baldwin plunges himself into the dreary waters of mid-twentieth-century America. This part of the narrative, in contrast to the personal and family episodes preceding it, abounds with experiences that suggest impersonality and superficiality in human relationships. After a long sojourn in France, Baldwin saw his school chum, now a U.S. post-office worker, whom he had not seen since graduation. At once Baldwin felt a sense of alienation that separated the one who was tormented by America's involvement in Vietnam and the one who blindly supported it. Baldwin felt no conceivable relationship to his old friend now, for "that shy, pop-eyed thirteen year old my friend's mother had scolded and loved was no more." His friend's impression of the famous writer, described in Baldwin's own words, is equally poignant: "I was a stranger now . . . and what in the world was I by now but an aging, lonely, sexually dubious, politically outrageous, unspeakably erratic freak?" What impressed Baldwin the most about this encounter was the fact that despite the changes that had occurred in both men, nothing had touched this black man. To Baldwin, his friend was an emblem of the "white-washed" black man who "had been trapped, preserved, in that moment of time" (15–18).

New York City, Baldwin's hometown, also struck him as emblematic of the impersonality and indifference that plagued American life. On his way to the South on a writing assignment, he stopped by the city to rest and to readjust his life—having spent nearly a decade on foreign soil—but all he heard was "beneath the nearly invincible and despairing noise, the sound of many tongues, all struggling for dominance" (51). This sound reminds one of what Stephen Crane in the guise of a tramp heard at the end of "An Experiment in Misery": "The roar of the city in his ear was to him the confusion of strange tongues, babbling heedlessly; it was the clink of coin, the voice of the city's hopes, which were to him no hopes" (Crane 258).

Baldwin's travel down the Southland brought a sense of terror he had never known. It was a time of racial turmoil in Little Rock, Arkansas—the late 1950s, when black children were attempting to attend school in the face of a hostile army and citizenry, confronting the white past and the white present. On this journey Baldwin encountered one of the most powerful Southern politicians, who made himself "sweating drunk" to humiliate another human being. Baldwin distinctly recalls the abjectness of this incident: "With his wet eyes staring up at my face, and his wet hands groping for my cock, we were both, abruptly, in history's ass-pocket." To Baldwin, one who had power in the South still lived with the mentality of a slave owner. This experience convinced Baldwin that black identity in the South was defined by the power of such a man and that a black person's humanity was placed at the service of his fantasies. "If the lives of those children," Baldwin reflects, "were in those wet, despairing hands, if their future was to be read in those wet, blind eyes, there was reason to tremble" (61–62). It is characteristic of the book's structure that the height of terror, as just described, is set against the height of love that the child Baldwin felt when his life was saved by his stepbrother. The narrative in this book moves back and forth with greater intensity and effect between the author's feelings of abjectness and exaltation, isolation and affinity.

Baldwin's style becomes even more effective as his tendency toward rhetorical fastenings and outbursts is replaced by his use of brief, tense images that reflects a control of the narrative voice. For instance, one summer night in Birmingham, Alabama, Baldwin met in a motel room the Reverend Shuttlesworth, a marked man as Martin Luther King, Jr., was. Gravely concerned with Shuttlesworth's safety and fearing that his car might be set with a bomb, Baldwin wanted to warn him as he was about to leave the room. But the minister would not let him. At first, there was only a smile on Shuttlesworth's face; upon closer observation, Baldwin detected that "a shade of sorrow crossed his face, deep, impatient, dark; then it was gone. It was the most impersonal anguish I had ever seen on a man's face." Only later did Baldwin come to realize that the minister then was "wrestling with the mighty fact that the danger in which he stood was as nothing compared to the spiritual horror which drove those who were trying to destroy him" (67). A few pages later, this shadow of darkness and sorrow is compensated for by light and happiness. Baldwin now reminisces about his Paris days—how little he had missed ice cream, hot dogs, Coney Island, the Statue of Liberty, the Empire State Building, but how much he had missed his brothers, sisters, and mother: "I missed the way the dark face closes, the way dark eyes watch, and the way, when a dark face opens, a light seems to go on everywhere . . ." (70–71).

By far the most penetrating image occurs when Baldwin is confronted with the time-worn racial segregation in the Deep South. One pleasant evening in Montgomery, Alabama, he found a restaurant on the corner only a block away from the black residential section of the town. Although the restaurant entrance for white patrons was not clearly marked as in the North, it was apparently recognized by all residents, but not by a stranger like Baldwin. So he went into the restaurant through the wrong entrance: "I will never forget it. I don't know if I can describe it. Everything abruptly froze into what, even at that moment, struck me as a kind of Marx Brothers parody of horror. Every white face turned to stone: the arrival of the messenger of death could not have had a more devastating effect than the appearance in the restaurant doorway of a small, unarmed, utterly astounded black man. I had realized my error as soon as I opened the door: but the absolute terror on all these white faces—I swear that not a soul moved—paralyzed me. They stared at me, I stared at them" (71–72).

In Baldwin's description of the scene, the terror he witnessed on the white faces evokes the poignant sense of isolation that African Americans feel. Then, he reports, one of the waitresses "rushed at me as though to club me down, and she barked—for it was not a human sound: 'What you want, boy? What you want in here?' And then, a decontaminating gesture, 'Right around there, boy. Right around there.'" Baldwin clinches the image of this woman: she had "a face like a rusty hatchet, and eyes like two rusty nails—nails left over from the Crucifixion" (72).

4.

The theme of estrangement dealt with in the first part of the book continues in the second, but greater emphasis is placed on the author's references to contemporary events in American society. Although "To Be Baptized" anticipates America's rebirth, the narrative here consists of scenes that signify a gloomier outlook than in "Take Me to the Water." This is why Baldwin appears obsessed with his memories of black martyrs such as Martin Luther King, Jr., and Malcolm X. But underneath this gloom and disillusionment, there is a sign of renewed hope that says: "these dead . . . shall not have died in vain" (89).

Despite the idea of creation suggested by the title "To Be Baptized," Baldwin's motifs in the latter portion of the book are derived from bitter personal experience. For example, the case of Tony Maynard, his former bodyguard, imprisoned on a murder charge arising from mistaken identity, provides the narrative with a sense of urgency and attests to Baldwin's personal involvement with contemporary affairs.[6] The length and recurrence of the episode throughout this part of the book further demonstrate that Baldwin refuses to remain a purely observant artist but instead becomes a passionate participant in a cause. Since Tony Maynard is treated as a victim of the indifference and hatred that exist in society, this episode also becomes a structural thread connecting to other episodes that otherwise appear fragmentary.[7]

The question still remains as to whether or not Baldwin had come away from the 1960s as a disillusioned American. Throughout *No Name in the*

Street he fluctuates between his feelings of love and hatred as shown by the episodes. From the perspective of his hatred and resignation, the book clearly bodes ill; from the perspective of his love and understanding, though avowedly less frequent, it nevertheless demonstrates that its author remains hopeful.

Only a person who had faith in America could assert at the end of his book: "A person does not lightly elect to oppose his society. One would much rather be at home among one's compatriots than be mocked and detested by them" (194–95). The reader also learns in *No Name in the Street* that Baldwin was in sympathy with black militants such as Huey Newton and black separatists such as Malcolm X. Even from the vantage point of hatred and estrangement which Malcolm X seemed to have represented, Baldwin persists in his usual doctrine of love and brotherhood. "What made him unfamiliar and dangerous," Baldwin writes, "was not his hatred for white people but his love for blacks" (97). When Baldwin declares in the epilogue, "the Western party is over, and the white man's sun has set. Period" (197), one can be puzzled, but at the same time one cannot rule out the possibility of Baldwin's meaning that the sun might also rise in America, this time for both African and European Americans.

CHAPTER 4

If Beale Street Could Talk:
Baldwin's Search for Love and Identity

No Name in the Street, discussed in the previous chapter, is a book of essays Baldwin wrote immediately before *If Beale Street Could Talk* (1974), a later novel. While *No Name in the Street* is a highly theoretical commentary on African American life in the city, the story of Beale Street is a realistic representation. Whereas *No Name in the Street* is a departure from Baldwin's earlier books of essays in expressing his theory of love, *If Beale Street Could Talk* goes a step further in showing how African Americans can deliver that love. In *No Name in the Street,* Baldwin does not talk like an integrationist; rather, he sounds as if he is advocating the ideals of a militant separatist who has no qualms about killing a white enemy. Whatever position he finally took in his polemics, he previously had not dealt with the issue more deliberately and quietly than in this novel. Although the book of essays turns out to be a far more sustained examination of the falsehood to which Americans try to cling than his previous works, it still falls short of Baldwin's universal, humanistic vision, in which love can be seized and re-created as it is in *If Beale Street Could Talk.*

Whenever Baldwin wrote about American society, he became the center of controversy, for his career coincided with one of the most turbulent eras in American history, marked by the Civil Rights movement at home and the Vietnam War abroad. As a realist, he was forced to take a stance in dealing with the current issues of society and of race in particular. He has been both extolled and denounced for his unique vision of racial harmony in America. Praise for his ideas is not difficult to understand because he was not only an eloquent writer but also an acute historian. Modern American society is predominantly urban; black and white people live and work together in the city. Those who looked forward to the future embraced him as a prophet; those who wanted to place politics over history and impose the past on the future dismissed him as a dreamer.

Some black readers also disparaged Baldwin's work. "The black writer," Joyce Carol Oates observed in her review of *If Beale Street Could Talk*, "if he is not being patronized simply for being black, is in danger of being attached for not being black enough. Or he is forced to represent a mass of people, his unique vision assumed to be symbolic of a collective vision" (1–2). An African American writer like Richard Wright is seldom assailed because he not only asserts being black but openly shows his anger as a black man. To Baldwin, Wright's portrayal of the lives of African Americans seems to be directed toward the fictional but realistic presentation of black men's anger. Though sympathetic to this rage, Baldwin sees a basic flaw in Wright's technique, contending that the artist must analyze raw emotion and transform it into an identifiable form and experience.[1] Baldwin cannot approve of Wright's use of violence, which he regards as "gratuitous and compulsive because the root of the violence is never examined. The root is rage" (*Nobody* 151).

This basic difference in vision and technique between Wright and Baldwin has a corollary to the difference between the two types of novels exemplified by *Native Son* and *If Beale Street Could Talk*. Both stories take place in the city—Chicago in the 1930s in Wright's novel and New York in the 1960s in Baldwin's. Bigger Thomas is accused of murder in the first degree for the accidental death of a white girl, and Fonny Hunts is imprisoned for the rape of a Puerto Rican woman, a crime he did not commit. Behind the scenes of racial prejudice, similar in the two novels, lie fundamentally different ideas about the existence of black people in American society. Bigger during his act of liberation becomes aware of his own undoing and creation, but he achieves his manhood at the expense of murdering his girlfriend. Fonny, an artist and an intellectual, consciously aware of the primacy of love, is able to revive the relationship with his girlfriend and achieve his deliverance. Wright's novel, whether it is *Native Son* or *The Outsider,* ends tragically with the death of its hero, and neither of the victims can lead others to the discovery of love. Fonny's search for love and liberation, on the other hand, is accomplished through his genuine sensibility of love, which others can emulate and acquire. Not only does he survive his ordeal, but also his child is to be born.

Baldwin's technique of elucidating this idea of love and deliverance differs from that of a protest novel. *Native Son* was intended to awaken the conscience of white society, and Wright's strategy was necessarily belligerent. To survive in his existence, Bigger is forced to rebel, unlike Fonny who defends himself within the interior of his own heart. Bigger learns how to escape the confines of his environment and gain an identity. Even before he acts, he knows exactly how Mary and, later, Bessie have forced him into a vulnerable position. It is no wonder, then, that he convinces himself not only that he has killed to protect himself but also that he has attacked civilization in its entirety. In contrast to *If Beale Street Could Talk, Native Son* departs from the principles of love and sympathy which people, black or white, have for their fellow human beings. In "How 'Bigger' Was Born," Wright admits that his earlier *Uncle Tom's Children* was "a book which even bankers' daughters could read and weep over and feel good about" ("How 'Bigger' Was Born" xxvii). In *Native Son,* however, Wright could not allow for such complacency. He warns that the book "would be so hard and deep that they would have to face it without the consolation of tears" (xxvii).

The salient device in *If Beale Street Could Talk* is the narrative voice of a nineteen-year-old black girl named Tish. She is Fonny's fiancée and is pregnant with his child. Not only is she a compassionate and lovable woman; her pregnancy also inspires others to have love and hope. Baldwin's concept of love and liberation is realistically conveyed by many of those involved in the story—her husband-to-be, his relatives and her own relatives, the lawyer, the landlord, the restaurant owner, and others regardless of their race. But what makes Baldwin's concept vibrant is Tish's voice, through which the story grows more enriched and spiritualized. Her manner of speech is warm but calm and completely natural. Only through her vision can the reader learn to know the meaning of love and humanity.

By contrast, Wright's authorial voice, as Baldwin noted, succeeds in recording the black anger as no black writer before him had ever done. But it is also the overwhelming limitation of *Native Son.* For Baldwin, what is sacrificed is a necessary dimension to the novel: "the relationship that Negroes bear to one another, that depth of involvement and unspoken recognition of shared experience which creates a way of life . . . it is this climate, common to most Negro protest novels, which has led us all to believe that in Negro life there exists no tradition, no field of manners, no possibility of ritual or intercourse, such as may, for example, sustain the Jew even after he has left his father's house" (Baldwin, *Notes* 27–28).

What Baldwin calls "ritual or intercourse" in African American life is precisely the catalyst for the attainment of love and deliverance in *If Beale Street Could Talk.* To view the relationship between Tish and Fonny as spiritual rather than sexual, genuine rather than materialistic, is commonplace, but to illustrate how it thrives on the strength of the communal bond in African American life is Baldwin's achievement. Baldwin seizes upon this kinship between family members, relatives, friends, and associates. Tommy in Saul Bellow's *Seize the Day,* like Fonny, falls victim to circumstance and changes his family name to Wilhelm. However, he retains his Jewish heritage in his battle of life. "In middle age," Bellow writes about Tommy, "you no longer thought such thoughts about free choice. Then it came over you that from one grandfather you had inherited such and such a head of hair . . . from another, broad thick shoulders; an oddity of speech from one uncle, and small teeth from another, and the gray eyes . . . a wide-lipped mouth like a statue from Peru. . . . From his mother he had gotten sensitive feelings, a soft heart, a brooding nature."[2]

The antithesis to Baldwin's idea of human bonding is the focus of the existentialistic novel *The Outsider*. Cross Damon in *The Outsider*, rejecting his heritage, wishes to be renamed. His mother, the product of the traditional Christianity in the South that taught black children subservient ethics, tries to mold her son's character accordingly. He rebels against his mother, who moans, "To think I named you Cross after the Cross of Jesus" (Wright, *Outsider* 23). As he rejects his mother because she reminds him of Southern Negro piety and racial and sexual repression, he, in so doing, discards her genuine motherly love altogether. Damon's action derives from his nihilistic belief that "man is nothing in particular" (135). At the end of the story, however, Wright expresses a sense of irony about Damon's character. Tasting his agonizing defeat and dying, Damon utters: "I wish I had some way to give the meaning of my life to others . . ." (439).

As if to heed Damon's message, Baldwin challenged the climate of alienation and estrangement that pervaded African American life. Not only did he inspire African Americans to attain their true identity, but, with a tenacity and patience seldom seen among radical writers, he also sought to build bridges between African and European Americans. In contrast to African American writers like Richard Wright and John A. Williams, who fled the Deep South to seek freedom and independence in northern cities, Baldwin always felt that he was a step ahead in his career. "I am a city boy," he declared. "My life began in the Big City, and had to be slugged out, toe to toe, on the city pavements" (*No Name* 59). For him the city was a place where a meaningful human relationship could evolve through both battle and dialogue. As in any confrontation of minds, there would be casualties, but eventually resolution and harmony would emerge. In *Another Country* (1962), a novel of African American life in the city, Rufus Scott, once a successful black drummer in a jazz band but now lonely and desperate, meets a poor white girl from Georgia. They are initially attracted to each other, but eventually she becomes insane and he commits suicide. Even though hate overrules love in their relationship, it is the traditional southern culture in which she was ingrained rather than the estranged environment of New York City that ruins their relationship.

Because *Another Country* is not a polemical tract but a powerful novel, as Granville Hicks recognized (21), it seems to express a subtle but authentic dilemma an African American man faces in America. The novel suggests not only that the South is not a place where black people can have peace of mind and happiness, but also that the city in the North is not a place where they can achieve their identity and freedom. And yet the novel is endowed with the ambivalent notion that America is their destined home. It is well known that Baldwin loved to live in another country. Paris was his favorite city, where he felt one was treated without too much reference to the color of skin. "This means," he wrote, "that one must accept one's nakedness. And nakedness has no color" (*No Name* 23). But Baldwin returned home, as did other American expatriates in the 1920s, and entrusted his fortune to America.[3] In "Many Thousands Gone," he stated, "We cannot escape our origins, however hard we try, those origins which contain the key—could we but find it—to all that we later become" (*Notes* 20).

In search of home, the African American writer naturally turns to the city in the North, where black and white citizens live side-by-side and talk to one another, as Baldwin observed in *No Name in the Street*. Black citizens were drawn to city living only because the interracial relationship in a melting pot could thrive on mutual respect and understanding, the lack of which has historically caused black people's exodus from the South. Such a relationship, as Baldwin quickly warns, is possible only if white people are capable of being fair and having goodwill and if black people themselves are able to achieve their true identity.

It was in the northern cities, as Baldwin witnessed in *No Name in the Street,* that African and European Americans came in close contact with one another. This observation, despite the turbulent, politically divided climate of the nation, contributed to his hopefulness and optimism in the 1970s. By then he had come to know that African Americans can free themselves as they learn more about European Americans. "The truth which frees black people," Baldwin argued, "will also free white people" (*No Name* 129). Baldwin's quest continues in *If Beale Street Could Talk,* for the novel is the catalyst for disseminating this truth. Even though Baldwin stresses the human bonds that exist within the black community, he also recognizes, in his imagination at least, the deep, universal bonds of emotion that tie the hearts of people regardless of their color of skin.

For Baldwin, the bonds that exist on Beale Street are scarcely visible from outside. City life, as depicted by American realists from Stephen Crane and Theodore Dreiser to James T. Farrell and Richard Wright, often creates isolation and loneliness in the residents. The city is a noisy, crowded place, yet people scarcely talk to one another. When Baldwin returned to New York City after a nearly decade-long stay abroad, the city struck him as impersonal and indifferent. Unlike an existentialist in search of individual autonomy in the face of the void of the chaotic and meaningless universe, Baldwin seeks order, meaning, and dreams in an individual's relation to others. A critic has dismissed *If Beale Street Could Talk* as "pretentious and cloying with goodwill and loving kindness and humble fortitude and generalized honorableness" (Aldridge 24–25). But, since Baldwin is a confirmed romantic, his concept of love and honor is expressed with idealism. Neither the turbulence that embroils city life nor the indifference that sweeps over it can destroy his dream.

It is ironic that the impersonality and estrangement that permeate Beale Street compel its residents to seek a stronger and more meaningful relationship with others. Tish, separated from her fiancé in jail, reflects her happy childhood days, "when Daddy used to bring me and Sis here and we'd watch the people and the buildings and Daddy would point out different sights to us and we might stop in Battery Park and have ice cream and hot dogs" (*Beale Street* 9). Later in the story, portraying the crowded subway, an epitome of city life, Baldwin suggests that city inhabitants are forced to protect themselves. When a crowded train arrives at the platform, Tish notices that her father instinctively puts his arm around her as if to shield her from danger. Tish recalls:

> I suddenly looked up into his face. No one can describe this, I really shouldn't try. His face was bigger than the world, his eyes deeper than the sun, more vast than the desert, all that had ever happened since time began was in his face. He smiled: a little smile. I saw his teeth: I saw exactly where the missing tooth had been, that day he spat in my mouth. The train rocked, he held me closer, and a kind of sigh I'd never heard before stifled itself in him. (52)

This image of human bonding also appears as a faint noise coming from Tish and Fonny's unborn child. Tish hears it in the loud bar where she and her sister Ernestine talk about their strategy to get Fonny out of jail:

> Then, we are silent. . . . And I look around me. It's actually a terrible place and I realize that the people here can only suppose that Ernestine and I are tired whores, or a Lesbian couple, or both. Well. We are certainly in it now, and it might get worse. I will, certainly—and now something almost as hard to catch as a whisper in a crowded place, as light and

as definite as a spider's web, strikes below my ribs, stunning and aston-
ishing my heart—get worse. But that light tap, that kick, that signal,
announces to me that what can get worse can get better. (122)

The bonding of African and European Americans in *If Beale Street Could
Talk* could also be solidified, as could the African American kinship, if the
relationship were based upon a mutual understanding of others as individual
human beings, rather than as blacks who have typically been victimized by
white society or as whites who have habitually oppressed blacks under the
banner of racial supremacy. No sooner does one treat another human being
for an economic or political purpose than such a relationship ceases to exist.
To show the possibility of a prosperous relationship between African and
European Americans in the city, Baldwin created many sympathetic portraits
of European Americans. The Jewish lawyer the black families hire to defend
Fonny is initially an ambitious man bent on advancing his career, but later he
becomes an altruistic individual. The Italian woman who owns a vegetable
stand informs the police of a racial harassment committed by a white hood-
lum, thereby helping Fonny, exonerated of his action, to protect Tish, a victim of the white man's insult. The owner of a Spanish restaurant willingly
allows Tish and Fonny to have dinner on credit out of his compassion for
their unjust plight.

For Baldwin, African Americans in the North, in contrast to those in the
South, can move freely and talk frequently with fellow residents. His white
characters, unlike those of Wright, for example, are seldom stereotyped.
Whether they are prejudiced or fair-minded, materialistic or humanistic, they
are always individuals capable of making their own judgments. It seems as
though the spirit of individualism with which they have grown up becomes,
in turn, contagious among black people. In *No Name in the Street,* Baldwin
shows why black men living in Paris were treated as individuals whereas
Algerians were not. "Four hundred years in the West," he argues, "had certainly turned me into a Westerner—there was no way around that. But four
hundred years in the West had also failed to bleach me—there was no way
around *that,* either" (42). The Westernization of African Americans, as
Baldwin would have agreed with Wright, has taken place at a by far swifter
pace in the North than in the South.

Unlike W. E. B. Du Bois and Jean Toomer, who viewed the South with
deep nostalgia, Baldwin, like Richard Wright and John A. Williams, was
repulsed by it. Even though he at times felt an affinity with African
Americans in the South and found his home there, he also found, as does
Richard Henry in *Blues for Mister Charlie* (1965), that once he had lived in

the North he could not go home again. Baldwin's quest for humanity in *If Beale Street Could Talk* is not merely to seek out affinity with African Americans; it is to search the interior of city life and find a human bond in the hearts and souls of the cities' people. The book stresses the conventional and yet universal bonding innate in human beings, a human affinity that can grow between man and woman, members of a family, relatives, friends—a group of any people united in the name of love and understanding.

Fundamental to Baldwin's concept of human bonds is the relationship of love between a man and a woman that yields posterity. What saves Fonny and Tish from loneliness and despair is that they are expecting a child. Every time she visits him in jail, their talk focuses on the unborn baby. Whenever he sees her face during the visit, he knows not only that she loves him but "that others love him, too. . . . He is not alone; we are not alone." When she looks ashamed of her ever-expanding waistline, he is elated, saying, "Here she come! Big *as two* houses! You sure it ain't twins? or triplets? Shit, we *might* make history" (162). While at home, she is comforted by Ray Charles's voice and piano, the sounds and smells of the kitchen, the sounds and "blurred human voices rising from the street." Only then does she realize that "out of this rage and a steady, somehow triumphant sorrow, my baby was slowly being formed" (41).

However crowded, noisy, and chaotic Baldwin's city may be, one can always discover order, meaning, and hope in one's life. The street talks as though conflict and estrangement among the residents compel them to seek their ties with smaller human units. Not only does the birth of a child—the impending birth of Tish and Fonny's baby—constitute the familial bond; it also signals the birth of new America. As noted earlier, Baldwin has theorized this concept in *No Name in the Street,* in which the first half of the book, "Take Me to the Water," depicts the turmoil of American society in the 1960s and the second, "To Be Baptized," prophesies the rebirth of a nation. In the epilogue he writes: "An old world is dying, and a new one, kicking in the belly of its mother, time, announces that it is ready to be born." Alluding to the heavy burden falling upon the American people, he remarks with a bit of humor: "This birth will not be easy, and many of us are doomed to discover that we are exceedingly clumsy midwives. No matter, so long as we accept that our responsibility is to the newborn: the acceptance of responsibility contains the key to the necessarily evolving skill" (196).

Baldwin's extolment of the relationship between Tish and Fonny also suggests that the interracial relationships of love and sex as seen in *Another Country* are often destroyed by the forces of society beyond their control. In such a relationship, genuine love often falls victim to society, a larger human unit. But in this novel Levy, Fonny's landlord, is a personable, happily married young man. Being Jewish, he values the closeness in family life and in the offspring marriage can produce. He willingly rents his loft to Fonny, who needs the space to work on his sculptures, because he is aware of his own happiness in raising children and wants his tenants to share the same joy. "Hell," Levy tells Fonny, "drag out the blankets and sleep on it. . . . Make babies on it. That's how *I* got here. . . . You two should have some beautiful babies . . . and, take it from me, kids, the world damn sure needs them." Out of sympathy for Fonny's situation, he even forgoes payment of the rent while Fonny is in jail, saying, "I want you kids to have your babies. I'm funny that way" (133–34).

As urban society disintegrates because of its indifference and impersonality, the love and understanding that can unite smaller communities—couples, families, relatives, and friends—become essential to the pursuit of happiness in America. Those who are deprived of such relationships cannot survive. Daniel Carty, Fonny's childhood friend, who is also arrested by the D.A.'s office, is a loner. Without ties to his family and relatives, he is doomed. Tony Maynard, Baldwin's former bodyguard, who appears in *No Name in the Street,* is reminiscent of Daniel Carty. Tony is imprisoned on a murder charge arising from mistaken identity.[4] Since the title "To Be Baptized" in *No Name in the Street* suggests the idea of rebirth, Baldwin's motif of alienation, which Tony's episode illustrates in the latter portion of the book seems incongruous. In any event, Tony is treated as a victim of the indifference and hatred that exist in society; like Daniel, he is without the protection of his family and relatives. Ironically, he is a professional bodyguard for a man, but no one else can guard him.

While Baldwin uses biblical references to evoke the idea of rebirth in *No Name in the Street,* he has a penchant to assail, in *If Beale Street Could Talk,* those who find their haven in the church. To him, a long history of the Christian church has partly resulted in slavery in America, and the African Americans "who were given the church and nothing else"[5] have learned to be obedient to the law of God and the land but have failed to be independent thinkers.[6] Mrs. Hunt, Fonny's mother, like Cross Damon's mother in *The Outsider,* has a blind trust in Christ. She even believes that Fonny's imprisonment is "the *Lord's* way of making my boy think on his sins and surrender his soul to Jesus" (64). Her doctor convinces Mrs. Hunt, who has a heart problem, that her health is more important than her son's freedom. By contrast, Fonny's father Frank is a defiant disbeliever. "I don't know," Frank tells his wife, "how God expects a man to act when his son is in trouble. *Your* God crucified *His* son and was probably glad to get rid of him, but I ain't like that.

I ain't hardly going out in the street and kiss the first white cop I see" (65). Although it is tragic that Frank commits suicide when he is caught stealing money to raise funds to defend his son, his actions suggest the genuine feelings of love and tenderness a father can have for his son.

Baldwin ends *If Beale Street Could Talk* on a triumphant note. Fonny is out of jail, however temporally, because of the efforts by those who are genuinely concerned about his welfare. Not only has he been able to endure his ordeal, but his experience in jail has also renewed his human spirit. The last time Tish visits him in jail, he tells her: "Listen, I'll soon be out. I'm coming home because I'm glad I came, can you dig that?" (193). The final scene once again echoes the voice that conveys Baldwin's idea of love and rebirth. Fonny is now a sculptor at work in his studio: "Fonny is working on the wood, on the stone, whistling, smiling. And, from far away, but coming nearer, the baby cries and cries and cries and cries and cries and cries and cries and cries, cries like it means to wake the dead" (197).

Baldwin completed this scene of freedom and rebirth on Columbus Day, October 12, as indicated at the end of the book. The reference to Columbus Day might easily remind the reader of Pudd'nhead Wilson's calendar note for that day in the conclusion of Mark Twain's classic novel of racial prejudice: "*October 12, the Discovery. It was wonderful to find America, but it would have been more wonderful to miss it*" (*Pudd'nhead* 113). While Twain's intention in the book is a satire on American society and on slavery in particular, Baldwin's in *If Beale Street Could Talk* is to discover a new America. In *No Name in the Street* he fluctuates between his feelings of love and hate, between racial harmony and conflict. In *If Beale Street Could Talk*, however, Baldwin's ambivalence has largely disappeared, and the book has painted a rosy cityscape for European and African Americans.

CHAPTER 5

Jazz and Toni Morrison's Urban Imagination of Desire and Subjectivity

1.

For African Americans the city has served as a historical and imaginative site of freedom. A crucial signifier in modern and postmodern African American literature, the city has been described in a rich variety of ways as a reflection of American life. LeRoi Jones cautioned against applying simplistic abstractions to African American cities like Harlem when he said that Harlem "like any other city . . . must escape *any* blank generalizations simply because it is alive, and changing each second with each breath any of its citizens take" (145). For Toni Morrison, the American city has often induced a sense of "alienation" in an African American writer like James Baldwin, but she nevertheless adds that modern African American writing is suffused with an "affection" for "the village within" the city, black neighborhoods which are repositories for life-sustaining "community values" ("City Limits" 37–38).[1] Langston Hughes saw in Harlem the coexistence of affection and alienation: "Harlem of honey and chocolate and caramel and rum and vinegar and lemon and lime and gall. Dusky dream Harlem rumbling into a nightmare tunnel" ("Early Days" 60). The perception of the city as a place of strife and conflict is derived from Thomas Jefferson, who warned that the city would breed corruption and injustice: while farmers were God-chosen people, manufacturers were likely to be greedy and materialistic.

Despite the paucity of humanity and love associated with city life, Harlem in the 1920s was full of joy and excitement. In this juxtaposition of alienation and affection, Morrison has found a dialectic vision, an interaction of conflicting emotions that ultimately leads to fulfillment of desire and attainment of subjectivity. In contrast to European Americans' pastoral idyll in the nineteenth century, Morrison's urban imagination necessarily involves racial difference and struggle. "Romance," Morrison argues, "offered writers not less but more; not a narrow a-historical canvas but a wide historical one; not escape but entanglement" (*Playing in the Dark* 37). To her, *pastoral idyll* was a romantic concept for nineteenth-century European American men, whereas what she reimagines in urban life is a romance for all Americans in the twentieth century and beyond.

Above all, Harlem in the 1920s was a city of paradox to African Americans. The negative aspects of urban life—alienation, antagonism, violence—did not necessarily become negativities in their lives. Because of the inhuman, materialistic atmosphere city life created, Harlemites built within the city a village of community, kinship, and love.[2] The dreams of freedom and subjectivity Harlemites cherished were so powerful that they submerged the frightening characteristics of the city. As Langston Hughes said: "What happens to a dream deferred? / . . . / Or fester like a sore— / . . . / Does it stink like rotten meat? / . . . / Maybe it just sags / like a heavy load. / *Or does it explode?*" (*Selected Poems* 268). The Harlem of the 1920s presented itself as a city of contradiction: while it was described as an extraordinarily exciting place with its legendary rent parties, it was also, as Cary D. Wintz has described, "half-buried beneath the filth and garbage of the city slum" (29).

Morrison suggests that because of this paradox, the African American dream of freedom and subjectivity could be achieved only if the racial struggle would squarely be confronted and conquered by all Americans: "The rights of man, for example, an organizing principle upon which the nation was founded . . . [were] inevitably yoked to Africanism. . . . Black slavery enriched the country's creative possibilities" (*Playing in the Dark* 38). Without the presence of racial difference, and of slavery in particular, American civilization, a culture known as an exemplar of freedom and democracy, would not have prospered. Granted, the massive movement of African Americans to northern cities in the early decades of the twentieth century created racial problems, but, in so doing, it also stimulated American culture.

In stark contrast to the situation in the South, where African Americans were not allowed to communicate freely with European Americans, the crowded, noisy apartments in the northern cities became hubs of interracial mingling and dialogue, a site where migrant African Americans came in contact with what Richard Wright called "the brisk, clipped men of the North, the Bosses of Buildings." Unlike southern landlords, city businessmen, intrigued with black people's life style, intermingled with African American

men (*12 Million* 100). As a result, the African American man of the industrial North was given a chance to shape his own life. Economically he was a
machine, and his production was measured not by his race but by his merit.
Despite the severe living conditions in which African Americans were placed,
the fierce competition they faced, and the traumas they suffered, the city nevertheless provided them with possibilities for equality and justice.[3]
Paradoxically, African Americans, subjected as they were to machine culture,
acquired in their urban living the practical concept of independence and
subjectivity.

2.

Just as most of her twentieth-century predecessors focused their racial discourse upon the city, Morrison too uses the city as a trope for freedom.
Although the American city in the nineteenth century is known for less
squalor and violence than in modern times, it is nevertheless described as a
place of conflict and friction. Those who were unable to endure such a social
environment sought to live in close contact with nature, as did Ishmael of
Moby-Dick and Huck Finn, where the Oceans and the River figured as signifiers of nature, peace of mind. In contemporary American fiction, as in *Jazz*
(1993), urban living dominates American life; people in the city try to live in
harmony or at least are conscious of diversity in the population. Just as
European Americans like Ishmael and Huck Finn looked for scenes of pastoral idyll, many contemporary Americans try to find their comfort in urban
living.

For Violet Trace in *Jazz,* living in the North "messed up" her own life: not
only did it oppress her life but it also prevented her from gaining a sense of
identity and individuality. Toward the end of the book Violet agrees with
Felice, who declares: "Living in the City was the best thing in the world.
What can you do out in the country? When I visited Tuxedo, back when I
was a child, even then I was bored. How many trees can you look at? That's
what I said to her. 'How many trees can you look at? And for how long and
so what?'" (207). Indeed, in *Jazz* Morrison poignantly portrays the city of the
Harlem Renaissance as a site of freedom and subjectivity, where the African
American was free to think and act as a subject in his or her spiritual, economic, social, and political life.[4] In fact, the African American of the Harlem
Renaissance was so mobile and interactive with others in the community that
the personal vision of life became impersonal, objective, and free of egotism.

In *Playing in the Dark: Whiteness and the Literary Imagination* (1993),

Morrison suggested that the city made it possible for African and European Americans to live side-by-side. Through the Africanist presence European Americans learned the truth about themselves, whose goal in life was pursuit of the American Dream, the faith and spirit that "rhetorically repudiated an adoration of the Old World and defined the past as corrupt and indefensible" (48). Just as Jim's freedom led to Huck's freedom and independence, European Americans, Morrison emphasizes, acquired the true vision of themselves, the recognition that they themselves were not truly free and that African Americans were "unfree" (48) in a free, democratic nation, a blatant contradiction in terms of the Constitution. It is also ironic that both European and African Americans, who sought individual freedom in rural communities, found it instead in urban life.

To stave off their isolation and boredom in the country, African American women like Violet and Felice seek excitement which the city offers. Their ultimate desire is to satisfy not merely their body but their need for social relationship. Morrison's discourse of urban life is based on history and conveyed by realism. In contrast to the feelings of conflict and loneliness from which Ishmael suffers at the outset of *Moby-Dick* as he finds himself in "a damp, drizzly November" (12) in his soul, the arrival of spring in Harlem in *Jazz* provides the residents with renewal of their spirit. "And when spring comes to the City," the narrator sees, "people notice one another in the road; notice the strangers with whom they share aisles and tables and the space where intimate garments are laundered" (117). Although she first finds spring in the city contradictory because it encourages people to buy food when they have no appetite, she finds it natural for "beat bricks" to warm up to the sun, tar to soften when they walk, "the darkness under bridges" to change from "gloom to cooling shade," and wet leaves and tree limbs to look like "wet fingers playing in woolly green hair" (118). The city even creates a condition in which the residents are made aware of what Richard Wright defines in *Black Power* as Africans' "primal outlook upon life" (266), an innate philosophy of life based on their awe of nature.[5]

Not only does much of the expression and representation in *Jazz* spring up from nature, but Morrison is also always concerned with nature's social implications. Critics and historians, as she has complained, tend to dilute her realism by attributing her writing to the magical in her work (*Conversations with Morrison* 226). Throughout the story, *Jazz* is replete with images of freedom. At the outset the narrator mentions, for example, that some of the city hospitals employ black surgeons and nurses (7–8). Violet lets her pet birds out when she goes to Dorcas's funeral with a knife (13). At the midpoint of the story the narrator calls the reader's attention to wage discrimination for black laborers in the city as well as in the country: "Rumor was the pay was ten cents for young women, a quarter for men. . . . It all had to be done in three weeks or less. Everybody with fingers in a twenty-mile radius showed up and was hired on the spot. Nine dollars a bale, some said, if you grew your own; eleven dollars if you had a white friend to carry it up for pricing" (102–3). Reflecting on Joe Trace's love of children, the narrator implies that African Americans' desire for kinship notwithstanding, they do not want "the trouble" of raising children and that they cannot bear their children's mistreatment by a racist society (107).[6] Toward the end of the story the narrator's blending of representations of nature and society continues. For Joe Trace, images of honey, shit, river holes, trout, and flies all evoke his feelings about nature as well as about society. The narrator says: "Nothing stirred and he could not persuade himself that the fragrance that floated over him was not a mixture of honey and shit" (177). In *Jazz*, not only do the images of nature and society mesh, but society also bears the mockery and wrath of nature.

Joe and Violet's motive to escape from the country was to establish in Harlem their latent kinship and friendship with their neighbors. Early on, the narrator traces their courtship and marriage: Violet chose to marry Joe "for him, helping him escape all the redwings in the country and the ripe silence that accompanied them" (30). As if to create the better of the two worlds, once they arrived in the city they actively sought social companionship but later occupied themselves with organic gardening. While such racial strife as white and black landlords' fighting over black renters for the high rents was taking place, Joe and Violet were eager to build an uptown urban pastoral of their own. "The buildings were like castles in pictures," Joe boasts, "and we who had cleaned up everybody's mess since the beginning knew better than anybody how to keep them nice. We had birds and plants everywhere, me and Violet. I gathered up the street droppings myself to fertilize them. . . . Pay was light, but the tips dropped in my palm fast as pecans in November" (127–28).

Morrison's representation of urban life as a trope for freedom and excitement also signifies nostalgia for the pastoral idyll people like Joe and Violet left behind as they moved to Harlem. On the one hand, the narrator mentions Violet's enjoyment of rent parties, a legendary form of exciting social life Langston Hughes vividly portrays in his autobiography *The Big Seas;* on the other, the narrator depicts Violet as a lonely woman "who speaks mainly to her birds" (24) and who used to enjoy watching trees and birds in the country.

While Morrison makes her signification expansive, she also reverses it. Whether she creates images of peace and harmony out of rural nature or out of the mood of pastoral idyll retrieved in urban living—her vision of the village within the city—*Jazz* becomes her deconstruction and transformation of the conventional, predictable discourse of nature, on which nineteenth-century American fiction thrived. Just as Stephen Crane in "The Open Boat" viewed nature as utterly indifferent and often hostile to humankind, Morrison warns the reader: "Nature freaks for you. . . . Spreads the limbs of lilac bushes low enough to hide you" (63). But the city,

> in its own way, gets down for you, cooperates, smoothing its sidewalks, correcting its curbstones, offering you melons and green apples on the corner. Racks of yellow head scarves; strings of Egyptian beads. Kansas fried chicken and something with raisins call attention to an open window where the aroma seems to lurk. And if that's not enough, doors to speakeasies stand ajar and in that cool dark place a clarinet coughs and clears its throat waiting for the woman to decide on the key. (63–64)

The negative aspect of nature in view, in turn, enhances the spirit of urban life: a dialectic vision of nature and society underlies Morrison's urban imagination.

What distinguishes her expression in *Jazz* from her earlier fiction is paradox. Any reader knows that the city is crowded and polluted, and earlier in the story the narrator says: "There is no air in the City but there is breath" (34). Although rural life can boast open space and natural beauty, to urban residents these images smack of loneliness and lack of human spirit. "I have seen the City do an unbelievable sky," reports the narrator. "Redcaps and dining-car attendants who wouldn't think of moving out of the City sometimes go on at great length about country skies they have seen from the windows of trains. But there is nothing to beat what the City can make of a nightsky. It can empty itself of surface, and more like the ocean than the ocean itself, go deep, starless" (35). Paradoxically the city, a "deep, starless," open space, is likely to accommodate what human beings most desire—freedom and love. "Close up on the tops of buildings, near, nearer than the cap you are wearing," the narrator says, "such a citysky presses and retreats, presses and retreats, making me think of the free but illegal love of sweethearts before they are discovered" (35). Strangers in Harlem, then, are not really strangers; they may become friends and lovers: "Dorcas and Felice are not strangers at the party—nobody is" (65).

Morrison's racial discourse in *Jazz* not only reads as paradoxical; it is also intent upon a deconstruction of Western discourse. At times her description of natural objects expresses a candid opposition to the traditional, hegemon-

ic worldview. Toward the end of the book, the narrator, describing in retrospect Joe Trace's search for Dorcas, focuses her representation on a tree that
is reminiscent of Dorcas:

> The third time Joe had tried to find her (he was a married man by then)
> he had searched the hillside for the tree—the one whose roots grew back-
> ward as though, having gone obediently into earth and found it barren,
> retreating to the trunk for what was needed. Defiant and against logic its
> roots climbed. Toward leaves, light, wind. (182)

For the reader used to the depiction of nature by transcendentalists like
Emerson and Thoreau or romantics like Hawthorne and Melville, Morrison's
description of the roots growing "obediently into earth" appears quite natural, for such an image conforms to the conventional worldview. On second
thought, however, the narrator realizes that the roots "grew backward as
though . . . retreating to the trunk . . . against logic," an action described not
only metonymically but critically, with a protesting voice.

"Below that tree," Morrison finally reminds the postmodern, postcolonial
reader, "was the river whites called Treason where fish raced to the line, and
swimming among them could be riotous or serene. But to get there you
risked treachery by the very ground you walked on." In *Jazz* the theme of
African American freedom is eloquently expressed by this passage:

> The slopes and low hills that fell gently toward the river only appeared
> welcoming; underneath vines, carpet grass, wild grape, hibiscus and
> wood sorrel, the ground was as porous as a sieve. A step could swallow
> your foot or your whole self. (182)

However conciliatory and inviting the white world may appear, it still hides
underneath its age-long condescension and complex of racial superiority.

3.

Jazz is intended to be not only a battle against racism but more importantly
a blueprint for fulfillment of African American desire. The book demonstrates that only when "the village within" is established in the city will
African Americans be able to fulfill their desire. Morrison's attempt to equate
desire with sexuality through jazz is corroborated by Richard Wright's view of
jazz. As Keneth Kinnamon and Michel Fabre have noted: "In Harlem

Richard Wright was familiarly known as 'Dick.' He was familiar with black music. Frank Tenot interviewed him for *Cahiers* a few days before his death" (242). He told Tenot: "Not to be a black bourgeois and to understand that the main gift that jazz has to offer the world today is an affirmation of *desire*. In spirituals and in Ray Charles—I repeat—there's the same erotic exultation. This aspect of black music has been denied for too long. The faith of mystics and of most blacks has a sexual ingredient which well meaning people are too timid to dare admit, but which must be proclaimed" (*Conversations with Wright* 242–43).

Whether one is consciously aware of desire or not, Morrison suggests, one must act upon it. If not acted upon, desire might desert the person. For Morrison, jazz is the best means of expressing not only desire itself but also its insatiability:

> I think about what Black writers do as having a quality of hunger and disturbance that never ends. Classical music satisfies and closes. Black music does not do that. Jazz always keeps you on edge. There is no final chord. There may be a long chord, but no final chord. (qtd. in McKay 429)

Violet Trace confides to Alice Manfred: "I'm fifty and I don't know nothing. What about it? Do I stay with him? I want to, I think. I want . . . well, I didn't always . . . now I want. I want some fat in this life." Alice responds in earnest: "Wake up. Fat or lean, you got just one. This is it" (110). The initial antagonism between them notwithstanding, their relationship has developed into one of deep kinship in search of the meaning of love, a true understanding of female desire that only women like them, in this stage of life, can share. Morrison urges, through Alice, that one must cling to a relationship of desire, however precariously it may come into one's life. And, for Morrison, the city is the perfect site to generate and keep fulfilling one's desire.

With his "wife . . . sleeping with a doll," Joe Trace, "a grown man," seeks love in Dorcas, "an eighteen-year-old girl" (129). As his unfulfilled desire and unrequited love seem to satisfy themselves with an act of utmost violence— the murder of his love—so do those of Violet transform themselves into jealousy and violence. Such actions of desire and love dramatized in this novel appear highly predictable, and yet the way in which Morrison represents them is not only metonymic—since Violet's name signifies desire and violence as Trace's does search and discovery—but also realistic. Morrison draws on the city as an open space large enough to contain virtue and vice, excitement and frustration: "The husband shot; the wife stabbed. Nothing. Nothing her niece did or tried could equal the violence done to her. . . .

Gambling. Cursing. A terrible and nasty closeness. Red dresses. Yellow shoes." Morrison sees all these excitements and frustrations powerfully expressed by jazz, what she calls "race music to urge them on" (79).

Above all, urban strife stimulates desire and generates love. To accommodate desire and love, the city must create more space for both the public self and the private world. Paradoxically, urban life, replete with social interaction and public gaze, creates more privacy. The narrator finds fifty-year-old African American women like Violet and Alice to be freer and more liberated than they realize, and she encourages them to fulfill their desire with a man like Joe Trace. "In a group such as this one," she says, "they could do with impunity what they were cautious about alone with any man, stranger or friend, who rang the doorbell . . ." (71). To these women, Joe is an attractive man both as a private and a public persona. In search of his love, Dorcas, Joe looks for "signs of her, recognizing none" (183), but he finally finds her at a place the narrator calls "a private place, with an opening closed to the public." Once you got inside, "you could do what you pleased: disrupt things, rummage, touch and move" (184). As public life stimulates desire, private life satisfies it. In this novel, desire and love are metonymically represented as both public and private.

Morrison's exploration of desire in *Jazz* reaches its climax at the midpoint of the story when spring arrives in Harlem. This timing strikes the reader as natural and spontaneous because spring in the Northern Hemisphere brings renewal of life on Earth. For young and old Harlemites, spring—perhaps a season of emotion just as autumn is a season of intellect—stimulates one's latent desire. Focusing on Dorcas, the narrator says: "Committed as Violet was to hip development, even she couldn't drink the remaining malt— watery, warm and flat-tasting. She buttoned her coat and left the drugstore and noticed, at the same moment as *that* Violet did, that it was spring. In the City" (114). Even children look as if they were crying for love: after a light rain, the "faces of children glimpsed at windows appear to be crying, but it is the glass pane dripping that makes it seem so" (118).

T. S. Eliot, imagining his cityscape as a wasteland, depicted April as "the cruellest month, breeding / Lilacs out of the dead land, mixing / Memory and desire, stirring / Dull roots with spring rain" (37). Whereas Eliot's representation, in keeping with the modernist temper, strikes the postmodern reader as overtly depressive—perhaps even cynical and conceited—Morrison reflects the sentiments of earlier American realists like Henry James and Theodore Dreiser as they drew upon urban life. In *The Ambassadors* James's voyeuristic gaze reveals, in its climactic episode, the fulfillment of desire by Chad Newsome and Mme de Vionnet as they ride on a boat near Paris in spring, however fleeting the moment might be. In *Sister Carrie* Hurstwood, who has fallen victim to the economic depression that has hit New York, reminisces about "the blissful spirit" of spring: when he saw Carrie "in the little park in Chicago—how happy he would be!" (316).[7]

Once the feeling of desire has been evoked by scenes of nature, Morrison's representation swiftly glides to reflections upon sexuality. As Dorcas lies dying, she is likened to Eve. Joe speaks to Dorcas:

> I told you again that you were the reason Adam ate the apple and its core. That when he left Eden, he left a rich man. Not only did he have Eve, but he had the taste of the first apple in the world in his mouth for the rest of his life. The very first to know what it was like. To bite it, bite it down. Hear the crunch and let the red peeling break his heart. (133)

Morrison's allusion is transparent and may strike the reader as contrived, but remarkably the representation immediately glides back to a realistic rendition of human action. Trying to convince Dorcas of his love for her, Joe tells her, "I didn't fall in love, I rose in it," expressing a genuinely spiritual and physical action of his desire. It is even more remarkable for Morrison to make her representation slide further back to the origin of its evocation, a realistic description of nature and character. In the same breath Joe tells Dorcas: "Those old people, they knew it all. I talk about being new seven times before I met you, but back then, back there, if you was or claimed to be colored, you had to be new and stay the same every day the sun rose and every night it dropped" (135).

Earlier in the story, desire is viewed as natural, arising spontaneously from spiritual and social interactions. "On those nights," Morrison tells us, "Joe does not mind lying awake next to his silent wife because his thoughts are with this young good God young girl who both blesses his life and makes him wish he had never been born" (40). Just as rest and boredom cause desire to stagnate, an active social life, which signals bodily interaction, generates desire. To many women of Harlem, like Violet, the notion of rest is comforting and peaceful, but they "are busy and thinking of ways to be busier because such a space of nothing pressing to do would knock them down" (16).

City living, then, creates desire in and love for everyone. The way Morrison draws on this process of creation is not analogous but extensive, not metaphoric but metonymic. When she talks about desire and love, she does so in terms of environment, an image of "blocks and lots and side streets" (9). *Jazz* begins its story with a discourse on the city, in which Morrison's imagination of desire and love is reified in what went on in the city of the Harlem Renaissance in the late 1920s before the great economic depression. "Nobody says," she declares, "it's pretty here; nobody says it's easy either. What it is is decisive, and if you pay attention to the street plans, all laid out, the City can't hurt you." To her the city creates autonomy, and its spirit is contagious: "I like the way the City makes people think they can do what they want and get away with it" (8). "All you have to do," she admonishes, "is heed the design— the way it's laid out for you, considerate, mindful of where you want to go and what you might need tomorrow" (9). One representation of desire in *Jazz* leads to another in time and space, thereby spreading its impact on the characters involved as the story unfolds. Desire leads to belief: Morrison finds that desire transforms into a sense of individuality and subjectivity.

Once subjectivity has been attained, it generates its own energy and, in turn, influences desire, its origin. Remindful of Ezra Pound's theory of imagism in his "Vorticism" essay, Morrison's image in *Jazz* is not a static, rational idea.[8] Because subjectivity, once achieved, is no longer a passive state of mind, it becomes an active image endowed with desire, its own energy. At the end of this initial discourse on the city, Morrison says: "Hospitality is gold in this City; you have to be clever to figure out how to be welcoming and defensive at the same time. When to love something and when to quit" (9). To Morrison, desire, yielding subjectivity, is in turn guided by willpower and judgment. Her imagination of the cityscape in *Jazz* also influences her treatment of the major characters. The ordeal and dilemma one individual experiences influences another in his or her attainment of subjectivity: as in Pound's vortex, one's desire influences another's and, in so doing, yields subjectivity for one another. At the outset of the story Alice Manfred and Violet Trace appear as victim and transgressor, respectively, but in the end they come to share the same female subjectivity and worldview.[9] As Alice comes to understand Violet's traumatic childhood, so does Violet sympathize with Alice's puritanical background. It is only in urban society that dialogue between strangers takes place and makes a crucial impact upon them in building character.

In Morrison's characterization, desire is also treated dialectically. In the beginning Violet becomes jealous of Joe's desire for Dorcas, but later Violet feels as if she is falling in love with Dorcas. To Violet the city functions as a site for inspiring desire in her life, that is, her love for an "adopted" daughter named Dorcas: "Not realizing that, bitch or dumpling, the two of them, mother and daughter, could have walked Broadway together and ogled the clothes. Could be sitting together, cozy in the kitchen, while Violet did her hair" (109). Whether Violet will be able to revive her love for Joe is unclear toward the end of the book, but they do continue to live together. At least,

Violet's desire for Dorcas is reified in retrospect. For Violet, desire was disguised as jealousy when Dorcas was alive, but it has now resulted in love for the woman she used to hate.

It is Morrison's urban imagination that has transformed desire into love. The city creates an open space large enough for love and hate to coexist. The most powerful vehicle to convey all these conflicting emotions and experiences in urban life is jazz. It is the jazz music reverberating in the city of the Harlem Renaissance that enables Morrison to challenge and erase the traditional oppositions of love and hate, success and failure, happiness and sorrow.

4.

Not only does *Jazz* concern African Americans' fulfillment of desire, but Morrison's ultimate intention is to inscribe in the memory of the Harlem-Renaissance city their achievement of subjectivity. "My project," Morrison has stated, "is an effort to avert the critical gaze from the racial object to the racial subject; from the described and imagined to the describers and imaginers; from the serving to the served" (*Playing in the Dark* 90). To destroy European Americans' racial prejudice and condescension and to establish their own individuality and autonomy, African Americans must create a discourse in which their life is envisioned not as a sociological case study but as an imaginative subject matter. The racial discourse in *Jazz,* as Morrison argues in *Playing in the Dark,* will not only enrich contemporary American culture but make her writing analytical and critical rather than polemical and political. "All of us, readers and writers," she concludes, "are bereft when criticism remains too polite or too fearful to notice a disrupting darkness before its eyes" (91). Her reimagination of the Harlem Renaissance in *Jazz* enables her to demonstrate African American subjectivity.

Her plan to use jazz music as a metonym for African American subjectivity is foregrounded by a quotation, the book's epilogue, from "Thunder, Perfect Mind," *The Nag Hammadi:*

> I am the name of the sound
>> and the sound of the name.
> I am the sign of the letter
>> and the designation of the division.

At the beginning of the book the concept of subjectivity is contrasted with that of objectivity, a view of African Americans as the racial object. Using the sound of jazz as a sign of subjectivity, Morrison says: "A city like this one makes me dream tall and feel in on things." It is the jazz music of "the City in 1926 when all the wars are over and there will never be another one" that inspired Harlemites to achieve their subjectivity. Not only does the African American woman "dream tall"; she feels "strong. Alone, yes, but top-notch and indestructible." But she notices that "[b]elow is shadow where any blasé, thing takes place: clarinets and lovemaking, fists and the voices of sorrowful women" (7). Just as the sound of sorrow and frustration is conveyed by the blues, that of joy and hope is expressed by jazz.

In *Jazz* Morrison creates Violet, the central character, portrayed in the beginning as a naive, inexperienced African American woman but in the end as one who achieves her subjectivity. As if in a female *Bildüngsroman,* Morrison traces Violet's development through her battle of life. As the story begins, Violet appears as a trope for shadowy women of unrequited love, frustration, and sorrow. Through her ordeal, however, she begins to realize that Dorcas, her archrival, is much like herself: she has failed to understand the values of independence and individualism.

Violet also gains her identity by confronting her other rival, Felice. To Felice, Dorcas is a woman who has succeeded socially but failed to establish autonomy in her life. As Felice tells the narrator, Dorcas "was always talking about who was good looking and who wasn't. Who had bad breath, who had nice clothes, who could dance, who was hincty" (200). By contrast, Felice was an individualist, a type of African American woman Violet should have emulated in her girlhood. "I didn't have a lot of friends in school," Felice recollects. "Not the boys but the girls in my school bunched off according to their skin color. I hate that stuff—Dorcas too. So me and her were different that way" (200–201). Felice's recollection of Dorcas's social life is ambiguous because it is not clear whether Dorcas, like Felice, detested the way in which social life among African Americans was determined by their skin color. But at least Violet becomes aware that her husband's desire for Dorcas is partly motivated by the fact that Dorcas is lighter in skin color than Violet. It is Felice who finally makes Violet realize that Violet, like Dorcas, is a social conformist. "My life," Violet is quoted as saying. "I just ran up and down the streets wishing I was somebody else" (208).

Early in the story Felice is introduced as a friend of Dorcas's, but toward the end she assumes the role of inspiring Violet with subjectivity.[10] At first, Felice is seen carrying "an Okeh record under her arm and a half pound of stewmeat wrapped in pink butcher paper in her hand although the sun is too hot to linger in the streets with meat" (197–98). Regarding her as a lazy girl, the narrator ironically remarks that her "arms are full but there is nothing much in her head" (198). To the reader, she seems a young woman interested only in contemporary music. Defying logic and common sense, she appears to possess a mind of her own. It is little wonder, then, that toward the end of the story the narrator thinks: "Now she is disturbing me, making me doubt my own self just looking at her sauntering through the sunshafts like that. Climbing the steps now, heading for Violent [Violet]" (198).

One of the salient characteristics of jazz music is the expression of happiness rather than of sorrow, as Felice's name itself implies. More importantly, however, jazz is used in this novel as a means by which African Americans are inspired to achieve their subjectivity.[11] "The Louis Armstrong catalyst," Morrison notes in *Playing in the Dark,* "was an addition to this file [her critical moments of discovery] and encouraged me to reflect on the consequences of jazz—its visceral, emotional, and intellectual impact on the listener" (viii). Jazz, as Morrison has recognized in her work, has a thematic as well as a technical impact on the listener—on both a fictional character and a novelist.

As the story unfolds in *Jazz,* Morrison explores the various events in which subjectivity finds its expressions and representations. Initially she focuses on the courtship of Violet and Joe. Tracing their country backgrounds in the South and their recent arrival in Harlem, she merely points out: "They were drawn together because they had been put together, and all they decided for themselves was when and where to meet at night" (30). For them subjectivity does not simply mean freedom from racial oppression in the South; it is a sign of creation and progression, the twin actions that urban mood and urban music are urging upon them. "Joe and Violet," Morrison remarks, "wouldn't think of it—paying money for a meal they had not missed and that required them to sit still at, or worse, separated by, a table. Not now. Not entering the lip of the City dancing all the way." Paradoxically, lack of space in the city creates more action and generates more desire: "Her hip bones rubbed this thigh as they stood in the aisle unable to stop smiling. They weren't even there yet and already the City was speaking to them. They were dancing." The rhythm of jazz represents an undulating movement that urges the listener into progression instead of regression. "However they came, when or why," Morrison emphasizes, "the minute the leather of their soles hit the pavement—there was no turning around" (32).

For Alice Manfred, the sound of drums she heard from a marching band in progress down Fifth Avenue on the Fourth of July, 1917, became a sign of liberty and pursuit of happiness, "a couple of promises from the Declaration of Independence" (53). To many of the listeners of the drums, however, the sound remained a sign, not an action, a natural objective image, not a Poundian subjective image as mentioned earlier. It is ironic that the drums could express "what the graceful women and the marching men could not" (53). As Alice marveled at the cold, quiet black faces despite a typically warm, sticky, but bright summer day, she was deeply moved by the power of the drums. The drums, she saw, were building a space into which the cold, quiet, beautiful black faces were moving. "The drums and the freezing faces hurt her," Morrison says, "but hurt was better than fear and Alice had been frightened for a long time" (54). Alice herself now learned how to conduct her own life and, in turn, help others:

> Now, down Fifth Avenue from curb to curb, came a tide of cold black faces, speechless and unblinking because what they meant to say but did not trust themselves to say the drums said for them, and what they had seen with their own eyes and through the eyes of others the drums described to a T. The hurt hurt her, but the fear was gone at last. Fifth Avenue was put into focus now and so was her protection of the newly orphaned girl in her charge. (54)

The sound of drums has the effect of urging on a mature, middle-aged African American woman like Alice to seek liberty and happiness, but more importantly it inspires her with a sense of individuality, responsibility, and altruism.

By contrast, for young women like Dorcas and Felice, the impact of music on their actions is illusive and paradoxical.[12] As they dance to the music, they "believe they know before the music does what their hands, their feet are to do, but that illusion is the music's secret drive: the control it tricks them into believing is theirs; the anticipation it anticipates" (65). What Morrison calls "a City seeping music" is urging them to generate a spirit of adventure, as if to say there will be nothing to lose but everything to gain: "Come," the music says. "Come and do wrong" (67). Jazz, an urban music, has the power of changing Dorcas's private self to her public self: Dorcas is likened to a swollen fish, an airship floating like "a private dream" (67). The spirit of liberty and autonomy felt by young and old women alike is contagious: "Even the grandmothers sweeping the stairs closed their eyes and held their heads back as they celebrated their sweet desolation" (67–68). Throughout *Jazz,* female subjectivity signifies not only racial freedom but also courage not fear, audacity not stoicism, involvement not isolation.

Violet's attainment of a sense of individualism and independence is more complex than Joe's. As he makes himself a subject, always trying to do what he desires for himself, he also wants Dorcas to be herself. Joe wishes that Dorcas would want to be a subject as well and gain her own identity, but she wants to be an object of male desire, what her lover Acton wants her to be. Violet now admits to Felice that Violet while young has been unable to attain her identity as a subject. Violet used to wish she had been whiter, lighter, younger than were her competitors so that she had been more attractive; she used to regard herself as an object of male desire. Her jealousy of Joe's desire for Dorcas and her violent attack on Dorcas's dead body transform her into one who understands the true meaning of individualism and independence. When Felice inquires her about how she has rid herself of an image that was not the real Violet, she replies, "Killed her. Then I killed the me that killed her" (209). If Joe's subjectivity means self-centeredness, egotism, and self-love, then Violet's subjectivity signifies self-mastery, altruism, and kinship.

More significantly, Violet's achievement of subjectivity suggests that Morrison's heroine has acquired a sense of transcendence. She has succeeded in transcending the traditional, sexist limits of regarding self either as a subject or as an object. Her new state of mind is akin to the state of nothingness, one of the doctrines in Zen philosophy. This enlightenment in Zen, which transcends even the consciousness of self, yields the state of nothingness. The state of nothingness, however, is not equated with a state of void, but it is instructive in that it has the function of cleansing the subject of egotism. Because this state of mind is free of self-centered, materialistic, and sexist desire, it is often likened to the spirit of nature.

Another doctrine in Zen calls for its follower to "kill Buddha." To attain the state of nothingness, one must annihilate not merely self but more importantly the self relying upon Buddha. Although Morrison's characterization of Violet toward the end of the book does not directly concern annihilation of Buddha, Violet's achievement of subjectivity bears a close resemblance to the doctrine of self-annihilation as prerequisite to attaining the state of nothingness. When Violet says, "Then I killed the me that killed her" (209), she means that she annihilated the old self to create the new one. Following Zen doctrine, one might argue that by both "the me" and "her," Violet means the old self. "I," the new self, then, signifies the state of nothingness. One might also construe what the old Violet, whom Morrison calls "Violent," has relied upon in her marriage as meaning Joe Trace. If Violet had relied upon Joe as her God, or Buddha, one might interpret her achievement of subjectivity in terms of Zen enlightenment.

Whether Violet's transcendence of subjectivity will lead to her happiness for the rest of her life is beyond the scope of the story. But the ending of the story clearly suggests that Felice has also achieved a sense of individuality and subjectivity. Although the narrator says, "I saw the three of them, Felice, Joe and Violet, and they looked to me like a mirror image of Dorcas, Joe, and

Violet" (221), the reader well remembers that Felice and Dorcas are developed as antithetical representations of female subjectivity. From Dorcas's tragedy, Felice has learned that she no longer wants to be an object of male desire as Dorcas was. It is debatable whether or not Felice at the end of the story is inclined to emulate Violet's transcendence of subjectivity. Zen teaches its followers that the state of nothingness will lead to happiness and peace of mind. It is also of interest to conjecture the motive behind Morrison's naming her Felice, "Happiness." By contrast, Dorcas represents a young African American woman who has fallen victim to male subjectivity. Morrison must have marveled at the love triangle of Dorcas, Joe, and Violet, pitted against that of Felice, Joe, and Violet; in fact Dorcas's tragic death led to Felice's happy life. The naming of Dorcas is also interesting, perhaps ironic, for it suggests a biblical allusion to selflessness as well as to altruism.

Morrison's ironic representations of Violet, Felice, and Dorcas notwithstanding, Joe Trace remains the most undeveloped character. By tracing Joe's background, however, the reader can discern his inability to see himself, let alone others.[13] Joe has turned out to be an African American man who, despite his struggle to fulfill his desire and attain his happiness, fails to transcend the limitation of the outdated tradition of male subjectivity. For this reason *Jazz* does sound postmodern and parodic. Joe is one character who has made himself victim of the patriarchal, sexist, and self-centered concept and practice of subjectivity.

Part II

European and African Cultural Visions

CHAPTER 6

Wright's *The Outsider* and French Existentialism

1.

Critics have largely regarded the Harper edition of *The Outsider* (1953) as existential. They have also noted parallels between Wright and European existentialist novelists in their treatment of the metaphysical rebel, calling Cross Damon's philosophy nihilistic.[1] It is well known that Wright lived and wrote *The Outsider* in France, where he maintained close contact with such influential writers as Camus, Sartre, and de Beauvoir. Moreover, these French existentialists can be conveniently placed side-by-side with Wright's protagonist, who contemplates human existence through his exhaustive reading of Nietzsche, Hegel, Kierkegaard, and Dostoevsky.

But Arnold Rampersad's edition of *The Outsider*, published by the Library of America in 1991, suggests that Wright's original intention for *The Outsider* was not as existential as critics had previously thought. In the Harper edition, as Rampersad has shown, the original length of 741 typescript pages was shortened to 620 pages, a 16.3 percent deduction of the original manuscript. The difference between the two versions is partly stylistic, but it is also related to Wright's intention for the book as racial discourse. Most of the block cuts suggest that the original novel was not so avowedly existentialist as critics have characterized the Harper edition. The original version suggests that Cross Damon represents more than simply a black man. Not only is his plight real, but all the incidents and characters he is involved with, which at times appear to be clumsily constructed symbols, nonetheless express well-digested ideas. He is not "pathetically insane" as a reviewer described him.[2] The novel bewildered black reviewers as well, not because Wright espoused a new philosophy but because he seemed to have lost contact with his native soil.[3] However, a detailed comparison of the two versions will show not only that Cross Damon as originally portrayed is not simply an embodiment of a half-baked philosophy, but that he is a genuine product of American society.

Wright's intention in the Harper edition of *The Outsider* is to express a version of existentialism in which human action is taken as the result of an individual's choice and will. Earlier in the novel Damon's wife Gladys complains to her husband that white people intimidate her. He in turn admonishes her that one must exert one's will to exist. "It's up to us to make ourselves something," he argues. "A man creates himself" (*Outsider* 51). Initially Damon is attracted to his Communist mentor Gil Blount for his ideology and his actions. After his death Damon realizes that Blount epitomized "a modern man." "Life, to him," Damon reflects, "was a game devoid of all significance except that which he put into it" (370). Damon, however, killed Blount because Blount had attempted to wield his Communist power over Damon's will.

Corollary to Damon's idea of self-creation is his abhorrence of human dependency on others. Damon loses his interest in Gladys because, as Wright observes, "it was the helplessness of dependence that made her fret so. Men made themselves and women were made only through men" (*Outsider* 51). In order to characterize modern man as self-reliant and autonomous, Wright deleted a number of passages in which people are portrayed as passive and dependent on others. Both editions of the novel begin with a scene where Damon, tired with his long work at the post office, tries to rest his body on one of his companions. But his friend, a short man, chides him, saying, "Hell, naw! Stand on your own two big flat feet, Cross!" (*Outsider* 1, *Later Works* 369). The opening scene is, indeed, identical in the two versions except for three sentences alluding to a racial feature of the black men: "Tiny crystals trembled whitely between their dark faces. The shoulders of their overcoats were laced with icy filigrees; dapples of moisture glowed diamondlike on their eyebrows where the heat of their blood was melting the snow" (*Later Works* 371). This passage was deleted because Damon and his black friends, conscious of their racial background, give the impression that their having been born black is responsible for their plight. Such an implication is in contrary to Wright's portrait of a self-made man.

Among the sequences and incidents cut out of the original manuscript, the extended Hattie episode, which runs fourteen pages in two scenes, is the longest. Hattie is a young black widow who is lost in her life and is trying to cling to others for help. Damon finds himself easily tempted by this lonely woman, but he staves off her temptation. Even before this event, Wright also deletes a sentence from Damon's conversation with Ely Houston, a district attorney he happens to meet on the train. Damon says to Houston: "The

American Negro, because of his social and economic situation, is a congenital coward" (*Later Works* 505). Even though Damon characterizes the African American as a helpless victim of society rather than a courageous, self-sufficient individual, he is not aware that he himself remains a coward. The irony in Wright's portrayal of Cross Damon rests in that fact that while Damon disparages African American women like Gladys and Hattie as weak and dependent, he himself does not always act like a strong man. The original manuscript includes an episode in which Damon, pursued by the Communist agents, desperately tries to save his life by begging Hattie to hide him in her apartment and promising to give her $250 for her help. An existentialist like Meursault in Camus's *The Stranger* and Raskolnikov in Dostoevsky's *Crime and Punishment* would not stoop to such an action as does Wright's protagonist.

Cross Damon as originally conceived strikes one as an egotist, a selfish individual, rather than an indifferent, audacious human being compelled to do nothing in the face of the void and meaningless universe. For this reason, Wright seems to have excised the two opening paragraphs of Book Four, entitled "Despair." In this passage Damon confesses his selfish motive for murdering Blount and Herndon. Damon accomplished his goal, Wright observes, "as much for a dawning reverence for her as for the protection of his own self-love" (*Later Works* 618).

In the original version of the novel, the character of Eva Blount, Damon's love, is strikingly similar to that of Damon. He falls in love with Eva because both have suffered from a loveless marriage. In stark contrast to an existentialist, Eva is as passionately in search of meaning in existence as is Damon. "Her sense of guilt," Wright says, "was throwing her on his side; she had long been wanting to be free of Gil and now that she was free she wants to unburden her guilt on to someone else, on to Herndon" (*Later Works* 642). In fact, Wright eliminates this passage to make Eva as selfless and passive a person as Damon: she is portrayed "as calm as marble. Balling a handkerchief in her right fist, she sat looking bleakly in front of her. His eyes caught hers and he saw in them a glint of recognition. Yes, she's with me. She thinks I'm a victim too . . ." (*Outsider* 253–54).

Despite the fact that Eva has fallen prey to the Communists as has Damon, Wright's aim in the Harper version is to endow her character with courage and autonomy. To strengthen her individualism, Wright omits two sentences from Eva's diary in which she expresses an outrage against the Communists: "The Party lifted me up in its hands and showed me to the world, and if I disown them, they'll disown me . . . What a trap!" (*Later Works* 594). Such a passage intimates that she has been deprived of freedom and independence and become a helpless victim of the Communists. Omitting this passage makes Eva akin to Damon and hence more attractive to him. His affinity for her, in turn, whets his craving for freedom and independence from a totalitarian philosophy. While his intimate relationship with Eva constitutes a credible event in *The Outsider* as a realistic protest novel, it also plays a crucial role in Wright's dialectics between oppression and freedom.

Wright's chief interest in *The Outsider* lies in an exposition of what freedom means to certain individuals. As Damon disparages Gladys and Hattie, he repudiates his own mother not only because she is the product of the traditional Christianity in the South but because she failed to challenge the lack of freedom and individualism that prevailed in African American life. To make Mrs. Damon freer of a religious dogma, Wright cuts out a long speech by her in which she admonishes her son to abide by God's law. "If you feel you can't master yourself," she warns him, "then take your problem to God. . . . Life is a promise, son; God promised it to us and we must promise it to others. Without that promise life's nothing. .. Oh, God, to think that at twenty-six you're lost . . ." (*Later Works* 391). It is only natural that he should find his peace of mind in a liberal woman like Eva. Wright also tries to show how religion gets in the way of achieving freedom. In his flight to New York he meets a priest he regards as "a kind of dressed-up savage intimidated by totems and taboos that differed in kind but not in degree from those of the most primitive of peoples." The priest's demeanor shows Damon as if good and evil are not discovered by "the edicts of any God" but by human actions, for it is only the individual who is responsible for the consequences of the actions (*Later Works* 494).

To Damon, law, like religion, is created to inhibit human actions. A truly liberated individual does not control the actions under the law. Instead one creates one's own law and abides by it. For this reason, Wright deletes a long passage in which Damon discusses how law has the capacity to inhibit individuality and creativity in human life but at the same time provide the freedom of choice. "Implied in law," Damon asserts, "is a free choice to each man living under the law; indeed, one could almost say a free challenge is embedded in the law" (*Later Works* 700). Since this ambivalence in Damon's interpretation of law is embodied in Houston, Wright also deletes several sentences that specifically refer to Houston: "Cross shrewdly suspected that Houston, a self-confessed outlaw, knew this, felt it; and it was what had made him become an active defender of the law; he *had* to represent the law in order to protect himself against his own weakness and fear" (*Later Works* 700). Wright makes such an omission to strengthen his argument that one's moral obligation is to the individual and not to society, as well as to justify his murder of the men who had deprived him of individual freedom.

Wright's emphasis on the autonomy of human action is also reflected in the style of the novel. While Wright partly intended the book to be a social protest, his chief aim was to mold an African American man's life upon existential tenets. As Damon's statement in the original manuscript that the African American is a victim of the social and economic environment is excised from the Harper edition, other descriptions of naturalistic determinism are also deleted. The subway accident in which he is involved makes him feel as if he were imprisoned in himself. He was "so swamped . . . by himself with himself that he could not break forth from behind the bars of that self to claim himself" (*Later Works* 488). A stranger who witnessed the accident tells Damon: "Brother, your blood is the tomato sauce. Your white guts is the spaghetti. And your flesh is the meat, see? You'd be surprised how like a plate of meatballs and spaghetti you look when you get minced up in one of those subway wrecks" (*Later Works* 470). Such a description is omitted, for it is a cynical remark about the gruesome condition of a human being.

To make *The Outsider* akin to existential novels by Sartre and Camus, Wright also eliminated much of the profane and sexually allusive language. The Harper edition, for instance, deletes an expression Eva writes in her diary as she accuses the Communists of having deceived her into marrying her husband: "Goddam this deception!" (*Later Works* 595). In describing the ground where Joe, a friend of his Damon kills, lies, Wright originally wrote: "some of the grounds spilled over a bloodstained Kotex which still retained the curving shape of having fitted tightly and recently against the lips of some vagina; there was a flattened grapefruit hull whose inner pulpy fibres held a gob of viscous phlegm" (*Later Works* 485). The quoted passage was changed to "some of the grounds spilled over a flattened grapefruit hull" (*Outsider* 115). Similarly, the passages including such sentences as "Sarah's breasts heaved" and "her lips hung open and she breathed orgiastically" are deleted (*Later Works* 556).

At a crucial point in the development of the story Wright is at the pains of revising the original manuscript to express an existential philosophy. On the one hand, Wright comes to recognize a close relationship between Damon's actions and his social and psychological backgrounds; on the other hand, he tries to demonstrate in Damon's life a nihilistic view of the world stated earlier in the book that "man is nothing in particular" (*Outsider* 135). As the story progresses, however, the feeling of isolation and loneliness increasingly dictates Damon's action. Reading Eva's diary makes him realize that Eva's love for him came out of her sympathy for his oppressed life just as his love for her was intensified by his compassion for her personal predicament. This revelation leads to his statement in his deathbed—"To make a bridge from man to man" (*Outsider* 439)—a clear contradiction to his earlier view of human beings.

Though Damon's final vision makes the Harper version of *The Outsider* less existential than originally intended, it suggests that Wright is ambivalent in expressing his view of human existence. In both versions, he intended to portray an outsider as an individual with courage and audacity, but as the story unfolds, Damon finds himself increasingly alienated and realizes that, however imperfect society may be, he cannot live without relating to others. It is ironic that Wright's hero is determined to be an outsider but in his heart he wants to be an insider. A character like Cross Damon is sometimes larger than the author's occasional philosophy and he is able to speak for himself. Wright the philosopher only gets in his way; Wright the artist remains true to him. In the end, the interest of the story lies not in Wright's mind but in his heart, the genuine feelings Wright himself had experienced in American society.

2.

A comparison of *The Outsider* with Camus's *The Stranger,* a typical French existentialist novel, further suggests that *The Outsider* is not as existential as it appears. Although the likeness in theme, character, and event between *The Outsider* and *The Stranger* has been pointed out, it has not been studied in any detail. In general, critics have regarded Wright's philosophy in *The Outsider* as nihilistic, as mentioned earlier. Charles I. Glicksberg, in "Existentialism in *The Outsider*" and "The God of Fiction," saw parallels between Wright and Camus in the treatment of the metaphysical rebel, calling Cross Damon's philosophy most consistently nihilistic.[4] More recently, critics have demonstrated Camus's influences on Wright in his conception of Cross Damon. According to Michel Fabre, Wright read *The Stranger* in the American edition at a very slow pace, "weighing each sentence, 'admiring' its damn good narrative prose," and remarked:

> It is a neat job but devoid of passion. He makes his point with dispatch and his prose is solid and good. In America a book like this would not attract much attention for it would be said that he lacks feeling. He does however draw his character very well. What is of course really interesting in this book is the use of fiction to express a philosophical point of view. That he does with ease. I now want to read his other stuff. (qtd. in Fabre, "Wright" 191)

Edward Margolies in his comparison of Damon and Meursault pointed out that "both men kill without passion, both men appear unmoved by the death of their mothers; both men apparently are intended to represent the moral and emotional failure of the age" (135).

It would be quite tempting to compare the two works if they were the products of the same age and the particular philosophy they dealt with was in vogue. Moreover Camus's indifferent philosopher can conveniently be placed side by side with Wright's protagonist, a self-styled existentialist. One suspects, however, that the comparison of the two novels would never have been made unless the two novelists were both caught up in the philosophical context of existentialism. This meant that the literary likeness was taken for granted. Meursault kills a man; he is charged with a murder, tried, and convicted in a world of court, jury, and judge. But Damon kills more than one man, not only an enemy but a friend, a mentor, and an ally, and is responsible for the suicide of a woman he loves. But he is never charged with a crime, brought to a trial, or convicted. Unlike Meursault, who encounters his death in the world of daylight in Algiers, Damon is himself murdered by two men, the agents of the Communist Party, on a dimly-lit street in New York. Such a comparison makes *The Outsider* fiction of a different order, brought together with *The Stranger* in an assumed definition of human existence in the modern world. Although the two novels are regarded largely as existentialist, giving attention to the crucial details that differentiate the narratives would make Meursault and Damon radically different in their ideology and action.

It is time to re-examine *The Outsider* as a discourse on race; that is, it is important to redefine the African American tradition and experience that underlies this work. Comparing this novel with an avowedly existentialist novel like Camus's *The Stranger* will reveal that Wright's novel is not what critics have characterized. A detailed comparison of this novel with *The Stranger,* a novel of another culture and another tradition, will show not only that Wright's hero is not simply an embodiment of a half-baked philosophy, but also that he is a genuine product of the African American experience. Such a re-evaluation of the book will also clarify misconceptions about his other books as well.

The disparity of the two books becomes even more apparent if it is seen in the light of the less fashionable literary philosophy, naturalism. To some American writers, such as Stephen Crane and Theodore Dreiser, naturalism is a doctrine that asserts the indifference of the universe to the will of human beings. The indifference of the universe is most poignantly described by Stephen Crane in "The Open Boat": "When it occurs to a man that nature does not regard him as important, and that she feels she would not maim the universe by disposing of him, he at first wishes to throw bricks at the temple, and he hates deeply the fact that there are no bricks and no temples. Any visible expression of nature would surely be pelleted with his jeers" (Crane 294). Dreiser describes the forces of nature in *Sister Carrie:*

> Among the forces which sweep and play throughout the universe, untutored man is but a wisp in the wind. Our civilisation is still in a middle stage, scarcely beast, in that it is no longer wholly guided by instinct; scarcely human, in that it is not yet wholly guided by reason. .. . As a beast, the forces of life aligned him with them; as a man, he has not yet wholly learned to align himself with the forces. In this intermediate stage he wavers—neither drawn in harmony with nature by his instincts nor yet wisely putting himself into harmony by his own free-will. (83)

Camus, though his naturalistic vision is not conveyed with Dreiser's massive detail or analyzed by Zola's experimental method, nevertheless constructs his novel to dramatize a climactic assertion of universal indifference. Wright's novel, on the other hand, is filled with the events and actions that exhibit the world's concerns with human affairs. The outside world is indeed hostile to Damon, a man of great will and passion. Refusing to be dominated by it, he challenges its forces. But Meursault, remaining much of a pawn, is not willing to exert himself against the forces that to him have no relation to existence.

Heredity and environment, the twin elements in naturalistic fiction, are more influential to human action in *The Stranger* than they are in *The Outsider.* Though heredity has little effect on Meursault's behavior, environment does play a crucial role. Meursault is consistently shown as indifferent to any of society's interests and desires: love of God, marriage, friendship, social status. He is averse to financial success or political power; he receives only what is given or acts when acted upon. He is, like Dreiser's Sister Carrie, "a wisp in the wind"; he is more drawn than he draws (*Carrie* 83–84). This explains his passivity. Camus painstakingly accounts for human action just as Zola or Dreiser demonstrates the circumstances under which it occurs.

Camus shows that Meursault, who had no desire to kill the Arab, merely responded to pressures applied by natural forces. The blinding sun and the glittering knife held by the Arab caused Meursault to fear and forced him to pull the trigger. If the man with the knife had been a Frenchman, Meursault would not have acted with such rashness. Given the history of Arab-French colonial relations in the background, Meursault's antagonism toward the Arabs might have subconsciously triggered his action. Camus's emphasis in this narrative, however, is placed on the elements of chance, that is, the blinding sun and the glittering knife, rather than on the social elements such as the disharmony between the French and the Arabs.

This idea of chance and determinism is absent in Wright's concept of human action shown in *The Outsider*. Each of the four murders committed by Damon is premeditated, the suicide of a woman is directly related to his actions, and his own murder is a reprisal to the actions he could have avoided. In each case it is made clear that Damon had control over his action; in each murder he was capable of exerting his will or satisfying his desire. In marked contrast to Meursault, Damon exerts himself to attain the essences of his own existence. They are the very embodiments of the abstract words of society—friendship, love, marriage, success, equality, and freedom—to which he cannot remain indifferent. Wright takes pains to show that they are not empty dreams. The fact that Damon has been deprived of them at one time or another proves that they constitute his existence.

The Outsider represents a version of existentialism in which human action is viewed as the result of an individual's choice and will. To Wright, the individual's action must be assertive and, if need be, aggressive. This is perhaps why he was more attracted to Sartre and de Beauvoir than to Camus. In an unpublished journal Wright wrote: "Sartre is quite of my opinion regarding the possibility of human action today, that it is up to the individual to do what he can to uphold the concept of what it means to be human. The great danger, I told him, in the world today is the very feeling and conception of what is a human might well be lost. He agreed. I feel very close to Sartre and Simone de Beauvoir" (Fabre, "Wright" 186).

If Wright's protagonist is considered an existentialist actively in search of an essence in the meaningless existence, Meursault seems a passive existentialist compelled to do nothing in the face of the void and meaningless universe. Focused on the definition of existence, their views are alike: Damon at one time says, perhaps uncharacteristically, "Maybe man is nothing in particular" (*Outsider* 135). The point of disparity in their worldview, however, is the philosophy of the absurd. While Meursault is convinced of the essential absurdity of existence, Damon is not. If one considers human life inherently meaningful as does Damon, then it follows that his action to seek love, power, and freedom on earth is also meaningful. Conversely, however, if one judges life absurd as does Meursault, then it follows that his action is also absurd.

What is absurd is this dilemma of Meursault between his recognition of chaos and his search for order. It is the conflict between his awareness of death and his dream of eternity. It is the disparity between the essential mystery of all existence and one's demand for explanation. The fundamental difference in attitude between Meursault and Damon is that Meursault seeks neither order, nor a dream of eternity, nor explanation, while Damon is passionately in search of such an essence. Meursault's passivity, moreover, stems from Camus's attitude toward his art. Camus tries to solve the existentialist dilemma by arguing that an artist is not concerned to find order, to have a dream of eternity, or to demand explanation, but to experience all things given. The artist describes; he does not solve the mystery of the universe that is both infinite and inexplicable.

Whereas Camus's hero resists action, Wright's is compelled to act. Wright endows his hero with the freedom to create an essence. Damon's revolt is not so much against the nothingness and meaninglessness of existence as it is against the inability of human beings' attempt to make illogical phenomena logical. In the eyes of the public, Damon is as guilty of his murder of the fascist as Raskolnikov is guilty of his murder of the pawnbroker in *Crime and Punishment.* As Damon's murder of the fascist Herndon is analogous to Raskolnikov's murder of the pawnbroker in *Crime and Punishment,* Damon's killing of his friend Joe is similar to Raskolnikov's killing of the pawnbroker's sister Lizaveta. In the case of Joe or Lizaveta the murderer has no malice toward the victim but intentionally kills the victim to protect himself from prosecution. Both crimes result from premeditated actions; Meursault's killing of the Arab is accidental.

Readers may find a contradiction in Damon's view of the world. Earlier in the story Damon considers human beings "nothing in particular" (135), but at the end of his life he asserts, "We must find some way of being good to ourselves. . . . Man is all we've got. . . . I wish I could ask men to meet themselves" (439). Likewise his inaction initially makes him see nothingness and meaninglessness in human existence but in the end his action results in his realization of loneliness and "horror" on earth (440). In short, what appears to be a contradiction in Damon's view of existence is rather a reflection of activeness and aggressiveness in his character.

The chief difference in philosophy between the two books derives from the differing philosophies of the two novelists, Wright and Camus. Though both characters are regarded as rebels against society, the motive behind the rebellion differs. Damon rebels against society because it oppresses him by depriving him of the values he and society share, such as freedom in association and opportunity for success. Meursault is aloof to society because he does not believe in such values. In fact, he does not believe in marriage or family loyalty. His obdurate attitude toward society is clearly stated in Camus's preface to the American edition of *The Stranger:*

> I summarized *The Stranger*—a long time ago, with a remark that I admit
> was highly paradoxical: "In our society any man who does not weep at
> his mother's funeral runs the risk of being sentenced to death." I only
> meant that the hero of my book is condemned because he does not play
> the game. In this respect, he is foreign to the society in which he lives; he
> wanders, on the fringe, in the suburbs of private, solitary, sensual life.
> And this is why some readers have been tempted to look upon him as a
> piece of social wreckage. A much more accurate idea of the character, at
> least one much closer to the author's intentions, will emerge if one asks
> just how Meursault doesn't play the game. The reply is a simple one: he
> refuses to lie. To lie is not only to say *more* than is true, and, as far as the
> human heart is concerned, to express more than one feels. This is what
> we all do, every day, to simplify life. He says what he is, he refuses to hide
> his feelings, and immediately society feels threatened.[5]

If Meursault is characterized by his refusal to play society's game, Damon is
a type of person who cannot resist playing such a game. If society is threatened by Meursault's indifference to it, it is Damon rather than society that
feels threatened.

   This estranged personality of Meursault is reflected in his relationship with
his mother. Some critics have used his calm acceptance of the bereavement as
evidence for his callousness.[6] But the fact that he does not cry at his mother's
funeral would not necessarily suggest that he is devoid of emotions. Had
Meursault thought her death would have spared her the misery of her life or
that death would be a happier state for human beings, he should not have
been aggrieved by the passing away of his mother. What makes him a peculiar character, however, is the fact that an experience which would be a traumatic one for others is for him devoid of any meaning. *The Stranger* opens
with the protagonist's unconcerned reaction to his mother's death: "Mother
died today. Or, maybe, yesterday; I can't be sure" (1). But as the story progresses he becomes a more sensitive individual. He is indeed disturbed during the vigil by the weeping of his mother's friend. And every detail, whether
it is the driving home of the screws in the coffin lid or the starting of the
prayers by the priest, is minutely described. Throughout the story there is no
mention of Meursault's disliking his mother. He fondly reflects on her habits
and personality; he affectionately calls her *Maman*.

   By contrast Damon's relationship with his mother betrays not only the
estrangement between them but also his hostility to the racist society that had
reared her. He rejects his mother not only because she reminds him of southern black piety but because she is an epitome of racial and sexual repression:

He was conscious of himself as a frail object which had to protect itself against a pending threat of annihilation. This frigid world was suggestively like the one which his mother, without knowing it, had created for him to live in when he had been a child. . . . This God's NO-face had evoked in his pliable boy's body an aching sense of pleasure by admonishing him to shun pleasure as the tempting doorway opening blackly onto hell; had too early awakened in him a sharp sense of sex by thunderingly denouncing sex as the sin leading to eternal damnation. . . . Mother love had cleaved him: a wayward sensibility that distrusted itself, a consciousness that was conscious of itself. Despite this, his sensibilities had not been repressed by God's fearful negations as represented by his mother; indeed, his sense of life had been so heightened that desire boiled in him to a degree that made him afraid. (17–18)

The young Damon's desire to free himself from such a bondage is closely related to his inability to love any black woman, as shown by his relationship with Gladys, his estranged wife, or Dot, his pregnant mistress. The only woman he loves is the white woman Eva. He feels an affinity with her, for he discovers that she, too, is a fearful individual and that she had been deceived into marrying her husband because of a political intrigue. He is, moreover, tormented by the envenomed abstraction of racial and political myths. Unlike the white phonograph salesman, who seduces the wife of a black man in "Long Black Song," he is permanently frustrated. Since *The Outsider* portrays a rich variety of racial and political animosities, his love life is defined in terms of the forces beyond his control. To him the consummation of his love for Eva means the ultimate purpose of his new existence. It is understandable that when that goal appears within reach and yet taken away from him, he finds only "the horror" that he has dreaded all his life (440).

Meursault's relationship with women, on the contrary, is totally uninhibited socially and psychologically. His relationship with Marie is free from the kinds of racial and political entanglements which smother Damon's relationship with Eva. Meursault, the perfectly adjusted man, does not suffer from any kind of repression. His action for love is motivated from within according to logic rather than convention or sentiment. In his life, love of woman is a natural instinct as is eating or resting; love is more akin to friendship than to marriage. He helps Raymond, for he says, "I wanted to satisfy Raymond, as I'd no reasons not to satisfy him" (41). Meursault is kind and benevolent as Damon is not; he is relaxed and content as Damon is tense and frustrated.

Meursault's indifference to existence is epitomized by his love life. His attitude toward Marie bears a sort of impersonal, superhuman mode of thought.

To the public such an attitude is inhuman, unconventional, and unethical. His view of love is no different from that of death; his sexual relations with Marie begin immediately after his mother's death. If death occurs beyond human control, so does love. His meeting with her takes place by mere coincidence and the relationship that develops is casual and appears quite innocent:

> While I was helping her to climb on to a raft, I let my hand stray over her breasts. Then she lay flat on the raft, while I trod water. After a moment she turned and looked at me. Her hair was over her eyes and she was laughing. I clambered up on to the raft, beside her. The air was pleasantly warm, and, half jokingly, I let my head sink back upon her lap. She didn't seem to mind, so I let it stay there. I had the sky full in my eyes, all blue and gold, and I could feel Marie's stomach rising and falling gently under my head. We must have stayed a good half-hour on the raft, both of us half asleep. When the sun got too hot she dived off and I followed. I caught up with her, put my arm round her waist, and we swam side by side. She was still laughing. (23–24)

Even when a marriage proposal is made by Marie, his indifference remains intact: "Marie came that evening and asked me if I'd marry her. I said I didn't mind; if she was keen on it, we'd get married" (52).

Meursault's indifference is also reflected in his reaction to the crime of which he is accused. Partly as a corollary to the nature of the crime, he is passive rather than active. Unlike Damon, he commits a crime without malice or intention. He kills the Arab not because he hates the victim but partly because he sympathizes with his friend Raymond, whose life has been threatened. Given this situation, it would be more natural for him to defend his friend than the hostile stranger. Meursault's crime is a crime of logic; it is not a murder. Camus's purpose for using crime in *The Stranger* is to prove that society, rather than the criminal, is in the wrong. Camus's intention is to prove that his hero is innocent, as well as to show that Meursault's logic is far superior to society's. When crime appears innocent, it is innocence that is called upon to justify itself. In *The Stranger,* then, it is society, not the criminal, that is on trial.

Because Meursault is convinced of his innocence, he attains at the end of his life his peace of mind, a Buddhist-like enlightenment. Despite the death sentence, he achieves a nirvana, through which he has liberated himself from the materialistic and egotistic pursuit of life:

> With death so near, Mother must have felt like someone on the brink of freedom, ready to start life all over again. No one, no one in the world had any right to weep for her. And I, too, felt ready to start life all over again. It was as if that great rush of anger had washed me clean, emptied me of hope, and, gazing up at the dark sky spangled with its signs and stars, for the first time, the first, I laid my heart open to the benign indifference of the universe. (154)

Damon is also convinced of his innocence at the end of his life. What the two novels share is not only that the hero is prosecuted by society, but that society—the prosecutor, jurors, and judge—seems to him to be always in the wrong. Because Camus's hero refuses to play society's game, he is sentenced to death by society. Society expects him to grieve over his mother's death and refrain from having a casual affair with a woman during the moaning. But Wright's hero, induced to play society's game, loses in the end. He is tempted to participate in the normal activities of society such as a love affair and a political association. Tasting his agonizing defeat and dying, he utters:

> I wish I had some way to give the meaning of my life to others. . . . To make a bridge from man to man . . . Starting from scratch every time is . . . is no good. Tell them not to come down this road. . . . We must find some way of being good to ourselves. . . . We're different from what we seem. . . . Maybe worse, maybe better . . . But certainly different . . . We're strangers to ourselves. (439)

The confession at the end of his life suggests that he, unlike Meursault, has always felt obliged to justify his actions. He has finally realized that they always collided with society's interests and values. As an outsider, he trusted no one, not even himself, nor did society trust him. While maintaining in his last breath that "in my heart . . . I'm . . . innocent" (440), he is judging society guilty. While Meursault is a victim of his own crime, Damon is a victim not only of his own crime but of society's. Meursault, who refuses to justify his actions, always feels innocent: "I wasn't conscious of any 'sin'; all I knew was that I'd been guilty of a criminal offense" (148).

Although both novels employ crime as a thematic device, the focus of the author's idea differs. Camus's center of interest is not crime but its consequences—its psychological effect on his hero. Before committing his crime Meursault is presented as a stranger who finds no meaning in life. After he is sentenced to death he realizes for the first time that his life has been enveloped in the elusive beauty of the world. "To feel it so like myself, indeed, so brotherly," he says, "made me realize that I'd been happy, and that I was happy still" (154). In *The Outsider* crime is used, like accidental death or suicide, to create a new life for the hero. He murders the fascist Herndon as a reprisal; he intentionally kills the Communist Blount out of his desire for a white woman. In contrast to Camus's hero, to whom death has brought life and happiness, Wright's hero in the end is once more reminded of his own estrangement and horror. The kind of fear Damon suffers at the end of his struggle is clearly absent in Meursault's life. A critic, in comparing Meursault to Clyde Griffiths, the hero of Theodore Dreiser's *An American Tragedy*, comments: "Passivity in *L'Étranger* is strength, and only the strong can be indifferent. When Meursault receives this almost Buddhist illumination, he loses the two great distractions from life: hope and fear. He becomes happy, rather than terrified, in the face of his expected execution; he no longer hopes for some wild chance to deliver him from it. This prisoner is alone and freed, from within" (Purdy 261).

The two novelists' divergent attitudes toward the problems of crime and guilt are also reflected in the style and structure of their works. *The Stranger* is swift in pace and dramatic in tone, and displays considerable subjectivity, involving the reader in the consciousness of the hero. The reader's involvement in the hero's dialectics is intensified because the book consists of two parts dealing with the same issue. The first part involves the reader in a few days of Meursault's life, ending with his crime; the second re-involves the reader in the same experiences through the trial in court. Since the hero's experiences are viewed from different angles, they never strike one as monotonous or repetitious. The chief reason for the juxtaposition is for the hero, and for Camus, to convince the reader that what appears to society to be a crime is not at all a crime in the eyes of an existentialist.

This juxtaposition also elucidates the discontinuity and unrelatedness of Meursault's experiences in the first half of the story despite the reordering and construing of those experiences in the second half. As the incidents and actions in the first half are discontinuous, so is time. No days are referred to in Meursault's life except for Saturday and Sunday, his days off. Of the months only August is mentioned since Meursault, Mason, and Raymond plan to have their vacation together; of the seasons only summer. By the same token, there is no mention of the day of the month. And Meursault's age is unknown; he is merely "young."[7] As there is nothing unique about his concept of time, there is nothing unique about his experience. As points in time are discontinuous, so are the experiences. At his trial the prosecutor accuses him of moral turpitude, for Meursault shed no tears at his mother's funeral and casually started an affair with Marie immediately after. To Meursault, his mother's death, his behavior at the funeral, and his love affair are not only devoid of meaning in themselves, but discontinuous, unrelated incidents.

Similarly, the threatening gesture of the Arab, the sweating in Meursault's eyebrows, the flashing of the sun against his eyes, and the firing of his revolver occur independently of one another. If his eyes were blinded by the sun and the sweating of his eyebrows, his pulling the trigger on the revolver would not have been a logical reaction. When he is later asked by the prosecutor why he took a revolver with him and went back to the place where the Arab reappeared, he replies that "it was a matter of pure chance" (110). If he does not believe that he is "morally guilty of his mother's death" (128), as charged by the prosecutor, it would be impossible for him to admit that he is morally guilty of the Arab's death. This is precisely the reason why he tells the priest that he is guilty of a criminal offense but that he is not a sinner (148).

Swift and intensive though Camus's probing of Meursault's character is, the reader is deliberately kept from coming to an easy conclusion about Meursault's guilt. By contrast, the reader is instantly made aware of Damon's guilt in unambiguous terms. In *The Outsider* truly heinous crimes are constructed in advance with all the plausible justifications. Before the reader is made aware of Damon's guilt, the author has defined in unequivocal terms the particular traits in Damon's character and the particular forces in society that had led to his crimes. In so doing Wright creates a clear pattern by which Damon's motives for crime are shown. Whereas there is no such relatedness in Meursault's motives for action, there emerges in *The Outsider* a chain of events that can scarcely be misinterpreted. The murder of the fascist is committed side by side with that of the Communist. Another example of this relatedness in Damon's actions is, as Edward Margolies observes, the pattern in which Damon rejects the African Ameican women as he destroys the Communists and fascist: "When Cross murders two Communists and a fascist, his motives seem to derive more from what he regards as his victims' desire to enslave him psychologically, rather than from any detached, intellectualized, conscienceless 'compulsion' on his part. What the Communists and fascist would do to Cross if they had him in their power is precisely what his mother, wife, and mistress had already done to him. In a sense, Cross murders his women when he crushes his enemies" (133). Damon kills both men with malice: he murders Herndon because of his hatred for the racist as he does Blount because of his passion for the white woman. Unlike Meursault, Damon is conscious of his guilt in the instant of committing crime.

Because Damon's actions are predetermined and interrelated, Damon is constantly made conscious of the passage of time. The problems in his manhood and marriage, for example, are related to those of his childhood. His desertion of his wife is analogous to his rejection of his mother just as the Communists' rule over workers in modern times is akin to slavery in the past. *The Outsider* opens with a scene at dawn in which Damon and his friends "moved slowly forward shoulder to shoulder and the sound of their feet tramping and sloshing in the melting snow echoed loudly" (1). Like Jake Jackson in *Lawd Today*, Damon, bored with routine work, finds the passage of time unendurable. In *The Stranger*, Meursault is least concerned with time; he never complains about the monotony of his work. In fact, he dislikes Sundays because he is not doing his routine job. Damon, on the contrary, wishes everyday were Sunday, or reminisces about Christmastime in a certain year. Damon's friend Joe Thomas reminds Damon of their happy days in the past. Joe speaks, "Remember that wild gag he pulled at Christmastime in 19 . . .? . . . When the hell was that now? Oh, yes! It was in 1945. I'll never forget it. Cross bought a batch of magazines, *Harper's, Atlantic Monthly, Collier's, Ladies' Home Journal*, and clipped out those ads that say you can send your friends a year's subscription as a Christmas gift" (*Outsider* 5). More importantly, Meursault says whether he dies at thirty or at seventy it doesn't matter. For him life has no more significance than death.

For Damon life is all that matters. If his earlier life is not worth living, a new one must be created. A freak subway accident, in which he is assumed dead, offers him another life and another identity. All his life he plans his action with hope for the future and with denial of the past. Such attitude is emblematic of the African American tradition, the deep-seated black experience, as expressed in the spirituals. While Edgar Allan Poe's writings sometimes smack of morbid romanticism, that erotic longing for death, the spirituals reverberate with energy and vitality and convey the sense of rejuvenation. However violent and destructive Damon may appear, he inherently emerges from this tradition. Meursault, on the other hand, is the very product of the nihilistic spirit that hovered over Europe, particularly France, after World War II.

Despite Wright's effort to relate Damon's actions to his social and psychological backgrounds, *The Outsider* remains an imperfect work as a novel, but as a racial discourse it closely reflects American social reality. Some of its faults are structural rather than philosophical. Given the kind of life Damon has lived, it is not difficult to understand his nihilistic view of the world stated earlier in the book that "man is nothing in particular" (135), or his conciliatory vision that man "is all we've got. . . . I wish I could ask men to meet themselves" (439). But, as some critics have pointed out, it is difficult to believe that a young man with such mundane problems, renewing his life through a subway accident, suddenly emerges as a philosopher discussing Nietzsche, Heidegger, and Kierkegaard. Saunders Redding considers *The Outsider* "often labored, frequently naive, and generally incredible." Another reviewer finds it impossible to relate Wright's "passionless slayer" to the Cross Damon of Book I, and says, "We can identify with the first Cross Damon, but not the later one. Wright goes out of his way to make this identification impossible."[8] While in *The Stranger* the two parts of the story are so structured that each enlightens the other, those in *The Outsider*, the hero's life before and after the accident, are constructed as though they were two tales.

This weakness notwithstanding, *The Outsider* is unquestionably a powerful statement made by an outsider who refuses to surrender his will to live. One can scarcely find among African American heroes in American fiction such a courageous and tenacious, albeit violent, man. As compared to Bigger Thomas, Wright's celebrated hero, Damon stands taller and poles apart simply because Damon is endowed with an intellectual capacity seldom seen in African American fiction. Small wonder that when the novel came out, critics in general, both white and black, who were unfamiliar with such a character, failed to appreciate Wright's intention and execution in the book. Orville Prescott's *New York Times* review was a typical white critic's reaction to *The Outsider*. With due respect for Wright's previous successes, Prescott politely insisted that Wright must have deplored Damon's moral weakness and irrational behavior at the end of the book, and further remarked, "That men as brilliant as Richard Wright feel this way is one of the symptoms of the intellectual and moral crisis of our times." Saunders Redding, quoted earlier, noted that Wright's brand of existentialism, instead of being a device for the representation of truth, "leads away from rather than toward reality." Arna Bontemps was even sarcastic: "The black boy from Mississippi is still exploring. He has had a roll in the hay with the existentialism of Sartre, and apparently he liked it."

The strengths of *The Outsider* become even clearer as this novel is compared with *The Stranger*. Although Damon professes to be a nihilist, as does Meursault, he is never indifferent to human existence as is Meursault. Camus's hero is called a stranger to society as well as to himself; he is indifferent to friendship, marriage, love, success, freedom. Ironically, Damon, who seeks them in life, fails to obtain them. It is ironic, too, that Meursault, to whom they are at his disposal, is indifferent to them. Wright's hero, an outsider racially as well as intellectually, struggles to get inside. Damon wants to be treated as an individual, not as a second-class citizen or a person whose intellectual ability is not recognized. By contrast, Camus's hero, an insider but a stranger, strives to get outside.

It is hardly coincidental that both novels are eloquent social criticisms in our times. *The Outsider* is an indictment against American society, for not only does Wright maintain Damon's innocence but he shows most convincingly that men in America "hate themselves and it makes them hate others" (439). *The Stranger,* on the other hand, is an indictment against French society, for Camus proves that while the criminal is innocent, his judges are guilty. More significantly, however, comparison of the two novels of differing characters and traditions reveals that both Wright and Camus are writing ultimately about a universal human condition in modern times.

CHAPTER 7

Pagan Spain:
Wright's Discourse on Religion and Culture

Upon publication, *Pagan Spain* (1957) appeared to signal a departure from Wright's earlier nonfiction and from *Black Power* (1954) and *The Color Curtain* (1956) in particular. While the two previous travelogues focused on the non-Western world—African and Asian cultures, respectively—*Pagan Spain* is primarily concerned with a Western culture. But what is common among the three works is, as *Black Power* and *The Color Curtain* have shown, that the narrator is distinctly an American. Although Wright claims African heritage, in *The Color Curtain* he does not speak like an African. Even though he speaks in *Pagan Spain* as a European resident, he still remains an American. If these works are read as travelogues—as commentaries on foreign cultures—his perspectives strike the reader as realistic, impartial, and critical.

That *Pagan Spain* contains many disparaging remarks about Spanish culture is partly responsible for the fact that the book has been published in such European countries as Germany, Holland, Sweden, and Italy, but not in Spain. Wright's aim at achieving objectivity is indicated by his interview with a magazine reporter in 1959: "*Pagan Spain* is about a journey—or rather it's a descriptive account of three automobile trips I made in Spain, the Spanish people I met, the fiestas, flamencos, bullfights, the feeling of the country, the warmth of the people and the incredible poverty" (Learned 185). As this statement suggests, his intention for the book, unlike that for *The Color Curtain,* in which the informants are predominantly intellectuals, what he calls "Asian elites," was to deal with all classes of the Spanish people, including aristocrats and gypsies, businessmen and workers, dancers and prostitutes, matadors and pimps, priests and shop clerks. As a result, *Pagan Spain* turns out to be not only a vivid portrayal of Spain after World War II but an acute cultural criticism just as *Black Power* and *The Color Curtain* served as highly insightful cultural criticisms of Africa and Asia, respectfully. Because Wright had established his reputation by the end of World War II, his later works, as Paul Gilroy has observed, attracted little critical attention.[1]

Just as Hemingway in the 1920s took Gertrude Stein's advice, which contributed to his writing such books on Spain as *The Sun Also Rises* (1926) and *For Whom the Bell Tolls* (1940), Wright eagerly listened to the legendary authoress when he arrived in Paris in 1946. "You'll see the past there," she told him. "You'll see what the Western world is made of. Spain is primitive, but lovely. And the people! There are no people such as the Spanish anywhere. I've spent days in Spain that I'll never forget. See those bullfights, see that wonderful landscape . . ." (*Pagan Spain* 1–2). Despite Stein's urging, however, Wright postponed his journey for nearly a decade. In the summer of 1954 at the urgings of his friends Alva and Gunnar Myrdal, the well-respected Swedish sociologists, he finally drove past the Pyrenees to Barcelona. In contrast to Gertrude Stein's romanticized, traditional, and ritualistic view of Spanish culture, *Pagan Spain* is dedicated to the Myrdals, *"who suggested this book and whose compassionate hearts have long brooded upon the degradation of human life in Spain."*

This dedication intimates that his immediate motive for the book was to explore the fate of Spanish exiles and victims under Franco's totalitarian regime. Reflecting on his own experience in America, he says: "I had never been able to stifle a hunger to understand what had happened there and why. . . . An uneasy question kept floating in my mind: How did one live after the death of the hope for freedom?" (2). What the Myrdals called "the degradation of human life in Spain" reminded him of his birth under a racist government in Mississippi, of his formative twelve years under the dictatorship of the American Communist Party, and of a year of his intellectual life under the terror of Argentine dictator Perón. "The author," as a reviewer noted, "gives his reader bitter, stark facts at the same time that he unwittingly reveals his own bitter, hurt self."[2] His avowed opposition to Franco's totalitarianism, evident throughout the text, contributed to the better reviews *Pagan Spain* received in the United States than did *Black Power* or *The Color Curtain*.

But some American readers "were shocked to see" a black writer discuss a white culture. Before Wright, the usual pattern had been for a Western anthropologist or a Western writer like Joseph Conrad to comment on Asian or African life. If Wright considered himself an African, his situation would have been the opposite of that of a Western writer. He declared: "I was reversing roles."[3] If, on the other hand, he regarded himself as an American writer, commenting on Europe as he did, indeed, signaled a reversal of commenting on America as did Alexis de Tocqueville and D. H. Lawrence, whose views of

American culture remain classic. Similarly, from today's vantage point, Wright's view of Spain remains a unique cultural criticism.

Three years after the publication of *Pagan Spain, L'Express,* in its interview with Wright, posed this question: "Is there in the United States an important output of Negro literature, and do you number many friends among these writers?" In response he stated:

> Yes, many. Negro literature in the United States is actually so important that it even preoccupies our government. American blacks are testifying against the most modern of Western countries. . . . In the United States, the tendency is to tell black writers: "Don't be preoccupied with your experience as Negroes. Don't be polarized by it. You are people. Write exactly as any other people would do on any other subject." I would be inclined to tell them, "On the contrary, take your ghetto experience as a theme, for this precisely is a *universal* topic. . . ." (emphasis added; *Conversations* 204–5)

Wright is suggesting that one's racial experience is a representation of universal experience. By analogy a Spaniard's experience represents not only Spanish culture but also universal experience. Not surprisingly, Wright's observations in *Pagan Spain* are closely related to those of African American experience.

1.

What underlies Wright's cultural discourse in *Pagan Spain* is the notion that Spain, despite its history, was not nearly as Christian as it looked. His chief interest lies not in the Catholic church as it became entangled with Franco's totalitarian regime, but in an exploration of the intriguing boundaries of Spanish religiosity. Initially he was puzzled by the Falangists, made up of "*half monks, half soldiers*" (60). He saw all of them worship the Virgin Mary, whose statue had been carved by St. Luke. "It is further claimed," Wright recounts, "that it was brought to Spain by St. Peter himself in A.D. 30. . . ." He was also told: "Hermán Cortés came here to ask blessings from the Black Virgin. Even Columbus made a pilgrimage here" (60). As his exploration of Spain's religious character delves into a comparison of the past political situation against the present, and into the interior of the Catholic church as a modern institution, his expressions become increasingly flexible, fluid, and dynamic. An anonymous reviewer interpreted *Pagan Spain* primarily as Wright's indictment against the machinations of the church and the state: "It is the Spain of the ready thumb of the church and the state, the thumb which twists and turns the lives of the poor mortals beneath it, shaping and moving the poor mortals in a way repugnant to much of the world."[4] While he relies on conventional metaphor, symbolism, and imagery in describing religious practices, he is bent on creating representations that strike the reader as unconventional, metonymical, and psychoanalytical.

Anyone commenting on the political situation of Spain in the 1950s could not help seeing the exploitation of the Catholic church by politicians whose strategy was to equate Spanish Catholicism with Spain's glorious past: Catholicism was pitted against Protestantism, which the majority of Spaniards perceived as a decadent, materialistic religion. "The average Spaniard," Wright says, "knows nothing of Protestantism." Even Spanish intellectuals felt "uneasy when the subject of Protestantism is mentioned" (137). Juan Perrone, S.J., in his catechism in 1950, asserted that Protestantism came into its existence in Spain to propagate Socialism and Communism. But from Wright's point of view, Spanish Protestantism was far more concerned with the lives of the poor and socially oppressed than was Catholicism. Reflecting on his own Protestant background, he sympathized with the Spanish Protestants for "the needless, unnatural, and utterly barbarous nature of the psychological suffering" they had undergone at the hands of the religious and political officials. What interested him was the uncanny psychological affinity that existed between the Protestants in Spain and African Americans, Jews, and other oppressed minorities in the United States. "It is another proof, if any is needed today," he argues, "that the main and decisive aspects of human reactions are conditioned and are not inborn" (138).

Economically, Catholicism in Spain fared worse than Protestantism. Protestants were known for their ability to cope with reality while Catholics were slow in adapting to changes in life in general and to industrialization in particular. To Wright, Protestantism, however suitable for industrialism and modernism, was rejected in Spain, just as was "the murderous rationalism of sacrificial Communism . . . in favor of an archaic collective consciousness based on family symbols: One Father, One Mother, One Spirit" (240). This definition of Spanish Catholicism as archaic, unrealistic, and impractical, however, is attributed only to a superficial characteristic of Spanish religiosity. Although Ferdinand and Isabel had driven the Moors out of Spain in 1492 under the banner of Catholicism, Spanish culture kept in tact, as Wright notes, "all the muddy residue of an irrational paganism that lurked at the bottom of the Spanish heart" (240). He maintains that the Spanish people would turn back the clock of history and cling to paganism. In this old, predominantly Catholic nation, the social, religious, and familial customs and rituals, as he shows throughout the book, reflect a religious philosophy that is not Catholic but primitive and primeval.

As for the sources of paganism in Spain, he relies on the commonly held view that "the pagan streams of influence flowing from the Goths, the Greeks, the Jews, the Romans, the Iberians, and the Moors lingered strongly and vitally on, flourishing under the draperies of the twentieth century" (193). From time to time, he also implies that paganism in Spain had also come from Asia through Buddhism and possibly Confucianism, both of which antedate Christianity by five hundred years or more. Spanish paganism, he speculates, was related to the Egyptian divinity, and the Akan God, which fascinated him when he traveled to West Africa, as discussed in *Black Power*.

But the most convincing argument for Spanish paganism is derived from his examination of the Black Virgin at Montserrat, one of the famous tourist attractions in Spain. "The ascent to Montserrat," he describes his own sensation, "was breath-taking. We climbed, spinning and circling slowly round the naked mountain peaks on tiny roads that skirted the sheer edges of cloud-filled chasms whose depths made the head swim" (60–61). The representations such a passage creates are avowedly Freudian, though Wright de-emphasizes it, and his approach to Spanish national character is unmistakably psychoanalytical:

> More and more nations of seriated granite phalluses, tumefied and turgid, heaved into sight, each rocky republic of erections rising higher than its predecessor, the whole stone empire of them frozen into stances of eternal distensions, until at last they became a kind of universe haunted by phallic images—images that were massive, scornful, shameless, confoundingly bristling, precariously floating in air, obscenely bare and devoid of all vegetation, filling the vision with vistas of a non- or super-human order of reality. (61)

The phallic images that dominate the geological environment of the Black Virgin do not allude to what Saunders Redding called "a paganism as gross and a venality as vulgar as the temples of Baal."[5] To Wright, such images represent not *prurience,* a physical, as opposed to psychological, emotion, but *procreation,* a "a non- or superhuman order of reality."

Wright indeed defines the genesis of the Virgin as non-Western. The Virgin in Spain is "a perhaps never-to-be-unraveled amalgamation of Eastern and African religions with their endless gods who were sacrificed and their virgins who gave birth perennially" (240). In portraying the statue of the virgin, he seized upon the Virgin's black face exhibiting "a kind of quiet, expectant tension" (62). Her facial feature recalled a mixture of the Roman and the Oriental. Moreover, the infant Christ seated on her lap, possessing "that same attitude of quiet, tense expectancy," resembled her (63). Wright continued to speculate: "Maya, the mother of Buddha, was supposed to have been a virgin. Chinese temples have long had their images of the Holy Mother sitting with the Child on her lap. The Egyptians worshiped Isis, mother of Horus, as a virgin, and she was called Our Lady, the Queen of Heaven, Mother of God" (65).[6] In all these religions, then, the image of the mother symbolizes how human beings feel about their birth. Divinity or superhumanity, as he maintains, "is inescapably bound up with sex." As human beings throughout history have worshiped the mother, "the female principle in life," Spaniards have worshiped the Black Virgin (65). A reviewer of *Pagan Spain,* an American Catholic priest, called Wright's interpretation of paganism in Spain heretic: "Montserrat, for him, can be accounted for according to the categories of Freud's pan-sexual theories. This attempt to explain religious phenomena in the crude terms of sexual sublimation has well been described as a type of Machiavellian denigration. There is no space here to expose the fallacy."[7]

Viewing religion in Spain, as Wright does, from the perspective of superhumanism reveals that Spaniards were scarcely conscious of class and racial differences. Rather than staying at a hotel, Wright chose to spend his first night with a Spanish family in a village. To his surprise the family took him into their Christian fellowship even before they knew his name. "To these boys," he remarks, "it was unthinkable that there was no God and that we were not all His sons" (9). Even the Falangists' book of political catechism includes such a dialogue:

ARE THERE THEN PEOPLE WHO WITHOUT BEING BORN IN SPAIN ARE SPANIARDS?

Yes; all who feel themselves to be incorporated in the destiny of Spain.

AND CAN THERE BE PEOPLE BORN IN SPAIN WHO ARE NOT SPANIARDS?

Yes; children of foreigners and those who disassociate themselves from the destiny of the Motherland.

THEN, DO YOU SEE CLEARLY THAT FOR US THE MOTHERLAND IS NOT THE LAND IN WHICH WE ARE BORN BUT THE FEELING OF FORMING PART OF THE DESTINY OR AIMS WHICH THE MOTHERLAND MUST FULFILL IN THE WORLD?

Yes.
WHAT IS THIS DESTINY?
To include all men in a common movement for salvation.
WHAT DOES THIS MEAN?
Ensure that all men place spiritual values before material. (23)

To the Western industrialized world, the primacy of the spiritual over the materialistic looked irrational and primitive. Wright calls Spanish paganism "an infantile insistence upon one's own feelings as the only guide and rule of living . . . to sustain their lives by being overlords to the 'morally' less pure, to the 'spiritually' inferior" (151). In Spain, it was not class and race but faith in universal superhumanism that determined one's superiority or inferiority.

2.

Pagan Spain concludes with a description of the lasting impression Wright had of the Virgin during his third and final visit to Seville. The hooded penitents in the procession were upholding the Virgin similarly to the way the Ku Klux Klan in the South were trying to protect white womanhood. But he says: "Some underlying reality more powerful than the glittering Virgin or southern white women had gripped these undeniably primitive minds. They were following some ancient pattern of behavior and were justifying their actions in terms that had nothing whatever to do with that pattern" (237). By "some ancient pattern of behavior" he means Spanish paganism, which has its psychological origin in the female principle of life. Though the Virgin in Spain was an established symbol of Catholicism, she was in reality a representation of paganism, the principle of eternal procreation: "A God died that man might live again, and the Virgin stood eternally ready to give birth to the God that was to die, that is, the Man-God" (238). Just as Wright was awed by the procreating image of the Virgin at Montserrat, he was struck again by what he witnessed in Seville: "The cross was held high and on it was the bloody, bruised figure of a Dying Man. . . . But behind the Dying Man was the Virgin ready to replenish the earth again so that Life could go on" (239), a spectacle remindful of the matriarchalism of the Ashanti, or the Sun-Goddess in Japanese Shintoism.

Spanish religiosity, based as it was on sexuality, betrayed another paradox. Toward the end of his travels Wright met a naturalized Spanish woman who told him: "The Church here will tell you that the people here love God so much that sex has been conquered. But all that you hear about here is sex.

When I first came here, I thought that the Spanish had just discovered sex—they talked so much about it, and they still do. Sometimes they act as if they invented sex" (212–13). To her, life was "upside down here" (213). Spaniards were obsessed with sex as much as with the Virgin; they were overly concerned with innocence as much as with sex. Such a contradiction revealed itself in all aspects of Spanish life. "Even the prostitution, the corruption, the economics, the politics," Wright observed, "had about them a sacred aura. *All was religion in Spain*" (192).

Although the pre-eminence of religion over sexuality suggests sexual repression on the part of Spanish men, it took a heavier toll on Spanish women. Anti-feminism was rampant in all segments of Spanish society. At home men dominated women: "The women ate silently with one eye cocked in the direction of their men, ready at a moment's notice to drop their knives and forks and refill the half-empty masculine plates" (90). In public, men tended to move away from women and vice versa, a common scene indicating the separation of the sexes. Young women, Wright saw, were always protected from contact with men so that virginity was guarded until marriage. At a hotel he found an American woman intimidated by the manager who claimed that she had refused to pay for baths she did not take. The Spaniard "smiled and explained . . . that men were not, perhaps, superior to women, but they were certainly more intelligent. His air was one of cynicism and his manner asked me to join him in his masculine game of domination" (74). As a fellow traveler, Wright admonished her not to be hysterical: "You are acting like a Negro. . . . Negroes do that when they are persecuted because of their accident of color. The accident of sex is just as bad. And crying is senseless" (76).

Not surprisingly, Franco's Falangists were bent on brainwashing young women. The government officials imposed a "moral" position on Spanish women. While women were protected, men were allowed to exploit prostitutes, a blatant anti-feminist contradiction. Under the Falangist doctrine, feminine heroism was defined as subservience to men: "*though for [women] heroism consists more in doing well what they have to do every day than in dying heroically.*" Women's temperament, the catechism continued, "*tends more to constant abnegation than to heroic deeds*" (77). Women under the Franco regime were called heroic if they sacrificed the pleasures of life for the sake of the dictatorship.

For Wright, the Falangist concept of the state, which denied the liberal doctrines of Jean Jacques Rousseau and the right of universal suffrage, was in direct opposition to superhumanism. This political repression, in turn, resulted in a sexual repression evident in the Flamenco dance. During his visit to the legendary Granada, Wright met an accomplished Flamenco dancer. He was deeply impressed by her performance as well as by the audience. "I pantomimed," he says, "what I wanted to say and they were willing to take time to imagine, to guess, and, in the end, to understand; and they were patiently determined to make others know and feel what they thought and felt." The dancer "began a sensual dance that made a kind of animal heat invade the room" (171). Even before the performance he was keenly aware of the frustration of the people. He assured the dancer, whose husband had died in the civil war fighting for the republic against Franco: "I shall tell [Americans] that the people of Spain are suffering" (170). Wright was also a witness to the orgiastic ecstasy of the gypsy dance, the emotion which Western culture in general and modern Spanish culture in particular had long suppressed. Though a tourist himself, he watched the audience: "The Germans, Swiss, Americans, Englishmen gazed open-mouthed at an exhibition of sexual animality their world had taught them to repress" (167), a spectacle that suggests Carl Jung's collective, unconscious repression.[8]

Whether sexual repression in Spain was viewed collectively or individually, its chief culprit was the church. The church, which condemned sex, made Spaniards more conscious of it. In Europe Spain had the highest rates of prostitution in the city as well as in the village. "To be a prostitute was bad," Wright quips at the church, "but to be a prostitute who was not Catholic was worse" (21). This collective, almost unconscious, sexual repression that permeated Spanish society manifested itself in a vicious circle of prostitution and the church. Spanish Catholicism was "a religion whose outlook upon the universe almost legitimizes prostitution" (151). The Spanish people largely acquiesced in a circular argument the church had maintained over the centuries: "Sin exists, so declares this concept. Prostitution is sin, and proof of sin. So prostitution exists." This universal prostitution, then, was not regarded as something that must be eradicated, a cynical sign that "the work of salvation is not yet complete" and that the church must make "a more strenuous effort" to save men as well as women in the name of God (152).

From a sociological perspective, the church and prostitution helped each other. The church took great pride in its generosity by accepting fallen women under any circumstances with open arms: "a prostitute can at any time enter a church and gain absolution" (152). Such generosity, however, was not always considered by Spanish men as a genuinely religious endeavor. Rumor ran rampant throughout the country that some priests openly took advantage of "lonely" women, including prostitutes who sought salvation in the church. Since sexual freedom was condoned by the church, Spanish laymen were jealous of the sexual lives of the priests. A Spanish man felt that "if they can do it and get away with it, so can I." Wright reflects: "I, for one, feel it naïve in our Freudian, twentieth-century world even to allude to the bruited sexual lives of priests and nuns. I do not know nor am I interested in whether they have sexual lives or not. I hope that they do, for their own sake; and I'm sure that God does not mind" (154). Given the paganism and super-humanism that characterized Spanish religion and culture, Wright's reflection emphasizes a conviction that human sexuality, as exhibited at Montserrat as well as in the Spanish Catholic church, was the best and absolute proof of the existence of God.

From an economic point of view, prostitution and poverty were intertwined in Spain. In the middle of the twentieth century, Spain was the poorest nation in Western Europe. As an American, Wright paid homage to Seville, where Christopher Columbus's body was held in the cathedral. Despite the surrounding lands rich with orange groves, olive gardens, and wheat and rice farms, "the impression of poverty was so all-pervading, touching so many levels of life that, after an hour, poverty seemed to be the normal lot of man." Recollecting the fertile southern landscape and the teeming city life in America he had left behind, and Paris and the peaceful southern provinces of France, Wright comments: "I had to make an effort to remember that people lived better lives elsewhere" (178). Not only was Seville, a capital of "white slave" trade, a glaring metonym, but the whole nation "seemed one vast brothel" (187). In Spain, poverty and sexuality indeed went hand in hand.

Wright observed that Spanish sexuality began in childhood. "No people on earth," he stresses, "so pet and spoil their young as do the Spanish" (152). A Spanish woman at an early age is trained to be a "seductress." Once married to a poor man, she can justify selling her body if it is for feeding her children. On a national level, sex is regarded as a medium of exchange for goods and services. Significantly as well, "white slavery between Spain and the bristling brothels of North Africa is a wide-scale, well-organized, and genially conducted business—prostitution being perhaps the biggest business in the Mediterranean world" (150). Just as a poor young mother in the village is tempted to become a prostitute for the sake of feeding her hungry children, a young domestic earning low wages in a coastal city is enticed to travel to North Africa as a prostitute rather than "to be an ill-clad, half-starved slave to some spoiled, bourgeois Spanish wench" (151). Prostitution flourished in Spain, for there was behind this indigenous poverty a persistent pagan outlook upon life, a love of ritual, dance, sex, and night life.

3.

Among the rituals, customs, and social activities Wright saw in Spain, bull-fighting created a profound impression on his understanding of Spanish culture and religion. On the surface, a bullfight was a representation of the Spaniard's love for ritual and ceremony, "a delight in color and movement and sound and harmony" (151). But to Wright, below the surface this cruel ritual smacked of the central paradox of Spanish religion. On the one hand, bullfighting as a religious ritual found its sanction and justification in the canons and practices of Spanish Catholicism. On the other, however, it was antithetical to Spanish paganism, what Wright calls superhumanism as represented by the Black Virgin at Montserrat, as noted earlier. Whereas Spanish Catholics believed in the sanctity of saving the human soul over protecting the nonhuman life, pagans, such as Buddhists and Hindus, made no distinction between human beings and the rest of the animate world because they believed that the soul resides in them as well as in animals.[9]

As the opening section of *Pagan Spain,* "Life after Death," reaches its apogee with the concept of eternal procreation—the female principle in life as represented by the Black Virgin of Montserrat—the following section, "Death and Exaltation," dramatizes a bullfight Wright attended in Barcelona. At the beginning of the journey into Spain he befriended a Catalan family with whom he stayed for a short period. They told him that Spaniards, and Catalans in particular, "don't shrink from dark skins" and that they were traditionally miscegenational (80). But once Wright went into a village, he was constantly stared at as if he were a total stranger, one who did not belong in Europe. "Amidst these naïve yokels," he felt, "I became something that I had never been before, an object that was neither *human* nor *animal,* my dark skin and city clothes attracting more attention than even the bullfighters" (emphasis added; 131–32). While Spaniards would consider him neither human nor animal, it seemed as though bullfighting was a religious ritual which reflected both Catholicism, a religion eminently concerned with the human soul, and paganism, a superhuman and pantheistic philosophy of life encompassing all forms of life on earth.

From this ambivalent point of view, Wright's description of the bullfight is a unique achievement. Above all, he was able to describe not only how the bullfighter faced death, but also how the bull himself felt:

> Chamaco's left hand now grasped the muleta firmly; he turned away from
> the bull, looking at him sideways, letting the red cloth drop below his left
> knee. He now lifted his gleaming sword chin high and sighted along the

length of it, pointing its sharp, steel tip at the tormented and bloody mound of wounds on the bull's back. . . . The bull's horns rushed past his stomach as Chamaco tiptoed, leaning in and over the driving horns, and sent the sword to its hilt into the correct spot in the bull's body.

The bull halted, swayed. Chamaco stood watching him, gazing gently, sadly it seemed, into the bull's glazed and shocked eyes. . . .

I watched the bull. He sagged, his eyes on his tormentor. He took an uncertain, hesitant step forward, and then was still. Chamaco lifted his right hand high above the bull's dying head; it was a gesture that had in it a mixture of triumph and compassion. The bull now advanced a few feet more on tottering legs, then his back legs folded and his hind part sank to the sand, his forelegs bent at the knees. And you saw the split second when death gripped him, for his head nodded violently and dropped forward, still. A heave shook his body as he gave up his breath and his eyes went blank. He slid slowly forward, resting on his stomach in the sand, his legs stretching straight out. He rolled over on his back, his four legs already stiffening in death, shot up into the air. (111–12)

Although Wright vividly depicts man's battle against beast—the triumph of man's will over nature's power as sanctioned by Catholicism—his implication is unmistakable: the bullfight is a crime against life, nature, and God. Viewed from any religious vantage point, it is a blatant representation of the depravity of the human soul. At the conclusion of the bullfight, he says: "The man-made agony to assuage the emotional needs of men was over" (112).

What Wright agonized over most about this ritual, as perhaps any humanist would, was the behavior of the audience in the bullring in the aftermath of the slaughter. He was appalled to see the spectators wildly rush to the dead bull, kick its testicles, stomp them, spit at them, and grind them under their feet, "while their eyes held a glazed and excited look of sadism" (134). Even though the bull was dead, they looked as though they were venting their own long-repressed feelings. Such behavior reflected the performance as well: "The peak of muscle back of his neck gushed blood. That was the way it had been planned. The means were cruel; the ends were cruel; the beast was cruel; and the men who authored the bloody drama were cruel. The whirlpool of discordant instincts out of which this sodden but dazzling drama had been projected hinted at terrible torments of the heart" (102). As noted earlier, the cruelty of a bullfight is a reflection of man-centered Catholicism, in which beast, part of nature, is regarded as man's adversary. In a pagan religion the followers are taught to respect man as well as beast. Wright was quick to point out that although the predominant sentiment of the crowd was sadistic, some people in the crowd had compassion for the bull: "the crowd began to howl, protesting, disapproving, fearing that the bull was being punished too much, would be too weak to fight well" (104–5). This sentiment of the spectators was a sign not only of paganism but also of universal humanism.

The sadism displayed on the part of the spectators also involved the bull-fighter. Harry Whitney, an American, who had gone to live in Spain to become a bullfighter, informed Wright that the bullfight "has the intensity of religious emotion" and that the bullfighter is expected to offer his life to the bull. "Without that, there is no bullfight," Whitney explained (130). "More and more, when you're in the ring, you're not fighting the bull; you're trying to live up to the legend the public has built up about you. They ask for risks and they boo you when you refuse to take them. When the bullfighter believes in his legend and tries to obey the crowd, he's on his way to the graveyard" (131). Such a testimony suggests that Spaniards were fascinated by the cruelty perpetrated not only on the bull but also on the bullfighter, a perverted psychology akin to one often seen among the spectators who enjoy watching race car accidents.

In Wright's description of the bullfight, the cruel treatment of the dead bull by the spectators is suggestive of the lynchings he had witnessed in the South. In his horrifying portrayal of a lynching in "Big Boy Leaves Home," the victim is hanged from a tree and is burned alive as the white mob chants in ecstasy.[10] In *The Long Dream,* Wright's last novel, Chris, the protagonist's friend, is lynched for having had sexual relations with a white girl; afterwards he is castrated by the mob, and white women were fascinated by his genitals.[11] Watching the bullfight, Wright was filled with horror at the sadism the ritual created: "It had been beautiful and awful and horrible and glorious," he thought, "and ought to have been forbidden. . . ." When he confessed, "I was revolted, but hungry for more . . . indignant, but bewitched, utterly" (109), he was also expressing the paradox of Spanish character.

This sadism, a sign of human selfishness, to which he thought Spaniards were prone, was in contrast to the African primal outlook upon life he saw among the Ashanti. As reported in *Black Power,* he was enormously impressed by the African reverence for the nonhuman life, an innate faith in nature which was absent in Christianity in general and Catholicism in particular. In his journey into Africa, Wright also found a strong resemblance between the Akan religion and pagan religions such as Buddhism. Africans, as he saw in Ghana, would not cut down a live tree without first appeasing its spirit: they identified its livelihood with theirs. Both the Akan religion and Buddhism share the faith that humankind occupies a mere fraction of the universe. It is no small wonder, then, that Wright, as he watched the bull being slaughtered, poured out his deepest sympathy for it; he was genuinely concerned about how it felt, just as most of the Spaniards were ecstatic about its tragic death.

Viewed as a uniquely Christian ritual, Wright felt, the bullfight was nothing more than a religious practice in which the followers were taught not only how to accept the inevitability of death, but also how to create death, a means of sacrificing animal life for the benefit of human life. Such human selfishness and egotism once more manifested itself in the drama enacted in the bullring: "*There was no doubt but that this beast had to be killed!* He could be allowed to linger along; he could be played with, teased even, but he had to go, for there was no possibility of coming to terms with him. . . . This beast had not only to be slain, but *ceremoniously* slain—slain in a manner that would be unforgettable" (97). For Wright, the drama signified the mystery and miracle of human life. The mystery rested upon "why the human heart hungered for this strange need"; the miracle involved "the heart's finding that a rampaging bull so amply satisfied that need" (98).

Just as a Catholic priest offered faithful prostitutes absolution, the matador as a lay priest offered a mass in front of a huge audience in the bullring, the guilty penitents. What the priest and the matador shared was a common practice in which they themselves gained salvation in their work. But Wright realized that the matador's work was far more disciplined than the priest's. Whitney, the American bullfighter, told him that bullfighters in Spain "are not supposed to touch women or liquor. This is not to help you in fighting the bull; it is to keep you in condition to recuperate when you are gored. And make no mistake, you will be gored" (130). When the lives of the priest and the matador were compared, Whitney's observation that a bullfight, buttressed as it was by intensely religious emotion, always risked the bullfighter's life seemed an ironic understatement.

Relying on Whitney's experience and understanding, Wright was fascinated by the emotional aspect of the bullfight. Whitney told him: "The essence of the bullfight is not in moving around, but in standing still. And that's a hard thing to do. When you're holding that muleta and facing a bull, your instinct prompts you to run. And if you do, you're dead, for the bull can outrun you. You must plant your feet in the sand and face death" (129). Whitney's understanding was derived from Juan Belmonte, the most celebrated matador in Spain. Wright was interested in Belmonte's characterization of bullfighting as, in Belmonte's words, "a spiritual exercise and not merely a sport. Physical strength is not enough." Wright interpreted this exercise as "the conquering of fear, the making of a religion of the conquering of fear. Any man with enough courage to stand perfectly still in front of a bull will not be attacked or killed by that bull" (113). Wright was told the local legend of a matador who stood still reading a newspaper while the bull ignored him. But Wright thought it humanly impossible and inconceivable for a man to remain still against a surging beast that weighs at least ten times more than he does.

While Juan Belmonte's concept of bullfighting was concerned with the emotional aspect of the sport, the test of courage in the face of death, Hemingway was interested in portraying the technical and artistic aspects of the rite. Hemingway describes Romero's bullfight in *The Sun Also Rises* as though he were drawing a painting:

> The bull did not insist under the iron. He did not really want to get at the horse. He turned and the group broke apart and Romero was taking him out with his cape. He took him out softly and smoothly, and then stopped and, standing squarely in front of the bull, offered him the cape. The bull's tail went up and he charged, and Romero moved his arms ahead of the bull, wheeling, his feet firmed. The dampened, mud-weighted cape swung open and full as a sail fills, and Romero pivoted with it just ahead of the bull. At the end of the pass they were facing each other again. Romero smiled. The bull wanted it again, and Romero's cape filled again, this time on the other side. Each time he let the bull pass so close that the man and the bull and the cape that filled and pivoted ahead of the bull were all one sharply etched mass. It was all so slow and so controlled. It was as though he were rocking the bull to sleep. He made four veronicas like that, and finished with a half-veronica that turned his back on the bull and came away toward the applause, his hand on his hip, his cape on his arm, and the bull watching his back going away. (216–17)

As Wright in *Pagan Spain* discusses the concept of Belmonte, who, fighting the bull closely, displayed his courage in facing death, Hemingway in *The Sun Also Rises* also refers to Belmonte's principle of always working close to the bull. "This way," Jake Barnes, Hemingway's mouthpiece, says, "gave the sensation of coming tragedy. People went to the corrida to see Belmonte, to be given tragic sensations, and perhaps to see the death of Belmonte" (214). Because Belmonte in the novel is neither a major character nor a representation of bullfighting as a religious rite, Hemingway underplays Belmonte's role and underscores Romero's bullfight as a central image of love making:

> The bull was squared on all four feet to be killed, and Romero killed directly below us. He killed not as he had been forced to by the last bull, but as he wanted to. He profited directly in front of the bull, drew the

sword out of the folds of the muleta and sighted along the blade. The bull
watched him. Romero spoke to the bull and tapped one of his feet. The
bull charged and Romero waited for the charge, the muleta held low,
sighting along the blade, his feet firm. Then without taking a step forward, he became one with the bull, the sword was in high between the
shoulders, the bull had followed the low-swung flannel, that disappeared
as Romero lurched clear to the left, and it was over. The bull tried to go
forward, his legs commenced to settle, he swung from side to side, hesi-
tated, then went down on his knees, and Romero's older brother leaned
forward behind him and drove a short knife into the bull's neck at the
base of the horns. The first time he missed. He drove the knife in again,
and the bull went over, twitching and rigid. (220)

Wright, on the other hand, depicts the bullfight as a test of one's courage in
the face of death. He watched this drama of life for man, or death for beast,
as it unfolded in the bullring. "Man and beast," he writes, "had now become
fused into one plastic, slow-moving, terrible, delicate waltz of death, the
outcome of which hung upon the breath of a split second" (*Pagan Spain*
109).

In contrast to Hemingway's treatment of the matador, Wright was interested in bullfighting as a profession. Compassionate as he was, Wright was
troubled to see that a young bullfighter was too young to risk his life, but
Wright was told by a Spanish informant that the boy, coming from a poor
family, had become rich: "Pain caused by a bull's horn is far less awful than
pain caused by hunger" (107). Such a fact of poverty recalls a social and economic environment that bred prostitutes who sold their own bodies for the
sake of feeding their hungry children. Observing the young matador's performance, Wright also felt that the young man "did not quite believe in the
value of what he had done . . . and harbored some rejection or doubt about
the Niagara of applause that deafened his ears" (113). The boy, in fact,
regarded the bullfight as nothing more than his livelihood: he was concerned
neither emotionally nor philosophically with his profession.

4.

Despite the deeply religious tradition, whether Catholic or pagan, that buttressed its culture, Spain in modern times revealed degradation at all levels of
society. Before Wright begins his discourse, he quotes two lines from Carl
Sandburg:

> *I tell you the past is a bucket of ashes.*
> *I tell you yesterday is a wind gone down,*
>   *a sun dropped in the west.*

Wright is alluding to his own observation that the vestiges of the glorious past were scarcely visible in modern Spain. Not only did Spain lose its political influences in the modern world; its spiritual tradition fell victim to materialism and a decadent commercialism. Even though Spain remained a vital part of the capitalist world, its development was hampered by its outdated social and economic policies and practices. *Pagan Spain* begins with a quotation from Nietzsche, "*How poor indeed is man. . . . ,*" and it ends with Wright's own statement, "How poor indeed he is. . . ." By "he," Wright means the twentieth-century Spaniard, the modern Spanish national character, who had lost touch with "the *rich* infinities of possibility looming before the eyes of men," the "hearts responding to the call of a high courage," and "the will's desire for a new wisdom" (emphasis added; 241). For Wright, the Spanish people were indeed economically poor, but more importantly they seemed *poor* at adapting themselves to a modern progressive culture.

Throughout the text Wright tries to demonstrate the conservatism that gripped Spanish life individually as well as collectively. He saw, for instance, a Spanish Communist leader carry a statue of the Virgin on his back in an Easter procession because the statue was from his own neighborhood. To Wright's informant, this act was a glaring contradiction. "I cannot support that kind of nonsense," the man uttered. "That man had sworn that he did not believe in God. Yet there he was carrying the Virgin. How can you fight with men who twist and turn like that?" (215).

Conservatism and traditionalism in Spain, on the other hand, had little effect on race relations in the country. Surprisingly, Wright found Spaniards free of racial prejudice. None of them he met during his travels showed a trace of the racism to which he had become so accustomed in America and by which he was on occasion disturbed in France. Not only was he welcomed by Spaniards personally and affectionately wherever he visited, but he also found them, and young intellectuals in particular, invariably anti-racist, anti-anti-Semitism, anti-Franco, anti-imperialist, anti-Russian, and anti-American.

For Wright, Spaniards as a whole possessed an innate virtue that enabled them to relate to their fellow human beings on a personal and spiritual basis rather than in terms of social and political relationships, a human-made trait that plagued race relations in America. Such a virtue notwithstanding, Spaniards were found as pecuniarily greedy as Americans; their materialistic outlook upon life also degraded their culture. Historically, Spanish colonialists had been regarded as less resistant to miscegenation than other Europeans, and yet, as a Spanish informant told Wright, "[w]e gave them our culture in a way that no other European nation ever did, and we meant it. But we were greedy; we were after gold. And that ruined us" (213).

One of the culprits responsible for Spain's cultural stagnation was the Catholic church. Spanish intellectuals were all in agreement that reforming archaic traditions must begin "at the cradle" and with "a new generation" (204). But the church, in collaboration with Franco, the Falange, and the Army, always stood in the way of change. Earlier in his discussion of Spanish character Wright posed this question:

> But why was Spain a dictatorship? I had long believed that where you found tyranny, such as exists in Russia, you would also find a confounding freedom secreted somewhere; that where you had a stifling bureaucracy, such as in France, there was a redeeming element of personal liberty; that where you had a police state, such as was in Argentina, you had under it, disguised, a warm comradeship; and that where you had a restrained and reserved attitude, such as is in England, you had, somewhere nearby, equalizing it, a licentious impulse to expression. *Did that principle hold true in Spain?* (12)

Wright's subsequent observation confirmed that a sense of freedom and open-mindedness existed in Spain only on the surface of its daily living.

Otherwise, as Wright recognized, the Spanish mind was stifled by its own uniquely religious and irrational consciousness. Indeed, Spanish culture was irrational just as Akan culture was irrational. And the sacredness and irrationality of Spain was in contrast to the secular that had liberated the rest of Europe from its past. Even compared with some part of Africa, and most of Asia, Spain lagged behind in its progress toward modernism. "The African," Wright notes, "though thrashing about in a void, was free to create a future, but the pagan traditions of Spain had sustained no such mortal wound" (193). Africa and Asia, as he saw, were endowed with seeds of modernism while Spain sadly was locked in tradition and religion.

Such a critical view of Spain notwithstanding, Wright was nevertheless sympathetic toward the energetic, maternal instinct of Spanish women, without which Spanish culture would not have survived after World War II. He discovered, for example, a strong affinity between the indigenous matriarchalism in the Ashanti, as discussed in *Black Power,* and the stalwart womanhood in Spain. Spain, beleaguered as it seemed by modernism and multiculturalism, withdrew into the past to regain its usable elements, however irrational and primeval they might have appeared in the eyes of the world. Over the centuries Spanish men had built a state but never a society, a fact of history that betrayed another paradox of Spanish culture. Wright was convinced above all that Spanish women, not Spanish men, had borne the burdens of an economically poor nation. As women worked and reared children, men idled away their time talking abstract nonsense in the countless establishments of entertainment that flooded an otherwise chaotic landscape. If there was a semblance of society, it was based only on the hearts and minds of women whose devotion to life stabilized Spain. This apotheosis of Spanish womanhood is derived from the female principle in life, a salient characteristic of pagan Spain.

CHAPTER 8

The African
"Primal Outlook upon Life":
Wright and Morrison

What Wright's travelogues and Morrison's *Beloved* (1987) have in common is that they reconsider Western discourse, which had been previously characterized solely by imperialism and a male-centered worldview. Schoolteacher in *Beloved*, for example, functions as an agent representing the most treacherous kind of institutional evil. Such a figure operates with the approval of a hegemonic culture under the guise of reason and enlightenment. This figure represents European imperialists and Christian missionaries in Wright's *Black Power*, just as it represents the Falange and the Catholic church in his *Pagan Spain*. The expedition that Sethe, Schoolteacher's pupil, makes outside of school teaches her to refute the lessons given by her teacher. In a similar vein, Wright, who had left America, where he was born and schooled, made an expedition into Africa and Spain. As a result, *Black Power* and *Pagan Spain* turn out to be not merely portrayals of African and Spanish cultures, but more importantly a penetrating cultural criticism of the West. Wright's travelogues and *Beloved* both examine the tradition-bound Western myths as enshrined in religious, political, and legal discourses and as reflected in such institutions as Christianity, slavery, and marriage.

In their efforts to displace Western discourse, Wright and Morrison try to reinstate what Wright calls "his [the African's] primal outlook upon life" (*Black Power* 266). "If my work," Morrison remarks, "is to confront a reality unlike the received reality of the West, it must centralize and animate information discredited by the West . . . because it is information described as 'lore' or 'gossip' or 'magic' or 'sentiment'" ("Memory" 388). Though fiction, *Beloved*, clearly informed by the tenor of the postmodern, thrives on its use of protesting voices to challenge political consensus and expand existing concepts of history. Morrison, in fact, takes pride in the political nature of her work. "The work," she has argued, "must be political. . . . The best art is political and you ought to be able to make it unquestionably political and irrevocably beautiful at the same time" ("Rootedness" 344–45). She is in agreement with Wright, who told James Baldwin: "*All* literature is protest. You can't name a single novel that isn't protest" (Baldwin, *Nobody Knows* 157).

In *Black Power,* Wright repeatedly shows that the primal outlook in African culture is buttressed by the African's "basically poetic apprehension of existence" (266) and "poetic humanity" (dedication). The vision Wright and Morrison come to share is postmodern in its recognition not only of political and historical situatedness but also of aesthetic discourse in order to contest and disrupt from within. During his journey into Africa, Wright discovered that in the face of European imperialism, the Ashanti had survived on the strength of familial and tribal kinship and love. His travels to Spain, as discussed in the previous chapter, revealed that Spanish religiosity was more pagan than Christian and that the pillar of Spanish culture was Spanish womanhood as represented by the Black Virgin of Montserrat. The communal kinship in Africa, epitomized by matriarchal society and symbolized by the Black Virgin, is also embodied in Sethe's enduring relationship with Beloved in Morrison's novel. The African's primal outlook indeed underlies the theme of *Beloved.* "Critics of my work," Morrison notes, "have often left something to be desired because they don't always evolve out of the culture, the world, the given quality out of which I write" (McKay 425).

1.

When Wright traveled to West Africa to write *Black Power,* he was struck by a culture in transition. The profound myths, traditions, and customs underlying African culture were in conflict with its modernization. In the eyes of Western anthropologists and imperialists, African culture seemed primitive and irrational. Wright, however, realized that the African always seemed a "savage" to the Westerner, just as the modern developments in the West were "fantastic" to the African. To Wright, the Western definition of the inferiority of the African race had derived from the hegemonic assumptions of academicians, assumptions that were scarcely related to the fundamental African beliefs. In short, African culture seemed irrational to Westerners just as Western culture did to Africans.

One of the African beliefs Westerners find difficult to comprehend is the

African concept of time—that time is not chronological and linear but cyclical. Believing in a circular movement of time, the African wishes what happened in the past to happen again. Africans, Wright thought, were capable of adapting to Western technology and industrialization, but their concept of time would be detrimental to the modernization of an old culture. Accra, the first city in Africa Wright visited en route to Kumasi, the Ashanti capital, reflected such a concept of time. The houses in Accra had no street numbers, a lack that not only indicated a chaotic urban development but also suggested a circular concept of time and space. Having no numbers assigned to individual houses meant that the houses had come into existence without regard for order and location and that the city functioned as a maze.[1]

Unlike the traditional journey motif, mainly concerned with the male narrator's worldview, Morrison's quest in *Beloved* is to acquire what Wright calls in *Black Power* the African's "primal outlook upon life" (266). Just as Wright in his journey into pagan Spain witnessed the energetic, maternal instinct of the Spanish woman and the female principle in life represented by the Black Virgin of Montserrat, Sethe in her journey from slavery to freedom seizes upon the maternal love of child innate in African culture. In stark contrast to the traditional slave narrative, *Beloved* features the heroic slave mother as a replacement of the figure of the heroic male fugitive.

Morrison's technique in *Beloved* is also innovative and strikingly postmodern. In a traditional gothic tale, the movement is either from the present to the past or from the past to the present. In Edgar Allan Poe's "Ligeia," for example, the first half of the story takes place as the narrator contemplates past events, and the latter half elaborates Ligeia's gradual return to the present. In *Beloved* the movement in time is extremely fluid: the story begins one day in 1873 at 124 Bluestone Road in Cincinnati and goes back not only to Sethe's slavery in Kentucky and the Middle Passage but also to her ancestors in Africa. Throughout the text, the story constantly goes back and forth between the present and the past. In *Black Power* Wright speaks of the African's concept of time: "His was a circular kind of time; the past had to be made like the present" (175). To Africans, time is cyclic rather than linear as in Western discourse. In *Beloved* Morrison uses this concept of time: the past and the present are intermingled to form one continuum. The movement in time, then, enables their "dead" ancestors to return to the present with their primal outlook intact as guiding forces.[2]

For Morrison as narrator, this concept of time allows her to convert the past to the present through memory. "Because so much in public and scholarly life," she has complained, "forbids us to take seriously the milieu of buried stimuli, it is often extremely hard to seek out both the stimulus and its galaxy and to recognize their value when they arrive." The value of Sethe's vision in the present, then, is determined by the intensity and quality of memory, the memory generated not only by one individual but also by her race and her culture. "Memory," Morrison underscores, "is for me always fresh, in spite of the fact that the object being remembered is done and past" ("Memory" 385).

Unlike the traditional journey narrative, *Beloved* does not make the identity of the two women, "the join" on their travel, its ultimate goal. Morrison's quest for that memory is open-ended: as Beloved reappears, Sethe disappears, and the thrust of the story in the end is toward the future, suggesting that the story must not "pass on," must not die, must continue. Morrison's concept of time allows the characters not only to reflect on the past but also to plan on the future. At the end of the novel Paul D reminds Sethe of their future. Their experiences suggest that African American life in the future must be strengthened by the African primal view of existence: communal and familial kinship.

Time in *Beloved* is not only cyclic as it is in African culture but also fluid and mysterious. Beloved's appearance at the beginning of the novel is contrasted to her disappearance in the end: "By and by all trace is gone, and what is forgotten is not only the footprints but the water too and what it is down there. The rest is weather. Not the breath of the disremembered and unaccounted for, but wind in the eaves, or spring ice thawing too quickly. Just weather" (275). Not only are such images as "wind in the eaves" and "spring ice thawing too quickly" signs of the future, but Morrison also brings home her worldview: the primacy of spirit over flesh, humanism over materialism, harmony over disruption. Her attainment of such vision is a nebulous affair, however, and Beloved's appearance and disappearance in particular can be interpreted psychoanalytically.[3] "Appearance/disappearance," Jacques Lacan theorizes, "takes place between two points, the initial and the terminal of this logical time—between the instant of seeing, when something of the intuition itself is always elided, not to say lost, and that elusive moment when the apprehension of the unconscious is not, in fact, concluded, when it is always a question of an 'absorption' fraught with false trails" (*Four Fundamental Concepts* 32).

Wright, on the other hand, appreciated the ancestral worship not only characteristic of African religion but also typical of other religions such as Hinduism, Buddhism, and Shintoism; even so, he was unable to penetrate the detail and symbolism of its mystery. He had no difficulty understanding, for example, the dedication of an African woman's life to preparing and serving food to the bones of a dead king, a ritual analogous to a Buddhist woman's service in offering food to statues of the Buddha. Similarly, just as a menstruating woman is feared in Ashanti life, a Shintoist woman in the same condition abstains from consecrating the food to be presented at the household shrine. But Wright found it difficult to appreciate the symbolism of the Golden Stool, shrouded in mystery. To him the stool represented the collected soul of a million people. Ashanti appeared Oriental, for a soul hidden behind the dark face "shrinks from revealing itself" (*Black Power* 273). Indeed, Western discourse is incapable of explaining the depth of the tribal culture. Africans, conscious of unwritten history, have created methods of representation to cast doubt upon the Westerners attempting to understand them.

The African primal outlook on life, in which a person's consciousness, as Wright and Morrison both believe, corresponds to the spirit of nature, bears a strong resemblance to the concept of enlightenment in Buddhism. To the African mind and to Buddhism, divinity exists in nature only if the person is intuitively conscious of divinity in the self. To American transcendentalists such as Emerson and Whitman, God exists in nature regardless of whether the person is capable of such intuition. Wright's discussion of the African concept of life is also suggestive of Zen's emphasis on transcending the dualism of life and death. As mentioned in the introduction, Zen master Dogen taught that life and death both constitute human experience and that there is no need to avoid death.[4] The funeral service Wright saw in an Ashanti tribe showed him that "the 'dead' live side by side with the living; they eat, breathe, laugh, hate, love, and continue doing in the world of ghostly shadows exactly what they had been doing in the world of flesh and blood" (*Black Power* 213).

Like a Buddhist text, Dr. J. B. Danquah's *The Akan Doctrine of God* persuaded Wright of the African belief that spirits reside in inanimate objects like trees, stones, and rivers, an innate African philosophy on which Morrison's narrative in *Beloved* is based. Wright also witnessed Africans' belief in ghosts and in the spirits of the dead, as Morrison used the concept in her fiction. Just as, in Zen, a tree contains satori only when the viewer can see it through his or her enlightened eyes, Wright saw in African life a closer relationship between human beings and nature than between human beings and their social and political environment:

> Africa, with its high rain forest, with its stifling heat and lush vegetation, might well be mankind's queerest laboratory. Here instinct ruled and flowered without being concerned with the nature of the physical structure of the world; man lived without too much effort; there was nothing

to distract him from concentrating upon the currents and countercurrents of his heart. He was thus free to project out of himself what he thought he was. Man has lived here in a waking dream, and, to some extent, he still lives here in that dream. (*Black Power* 159)

Wright created here an image of the noble black man: Africa evokes in one "a total attitude toward life, calling into question the basic assumptions of existence," just as Zen teaches one a way of life completely independent of what one has been socially and politically conditioned to lead. As if echoing the enlightenment of Zen, Wright says: "Africa is the world of man; if you are wild, Africa's wild; if you are empty, so's Africa" (159).

Wright was moreover fascinated by the African reverence for nonhuman beings, a primal African attitude that corresponds to Buddhist belief:

> The pre-Christian African was impressed with the littleness of himself and he walked the earth warily, lest he disturb the presence of invisible gods. When he wanted to disrupt the terrible majesty of the ocean in order to fish, he first made sacrifices to its crashing and rolling waves; he dared not cut down a tree without first propitiating its spirit so that it would not haunt him; he loved his fragile life and he was convinced that the tree loved its life also. (*Black Power* 261–62)

The concept of unity, continuity, and infinity underlying that of life and death is what the Akan religion and Buddhism share.[5] When Wright was among the Ashanti, he was not conscious of an affinity between the two religions, but as he later read R. H. Blyth's explanation of Zen and its influence on haiku, he found both religious philosophies fundamentally alike.

This unity and continuity between life and death, a quintessential African outlook, is fictionalized in *Beloved* with much intricacy and in depth. At times Morrison freely lets time elapse for generations and centuries. Sethe remembers the dancing feet of her dead mother as she feels the kicking legs of Denver in her womb. The pain caused by Denver's movement makes her feel as if she were rammed by an antelope, a wild animal roaming in Africa centuries earlier. Even though she has never seen an antelope, the creation of this image bridges the gap between the occurrences of the present and those of the past. "Oh but when they sang," Morrison writes. "And oh but when they danced and sometimes they danced the antelope. . . . They shifted shapes and became something other. Some unchained, demanding other whose feet knew her pulse better than she did. Just like this one in her stomach" (31). Morrison bridges the gap between Denver's generation and her grandmother's, as well as that between American history and African history, by merging the images of the antelope, the grandmother's dancing, and Denver's kicking into a unified image. Later in the story Beloved recalls her traumatic experiences on a slave ship in which the captured Africans were herded into a crammed space: "All of it is now it is always now there will never be a time when I am not crouching and watching others who are crouching too   I am always crouching   the man on my face is dead" (210). A slave woman's crouching in the confined space immediately evokes the image of a free woman's crouching in an open field on the African continent, "where a woman takes flowers away from their leaves and puts them in a round basket   before the clouds   she is crouching near us   but I do not see her until he locks his eyes and dies on my face" (211–12). This image unifies Beloved's stream-of-consciousness rememberings of the two women from the different centuries.

On the surface of the story the distinction of present and past reflects that of outside and inside, the outer world and the character's mind. But the story cannot distinguish the present from the past. Denver, for example, views the present in terms of the past because she is obsessed with the premonition that Beloved is her ghost sister. The character's inability to distinguish between his or her inner mind and the outer world, the past and the present, manifests itself in Sethe's relationship with Beloved, Morrison's central theme. At a climactic moment Morrison depicts the mother and daughter's reunion:

> I have to have my face   I go in   the grass opens   she opens it   I am in
> the water and she is coming   there is no round basket   no iron circle
> around her neck   she goes up where the diamonds are   I follow her   we
> are in the diamonds which are her earrings now   my face is coming   I
> have to have it   I am looking for the join   I am loving my face so much
>   my dark face is close to me   I want to join (213)

As Beloved sees her own face reflected in the water, she at once identifies with her mother.

2.

The primacy of kinship over individualism, a social practice based on the African primal view of human existence, is also conveyed in Morrison's fiction. Morrison takes pains to express this African idealism in terms of place as well as of time. As time plays a crucial role in unifying various planes of existence in *Beloved,* so does the word *place.* Morrison's use of such a word is so powerful that it imbues the text with a postmodern sense of situatedness. Just as Wright explains the Akan doctrine of God, in which the deceased live exactly as do the living, Morrison portrays spirits and ghosts as if they were alive. When Sethe smiles at Beloved, for instance, her smile is reflected on Beloved's face: "I see her face which is mine it is the face that was going to smile at me in the *place* where we crouched" (212–13; emphasis added). Beloved's use of the words *face* and *place* suggests her inability to separate her own body from that of her mother. Earlier in the story, Sethe reminisces about a woman named Nan who "used different words," the same language her own mother spoke. Although she does not remember the language, "the messages—that was and had been there all along" (62) links her back to her mother and to her mother's land, the place where women picked flowers in freedom before the slave traders invaded their place.

As the function of time in *Beloved* is fluid, so is Morrison's use of the word *place.* The characters journey from place to place freely and abruptly as they please. They constantly traverse the boundary between the visible and the invisible, the physical and the spiritual, the conscious and the unconscious. Baby Suggs, for example, expresses primal human sensations:

> "Here," she said, "in this here place, we flesh; flesh that weeps, laughs; flesh that dances on bare feet in grass. Love it. Love it hard. . . . Love your hands! . . . Touch others with them, pat them together, stroke them on your face. . . . The dark, dark liver—love it, love it, and the beat and beating heart, love that too. More than eyes or feet. More than lungs that have yet to draw free air. More than your life-holding womb and your life-giving private parts, hear me now, love your heart. For this is the prize." (88–89)

In her exhortations that emphasize *this* place and *this* time, Baby Suggs is calling not only for self-love but also for communal kinship. Her use of words is reminiscent of those of a transcendental poet, such as Whitman in "Song of Myself."[6]

Morrison's use of *place* varies from character to character, from the dead to the living in particular. The referents of a place for Baby Suggs are characterized by their concrete and contemporaneous existence: *flesh, feet, grass, hands, face, backs, shoulders, arms, womb, lungs, heart.* By contrast, Beloved's referent for a place is not only abstract but elusive, as a dialogue between Beloved and Denver illustrates:

"What is it?" asks Denver.

"Look," she points to the sunlit cracks.

"What? I don't see nothing." Denver follows the pointing finger. . . .

Beloved focuses her eyes. "Over there. Her face."

Denver looks where Beloved's eyes go; there is nothing but darkness there.

"Whose face? Who is it?"

"Me. It's me."

She is smiling again. (124)

Moreover, Morrison's language in *Beloved* is strikingly postmodern in its use of contestatory voices and ironic, parodic modes of expression. It challenges Western discourse and expands concepts of history. Stamp Paid, for example, parodies the anthropological observation, as Wright in *Black Power* assails Western anthropologists, that the "jungle" life of black people originated from African culture: "Whitepeople believed that whatever the manners, under every dark skin was a jungle." He challenges such a notion by articulating fact and history: "The more coloredpeople spent their strength trying to convince them how gentle they were, how clever and loving, how human, the more they used themselves up to persuade whites of something Negroes believed could not be questioned, the deeper and more tangled the jungle grew inside. But it wasn't the jungle blacks brought with them to this *place* from the other (livable) *place*. It was the jungle whitefolks planted in them" (*Beloved* 198; emphasis added).

The most poignant use of *place* is reserved for Morrison's expression of the central theme. Her aim in this narrative is to deconstruct and reconstruct history about an incident in 1855 in which, out of her innate love of child— what Stamp Paid calls "how gentle . . . and loving, how human . . . something Negroes believed could not be questioned"—a slave mother ran away to Cincinnati with her four children and attempted to kill the children when they were chased and then caught by her owner.[7] Sethe, faced with this genuinely human dilemma, opts for murdering Beloved. The text Morrison creates to dramatize Sethe's dilemma and action reverberates the morally unquestionable ideology that, for human beings, the place of death is better than that of slavery. From the beginning of the story Morrison is intent upon creating a parody to drive home the meaning of slavery. Early in the story, Sethe reminisces about her experiences at Sweet Home. "After choosing Halle for her husband," she wonders about their wedding: "Mrs. Garner," Morrison describes the scene, "put down her cooking spoon. Laughing a little, she touched Sethe on the head, saying, 'You are one sweet child.' And then no more" (26). It is utterly ironic that the kinship of Sethe and Beloved, the mother-daughter relationship that has overcome slavery, is inherently stable and permanent whereas the mother-daughter relationship Mrs. Garner and Sethe forged at Sweet Home is not.

What motivates the African American characters in *Beloved* is their primal outlook on life: spiritualism and kinship. Searching for their "beloved," Sethe and Denver try to reconnect their kinship with all sixty million women, and they deny any boundary between the individual and the group. Such action disrupts the Western and American character of individualism and self-reliance. Sethe's and Denver's quest is further intensified by Paul D's appearance on the scene. Trying to revive Sethe with the words and images both remembered, Paul D reconnects her with the community. In Morrison's fiction, alienation from community and kinship leads to tragic consequences; the reassertion of this bond makes possible the recovery of order and wholeness.

As pointed out earlier, Wright discovered in Ashanti's tribal culture the primacy of kinship and community over individualism. For the Ashanti, this solidarity, a defense mechanism to fend off industrialism and imperialism, was a form of African nationalism that challenged the cross-cultural politics in modern Africa. Wright's Marxist stories in *Uncle Tom's Children* are endowed with this communal spirit. In "Long Black Song" Silas's individualistic spirit in competing with white farmers is negated by the lack of solidarity with his black community: one individual's liberation is not accomplished until all oppressed people are liberated. In a similar vein Morrison has stated that African American communal kinship is rooted in African culture. "The contemporary autobiography," she says, "tends to be 'how I got over—look at me—alone—let me show you how I did it.' . . . I want to point out the dangers, to show that nice things don't always happen to the totally self-reliant if there is no conscious historical connection" ("Rootedness" 339–40, 344).

Contrary to Morrison's view of self-reliance, however, Wright's is ambivalent. In *Black Power,* while Wright admired close relationships that bonded the Ashanti family and tribe, he was troubled by the denial of individualism. All his life he believed in the twin values of American life: individualism and freedom. Not only did he remain ambivalent on the subject, but to him the tribal solidarity and the lack of individualism in African life signified the African paradox in modern times. The open letter he wrote Nkrumah on his way home reflects his ambivalent feelings about African culture in general and this African pioneer's political strategy in particular.[8]

In fact, Paul D's advice to Sethe bears a striking resemblance to Wright's to

Nkrumah. Reviewing Sethe's ordeal in slavery, Sethe and Paul D are engaged in this dialogue:

> "It ain't my job to know what's worse. It's my job to know what is and to keep them away from what I know is terrible. I did that."
> "What you did was wrong, Sethe."
> "I should have gone on back there? Taken my babies back there?"
> "There could have been a way. Some other way."
> "What way?"
> "You got two feet, Sethe, not four," he said, and right then a forest sprang up between them; trackless and quiet. (165)

Reminding Sethe of having two feet rather than four, Paul D admonishes her against reliance on others. At the end of the novel, however, he abandons his earlier doctrine of individualism and self-reliance and comes to believe in communality as the most powerful weapon in the battle of life. "Look," he calls her attention, "Denver be here in the day. I be here in the night. I'm a take care of you, you hear? Starting now. First off, you don't smell right. Stay there. Don't move. Let me heat up some water . . . Is it all right, Sethe, if I heat up some water?" Quipping at the conversion, she asks him, "And count my feet?" (272).

3.

As the title of Morrison's novel suggests, this insistence on communal kinship, the African primal view of existence, permeates the entire text. It is a mother's love for her child that constitutes the deepest layer of human relationship. As Sethe's story unfolds, Denver gradually comes to understand the paradox that compelled her mother to kill Beloved. Sethe convinces Denver that her act of murder was justified because it came from spiritual love.[9] Pitted against the male-female relationship such as that of Paul D and Sethe, how strong and deep this mother-child bond remains becomes evident as the narrative develops. From time to time Morrison emphasizes the depth and permanence of mother-child kinship with such images as baby blood, mother's milk, and growing trees. At the end of the novel Paul D tries to negotiate his future with Sethe, but his attempt fails because spiritual love does not exist between them. By the time Beloved has chased Paul D out of Sethe's house and lured him into spiritless sex in the cold-house, she deals the relationship of Paul D and Sethe permanent separation. When he goes to live in the cellar of the church, Stamp Paid tries vainly to rectify the situation by pleading with him: "She ain't crazy. She love those children. She was trying to outhurt the hurter" (234).

The mother-daughter kinship that dominates Sethe's story is remindful of the female principle in life represented by the Black Virgin in Wright's *Pagan Spain.* Instead of applying Freudian psychoanalysis,[10] which overemphasizes male sexual desire, Wright views the Black Virgin in terms of what he calls "superhuman order of reality" (*Pagan Spain* 61). Contrary to the male principle of life, which smacks of Christianity,[11] he defines the genesis of the Virgin in Spain as pagan, for in Eastern and African religions the Holy Mother, the perennial life-giver, is a representation of nature. In *Beloved,* mother's irresistible urge to feed milk, child's insatiable sucking of mother's nipple, "no stopping water breaking from a breaking womb" (51)—all such natural actions establish the strongest, undeniable nexus between mother and child. At the triumphant moment of her maternal quest, Sethe declares: "I was big, Paul D, and deep and wide and when I stretched out my arms all my children could get in between. I was *that* wide" (162).

As shown in *Black Power,* the African concept of society is derived from kinship and love in the family. Just as the Akan God is a woman, the state is owned by a female king and a child is under the custody of its mother, while the state is ruled by a male king and a family is managed by a father. Because the state is supported by women, the family is matrilineal in its inheritance. The supremacy of woman in the African state and family reflects the universal idea of Mother Nature. Womanhood in *Black Power* constitutes an innate representation of African character. Just as Wright in his journey into pagan Spain witnessed the energetic maternal instinct of the Spanish woman and the female principle in life represented by the Black Virgin of Montserrat, Sethe in her journey from slavery to freedom seizes upon the maternal love of child innate in African culture. In contrast to the traditional slave narrative, *Beloved* features the heroic slave mother to replace the figure of the heroic male fugitive.

The mother-daughter bond in *Beloved,* representative of superhumanism, originated in African religiosity. According to the Akan doctrine of God, as reported in *Black Power,* Africans believed in reincarnation just as do Buddhists: ancestors freely return to the present, and their spirits reside in nonhuman objects. Africans indeed denied the Western dichotomy of life and death. For them life in the spiritual world exactly reflected that in this world: the dead carry on their lives exactly as do the living in the present world. Given this vision of existence, not only can we understand a slave mother's infanticide in *Beloved*; we are also painfully reminded of humankind's worst crime—slavery.

Part III

Eastern and African American
Cross-Cultural Visions

CHAPTER 9

The Poetics of Nature:
Wright's Haiku, Zen, and Lacan

1.

While Wright is acclaimed for his powerful prose in such books as *Native Son* and *Black Boy*, critics and readers alike have paid little attention to his poetry and, in particular, to his haiku, even though they have been in print for nearly a decade. In "Blueprint for Negro Writing" (1937) Wright argued that "the Negro writer who seeks to function within his race as a purposeful agent has a serious responsibility. In order to do justice to his subject matter, in order to depict Negro life in all of its manifold and intricate relationships, a deep, informed, and complex consciousness is necessary; a consciousness which draws for its strength upon the fluid lore of a great people, and moulds this lore with the concepts that move and direct the forces of history today." Despite the context of that idea, drawn from his discussion "Social Consciousness and Responsibility," the concept of an individual consciousness dependent on the "fluid lore" of a people raises, as Wright noted, "the question of the personality of the writer. It means that in the lives of Negro writers must be found those materials and experiences which will create a meaningful picture of the world today." Wright felt that in his new role the black writer must "create values by which his race is to struggle, live and die." In his discussion "The Problem of Theme," he added that "this does not mean that a Negro writer's sole concern must be with rendering the social scene"; instead, he must have a sense of "the *whole* life" that "he is seeking" and that needs to be "vivid and strong in him" ("Blueprint" 43–44, 46).

What was "vivid and strong" in Wright, and had been from his childhood on, is reflected in his poetry. To Wright, being a responsible agent for his people meant that he had to draw on the materials of his own life, much of which was deeply involved with his feelings about nature. To have a sense of "the *whole* life" and to "create values" for his people meant that Wright had to contend with his deepest yearnings about a harmonious union between human beings and nature. In writing poetry he must have found echoes of all he believed in and desired, both in the form pleasurable and challenging to him as an artist and in the content so strongly appealing to his inner self.

The evidence of Wright's identification with nature and his use of its motif stretch from "Big Boy Leaves Home," with its rural events around the swimming hole, to *Black Boy,* but the poetics of nature culminates in his haiku. In *Black Boy* he expresses his delight "in seeing long straight rows of red and green vegetables," and he expresses nostalgia when he hears "the crying strings of wild geese winging south against a bleak, autumn sky." Wright, in fact, used this portrayal as one of the haiku selected in *This Other World: Projections in the Haiku Manner:*

> 581.   Don't they make you sad,
> Those wild geese winging southward,
>   O lonely scarecrow?
>   (Wright)

He even wishes to "imitate the petty pride of sparrows" and finds an "incomprehensible secret embodied in a whitish toadstool hiding in the dark shade of a rotting log." Most revealing, perhaps, is his yearning for identification when he sees "a solitary ant carrying a burden upon a mysterious journey" (*Black Boy* 14). The evidence is a record of his early childhood days and sensations, transformed beyond the expansive symbolism of *Black Boy* into those patterns from Mississippi days when the young Wright learned to identify his mood and self with specific aspects of nature. The domain of nature was a space he wanted to inhabit.

Sometime during the summer of 1959, Wright was introduced to haiku by Sinclair Beiles, a young poet who loved its form (Fabre 505). Only recently has Beiles been identified as a poet from South Africa living in Paris and associating with other poets of the Beat generation, such as Jack Kerouac, Allen Ginsberg, William Burroughs, and Gary Snyder.[1] Later in the 1960s, after Wright's death, Ginsberg and Snyder, for example, became so fascinated with Zen and Zazen, a kneeling meditation, that they studied Zen philosophy and practice in earnest with priests living in celebrated medieval monasteries in Japan. Wright, on the other hand, borrowed from the South African poet R. H. Blyth's four volumes on the art and history of haiku and its relationship to Zen philosophy, and he settled down to rediscover his old dream of oneness with all life. By March 1960 he was so captivated by the beauty of haiku that he was already in the midst of composing what turned out to be over four thousand separate haiku.[2]

2.

In studying Blyth's analysis and reading of classic haiku, Wright learned that haiku masters were able to present in direct statement the paradox of human union with nature, expressing the desire to be a part of nature while simultaneously maintaining their separate identity. Born and trained in Western culture and tradition, Wright as an artist must have struggled to develop such a characteristic in his haiku. Above all, as Blyth emphasizes, great haiku call for a strict Zen discipline on the part of the poet, much like a Zen priest. Such haiku call for simplicity of language, thought, and image, a lack of complication often revealed in the spontaneous joy of human union with nature. The joy, Blyth points out, comes from "the (apparent) re-union of ourselves with things" (*Haiku* 9), our being ourselves. Austerity on the part of the poet, a Zen discipline, is not only a lack of intellectualization; it is almost a wordlessness, a condition in which words are used not to externalize the poet's state of feeling but to "clear away something that seems to stand between" the poet and real things. Because the real things are not actually separate from the poet, they "are then perceived by self-knowledge" (176). "Zen," as Blyth observes, is "*non-intellectual*" (182). Classic haiku, as Wright learned, remove as many words as possible, stressing non-intellectuality, for thought, like passion, must depend upon and not substitute for intuition. Blyth finds joy in Zen-inspired haiku, in the humor, the lightness, the lack of sentimentality: "The humour of haiku and Zen . . . goes down to something deeper than the unconscious where repressions wait with ill-concealed impatience. It goes beyond this into the realm where a thing is and is not at the same time, and yet at the very same time *is*" (199).

Another major characteristic of haiku Wright learned is a love of nature that is inseparable from the ordinary. A love of nature without humanizing or sentimentalizing it, as Blyth notes, stems from the Taoist belief in the unity and harmony of all things, a sense of kinship among all things. For Blyth this characteristic is explained in terms of selflessness, meaning that the poet has identified with nature. The loss of the poet's individuality, or what postmodern psychoanalysts would call "loss of subjectivity," within the union with nature involves a generalized melancholy aspect or loneliness as an underlying rhythm. It represents a state of Zen, of "absolute spiritual poverty in which, having nothing, we possess all" (162). In Zen-inspired haiku, the material or the concrete is emphasized without the expression of any general principles of abstract reasoning. Animate and inanimate lose their differences so that one might say haiku are not about human beings but about things. Zen teaches, as Blyth observes, that the ordinary thing and the love of nature are reduced to a detached love of life as it is, without idealistic, moralistic, or ethical attachments. Things are equal to human beings; both exist through and because of each other.

The most important principle for writing haiku, as Blyth demonstrates with the classic examples he quotes in the original in Japanese and in his translation, is that a haiku poet views nature from a perspective devoid of human subjectivity. Unlike Western romantic poetry and even the earlier Japanese poetry called *waka,* haiku, Blyth observes, "is as near to life and nature as possible, as far from literature and fine writing as may be, so that the asceticism is art and the art is asceticism" (*History of Haiku* 1: 1). Blyth's definition of haiku as an ascetic art means that classic haiku by such masters as Basho, Buson, and Issa, whom Wright emulated, strictly concern objects and phenomena in nature. A haiku is not a haiku if it is an expression or representation of human subjectivity. In composing a haiku the poet must first observe an object or phenomenon in nature from a perspective devoid of thoughts and feelings. Only after the poet attains that stance and vision will he or she be able to achieve a harmonious union with nature.

The absence of the subject as a first step in composing haiku is akin to Lacan's concept of the subject. Lacan, as a postmodern psychoanalyst, challenges this traditional concept of human subjectivity. Based on his own experience, he defines human subjectivity merely as a concept that concerns neither the autonomy of the self nor the ability to influence the other. Subjectivity, as he demonstrates, is deficient because of the deficiencies inherent in language:

> The effects of language are always mixed with the fact, which is the basis of the analytic experience, that the subject is subject only from being subjected to the field of the Other, the subject proceeds from his synchronic subjection in the field of the Other. That is why he must get out, get himself out, and in the *getting-himself-out,* in the end, he will know that the real Other has, just as much as himself, to get himself out, to pull himself free. (*Fundamental Concepts* 188)

Because the subject, an infinitesimal fraction in time and space, is isolated from the world, the subject is capable only of imagining the other: society, nature, and life. Only when the subject is conscious of the deficiencies of language, as Lacan theorizes, does the subject of the unconscious emerge. Only then is the subject able to approach and encounter the truth of life, what Lacan calls "the real" and "the unsymbolizable."

To Lacan, the motive for subjectivity aims at the symbolic—what constitutes tradition, religion, law—whereas the motive for absence of subjectivity aims at the unconscious, a state of consciousness partly derived from the imaginary on the part of the subject. The unconscious, then, is closer to the real than it is to the symbolic; the imaginary is closer to the real than is the symbolic. Lacan posits that "there exists a world of truth entirely deprived of subjectivity," universal truth, "and that . . . there has been a historical development of subjectivity manifestly directed towards the rediscovery of truth," historically subjective truth, "which lies in the order of symbols" (*Seminar II:* 285). Lacan sees a door as language. When a door is open to the real, the door is closed. When a door is open to the imaginary, the door is closed; that is, language is either the real or the imaginary. In short, Lacan considers language either objective or subjective.

Lacan, moreover, envisions a domain of the real beyond "the navel of the dream, this abyssal relation to that which is most unknown, which is the hallmark of an exceptional, privileged experience, in which the real is apprehended beyond all mediation, be it imaginary or symbolic." Lacan equates this domain with "an absolute other . . . an other beyond all intersubjectivity" (*Seminar II:* 176–77).[3] In Lacanian terms, the haiku poet is motivated to depict the real directly, without using symbols. In this process the poet relies on the imaginary, a domain that is closer to nature, where subjectivity is suppressed or minimized, than it is to language. The reason for shunning symbols in writing haiku comes from the poet's attempt to be objective and yet creative. "If the symbolic function functions," Lacan laments, "we are inside it. And I would even say—we are so far into it that we can't get out of it" (*Seminar* II: 31).

That symbolism is an obstacle to avoid in writing haiku can be explained in terms of Lacan's definition of the symbolic order. Lacan observes that language symbolizes things that do not exist, non-being: "The fundamental relation of man to this symbolic order is very precisely what founds the symbolic order itself—the relation of non-being to being . . . What insists on being satisfied can only be satisfied in recognition. The end of the symbolic process is that non-being came to be, because it has spoken" (*Seminar* II: 308). To Lacan, then, language makes non-being become being. Because haiku represent being rather than non-being, what Lacan calls "language" or what is "spoken" does not apply to the language of haiku.

Another discipline in haiku composition calls for shunning the expression of desire. "Desire," as Lacan observes, "always becomes manifest at the point of speech, where it makes its appearance, its sudden emergence, its surge forwards. Desire emerges just as it becomes embodied in speech, it emerges with symbolism." To Lacan, symbolism means "the symbolizing *Merken* which make what doesn't exist exist" (*Seminar* II: 234). In Zen philosophy, desire emerges with nature rather than with symbolism; that is, desire is made aware by natural instincts rather than by language. Lacan's theory relies more heavily on language than does Zen on nature.

In his first published seminar, Lacan, fascinated by Zen ontology, emulated the practice of a Zen master:

> The master breaks the silence with anything—with a sarcastic remark, with a kick-start.
>
> That is how a buddhist master conducts his search for meaning, according to the technique of *zen*. It behooves the students to find out for themselves the answer to their own questions. The master does not teach *ex cathedra* a ready made science; he supplies an answer when the students are on the verge of finding it. (*Seminar* I: 1)

Lacan's aim in his work was to become the ultimate master of psychoanalysis, as many critics have suggested,[4] but he was absolutely critical of any kind of human mastery. Lacan's interest in Zen, as evident throughout his writing, suggests that Lacan is as highly critical of human egotism as is a Zen master. Along with Lacan, Roland Barthes, who traveled to Japan, was also fascinated by Zen ontology, as shown in his *Empire of Signs*. Barthes demonstrated that haiku, a Zen-inspired poetic genre, is a decentered writing in which the poet is dethroned; and Lacan would have thought that the Zen master is "kicked out," let alone expressing the ego.[5]

The most famous haiku by Basho (1644–94), "The Old Pond," has served in haiku criticism as a model for Zen-inspired haiku. To explain the poetics of nature in contrast to that of subjectivity, which characterizes much nineteenth-century English romantic poetry, Yone Noguchi, a noted bilingual poet and critic, quoted "The Old Pond" in his criticism:

Furu ike ya	The old pond!
Kawazu tobikomu	A frog leapt into—
Mizu no oto	List, the water sound!
	(Noguchi's translation)

One may think a frog an absurd poetic subject, but Basho focused his vision on a scene of autumnal desolation, an image of nature. The pond was perhaps situated on the premises of an ancient temple whose silence was suddenly broken by a frog plunging into the deep water. As Noguchi conceived the experience, Basho, a Zen Buddhist, was "supposed to awaken into enlightenment now when he heard the voice bursting out of voicelessness, and the conception that life and death were mere change of condition was deepened into faith" (*Selected English Writings* 2: 73–74).

Noguchi's definition of life and death as a mere change in the human condition is similar to that of Lacan, who defines this change from life to death as "human experience, human interchange, intersubjectivity" (*Seminar II* 80). Unlike Freud, who believed that death is the opposite of life and that a human being, an animate organism, turns into an inanimate element in nature, Lacan believes in continuity of life in death. For Lacan, death is a concept that involves the imaginary as well as the symbolic, the conscious as well as the unconscious. The definition of death in terms of intersubjectivity bears a close resemblance to the observations of Dogen (1200–1254), the most revered Zen priest in Japanese history. Not only is he celebrated as the most prolific theologian, as his life work, the 87-volume *Shobogenzo*, indicates, but he is also known for his practical wisdom. As Kodo Kurebayashi remarks: "*Shobogenzo* remains a work solely based on his religious experience and is not the product of his thought" (2). One of his well-known observations about human life is that because life and death are beyond human control, one must not avoid them, nor must one divide them.

Basho, who was deeply influenced by Dogen, was not suggesting in the haiku that the tranquility of the pond meant death or that the frog symbolized life. He had the sensation of hearing the sound bursting out of soundlessness. A haiku is not a representation of good, truth, or beauty; there is nothing particularly good, true, or beautiful about a frog's jumping into water. Just as Basho focused his attention on natural objects and phenomena by suppressing subjectivity, in Zen one is taught to annihilate one's thoughts or feelings before *satori* is attained: *satori* is the achievement of a state of *mu,* nothingness. The state of nothingness is free of human subjectivity; it is so completely free of any thought or emotion that such a consciousness, or "the unconscious" in Lacanian terms, corresponds to the state of nature.

As Basho, directly concerned with objects and phenomena in nature, suppresses subjectivity, so does Wright in most of his haiku. Wright's interest in this doctrine in Zen is reflected in haiku 508:

508.   It is September,
The month in which I was born;
And I have no thoughts.
(Wright)

In the first haiku in *Haiku: This Other World,* Wright as the subject, as well as the narrator, describes himself deprived of both his name and his subjectivity:

1.   I am nobody:
A red sinking autumn sun
Took my name away.
(Wright)

The state of nothingness, however, is not synonymous with a state of void but is functional. And its function is perceived by the senses. If, for example, the enlightened person sees a tree, that person sees the tree through his or her enlightened eye. The tree is no longer an ordinary tree; it now exists with different meaning, as shown in Wright's haiku 809:

809.   Why did this spring wood
Grow so silent when I came?
What was happening?
(Wright)

In the following haiku (721), Wright tries to suppress egotism and attain a state of nothingness:

721.   As my anger ebbs,
The spring stars grow bright again
And the wind returns.
(Wright)

As he relieves himself of anger, he begins to see the stars "grow bright again" and "the wind" return. Only when he reaches a state of nothingness and what he calls in *Black Power* "a total attitude toward life" (159) is he able to perceive nature with his enlightened senses.

Wright's attainment of *mu* is reminiscent of Emily Dickinson's poems on life after death. In her poem 280, "I felt a Funeral, in my Brain," the state of nothingness is signified by the collapsing of the floor of reason:

And then a Plank in Reason, broke,
And I dropped down, and down—
And hit a World, at every plunge,
And Finished knowing—then—

                              (1: 200)

The last line, "And Finished knowing—then—," signifies in Lacanian terms
the subject's achievement of the unconscious. For Dickinson, this unconscious state means all the states intertwined in her imagination: death, eternity, nature, and truth. For Lacan, such states constitute the real and the
unsymbolizable. In poem 465, "I heard a Fly buzz—when I died—," the
state of nothingness is suggested by the disappearance of the windows:

With Blue—uncertain stumbling Buzz—
Between the light—and me—
And then the Windows failed—and then
I could not see to see—

                              (1: 358)

Just as Wright suppresses subjectivity, Dickinson becomes unconscious as she
approaches death. In Lacanian terms, these poems by Dickinson, as do some
of Wright's haiku, represent the subject's movement away from the symbolic
toward the unconscious by way of the imaginary.

This interchange and interaction between the imaginary and the unconscious can also be seen in modernist poetics. In Zen poetics, as Basho's haiku
show, there is little distinction between human and nature, the subjective and
the objective, or in Lacanian terms between the imaginary and the unconscious. In Ezra Pound's early poetics, an image, though created by the subject, is based on a Zen-like, instantaneous response to pure nature. Pound
writes: "It is the presentation of such a 'complex' instantaneously which gives
that sense of sudden liberation; that sense of freedom from time and space
limits; that sense of sudden growth, which we experience in the presence of
the great works of art" (*Literary Essays* 4). This sense of liberation suggests an
impersonal conception of poetry, for it focuses attention not upon the poet,
the subject, but upon the other, the image that closely represents nature.

3.

Many of Wright's haiku, on the other hand, focus their poetic vision on the subject's interaction and union with nature. In some of these pieces, as the following examples show, Wright offers simple, direct scenes where human beings and nature exist in harmony, in contrast with those complex, intriguing scenes in society where people are always at strife.

> 42.   Seen from a hilltop,
>   Shadowy in winter rain,
>   A man and his mule.
>   (Wright)

> 377.   In the winter dusk
>   A thin girl leads a black cow
>   By a dragging rope.
>   (Wright)

> 541.   After the sermon,
>   The preacher's voice is still heard
>   In the caws of crows.
>   (Wright)

"Seen from a Hilltop" (42) finds unity in humankind and nature: a man, a mule, rain, a meadow, and a hill. "In the Winter Dusk" (377), like "Seen from a Hilltop" (42), is a direct description of a scene where a girl lives in harmony with nature. It is not clear whether a girl leads a cow or a cow leads her; creating such an ambiguous image intensifies the unity and harmony between them. In "After the Sermon" (541), the seasonal reference is ambiguous, but Wright finds unity and an analogy between humanity and nature, "the preacher's voice" and "the caws of crows."

Whether perceiving nature in its own sake or in its relation to humankind, Wright's haiku thrive on the subtle interactions of the senses captured in seventeen syllables. For instance, in haiku 47, the poet seems to detach himself from a natural scene:

> 47.   The spring lingers on
>   In the scent of a damp log
>   Rotting in the sun.
>   (Wright)

The feeling of the warm sun, the scent of a damp log, the sight and silence of an outdoor scene, all coalesce into an image of spring. In the process the overall image has evolved from the separate visual images of the sun, of the log, and of the atmosphere. The three images of sight, moreover, are intertwined with the images of warmth from the sun and the rotting log, as well as with the image of smell from the log; all five images are interacting with one another.

In trying his hand at haiku, Wright initially modeled after classic Japanese poets such as Moritake (1472–1549), Basho (1644–94), Kikaku (1661–1707), Buson (1715–83), and Issa (1762–1826). Two of the haiku in Wright's *This Other World* have a thematic resemblance to Moritake's famous *hokku:*

> 626.   Off the cherry tree,
> One twig and its red blossom
> Flies into the sun.
> (Wright)

> 669.   A leaf chases wind
> Across an autumn river
> And shakes a pine tree.
> (Wright)

Moritake's poem, quoted in Blyth's book of haiku, is as follows in Japanese and in Blyth's translation:[6]

Rakka eda ni	Fallen petals
Kaeru to mireba	Seemed to return to the branch,—
Kocho kana	A butterfly!
(Moritake)[7]	

Both of Wright's haiku "Off the Cherry Tree" (626) and "A Leaf Chases Wind" (669) create an illusion similar to that in Moritake's haiku. In "Off the Cherry Tree" a twig with its red blossom flies into the sun as if a bird flew off the cherry tree. Likewise "A Leaf Chases Wind" captures a scene as though a leaf were chasing wind and shaking a pine tree rather than the other way around.

It is this haiku by Moritake that influenced Ezra Pound's composition of the famous metro poem, "In a Station of the Metro." Pound acknowledged for the first time in his career his indebtedness to the spirit of Japanese poetry in general and the art of haiku in particular. In the "Vorticism" essay, he quoted Moritake's haiku, "The fallen blossom flies back to its branch: A butterfly," just before discussing his "In a Station of the Metro," often regarded as the first published haiku written in English.[8] What impressed Gwendolyn Brooks, who called Wright's haiku "a clutch of strong flowers,"[9] was that the imagery in Wright's haiku is charged with energy. According to Margaret Walker, Wright was fascinated by the American modernist poets, including Pound.[10]

As Pound explained in his essay, the image is not a static, rational idea: "It is a radiant node or cluster; it is what I can, and must perforce, call a VORTEX, from which, and through which, and into which, ideas are constantly rushing. In decency one can only call it a VORTEX. And from this necessity came the name 'vorticism'" ("Vorticism" 469–70). A year later Pound defined the form of an image by stating that the image "may be a sketch, a vignette, a criticism, an epigram or anything else you like. It may be impressionism, it may even be very good prose." An image, he argued, does not constitute simply a picture of something. As a vortex, the image must be "endowed with energy" ("Imagisme" 349). Since Pound's image is endowed with the energy of nature, it can be considered, in Lacanian terms, the product of the imaginary rather than of the symbolic. To Pound, haiku relies on an image that conveys objective, impersonal truth rather than subjective, personal point of view. Imagism, in turn, is likened to the painter's use of pigment. "The painter," Pound wrote, "should use his colour because he sees it or feels it. I don't much care whether he is representative or non-representative. . . . It is the same in writing poems, the author must use his *image . . . not* because he thinks he can use it to back up some creed or some system of ethics or economics" ("Vorticism" 464). The poet's image and the painter's color, Pound believed, are the most direct means by which to represent the unconscious and unsymbolizable truth rather than reflect the conscious, subjective artist.

To demonstrate his poetic theory, Pound thought of an image not as a decorative emblem or symbol but as a seed capable of germinating and developing into another organism. As an illustration, he presented what he called "a *hokku*-like sentence" he had written:[11]

> The apparition of these faces in the crowd:
>   Petals, on a wet, black bough.

"In a poem of this sort," he explained, "one is trying to record the precise instant when a thing outward and objective transforms itself, or darts into a thing inward and subjective" ("Vorticism" 467). The image of the faces in the crowd is based in immediate experience at a metro station in Paris; it was "a thing outward and objective." Not only did Pound actually see the "thing," but it also generated such a sensation that he could not shake it from his mind. This image, he emphasizes, "transforms itself, or darts into a thing inward and subjective," that is, the image of the "Petals, on a wet, black bough." Imagism is further contrasted to symbolism: "The symbolist's *symbols* have a fixed value, like numbers in arithmetic, like 1, 2, and 7. The imagiste's images have a variable significance, like the signs *a*, *b*, and *x* in algebra" ("Vorticism" 463).

Pound's point about symbolism in poetry suggests that the symbolic description of a natural object or event, as opposed to imagism, is always through the mediation of language. In Wright's haiku, as in Pound's imagistic poems, the description of nature is an imagistic one that directly derives from a natural object or event itself without the mediation of language, that is, the poet's thought, emotion, and point of view. As a result, the instantaneity and spontaneity in the construction of haiku images fend off the interference of subjectivity.[12]

Whether Wright was directly influenced by Pound's imagism is difficult to determine, but many of Wright's haiku bear a close resemblance to classic Japanese haiku. A pair of his haiku in *This Other World,* in their style and content, are reminiscent of two of Basho's most celebrated haiku. Wright's "In the Silent Forest" echoes Basho's "It's Deadly Quiet":

316.   In the silent forest
        A woodpecker hammers at
           The sound of silence.
                    (Wright)

           It's deadly quiet
           Piercing into the rocks
           Shrills of cicada.
                    (Basho)[13]

Just as Basho expresses awe for quietude, Wright juxtaposes silence in the forest to the sound of a woodpecker. Similarly, Wright's "A Thin Waterfall" is akin to Basho's "A Crow":

569.   A thin waterfall
        Dribbles the whole autumn night,—
           How lonely it is.
                    (Wright)

A crow
Perched on a withered tree
In the autumn evening.
(Basho)[14]

Basho focuses upon a single crow perching on a branch of an old tree just as Wright focuses upon a thin waterfall. In both haiku, the scene is drawn with little detail, and the mood is provided by a simple, reserved description of fact, a phenomenon in nature that has nothing to do with the poet except for his attempt to describe the scene for its own sake. In Lacanian psychoanalysis, both haiku are expressions of the imaginary derived directly from nature rather than expressions of the symbolic mediated by language and subjectivity. In both haiku, just as parts of the scene are painted in dark colors, so is the background. Both haiku create the kind of beauty associated with the aesthetic sensibility of *sabi* that suggests loneliness and quietude, the salient characteristics of nature, as opposed to overexcitement and loudness, those of subjectivity.[15] Whether Wright and Basho themselves felt lonely when writing the haiku, however, is moot.

It is legend that Basho inspired more disciples than did any other haiku poet and that Kikaku is regarded as Basho's most innovative disciple. Two of Wright's haiku (106 and 671) bear some resemblance to Kikaku's "The Bright Harvest Moon"[16] since both poets emphasize an interaction between humanity and nature in the creation of beauty:

106.   Beads of quicksilver
          On a black umbrella:
               Moonlit April rain.
                    (Wright)

671.   A pale winter moon,
          Pitying a lonely doll,
               Lent it a shadow.
                    (Wright)

The bright harvest moon
Upon the tatami mats
Shadows of the pines
(Kikaku)

In Kikaku's haiku the beauty of the moonlight is not only humanized by the light shining on the human-made object but also intensified by the shadows of a pine tree that fall upon the mats. The beauty of the shadow reflected on the intricate pattern of an ageless pine tree as it stamps the dustless mats intensifies the beauty of the moonlight. Not only does such a scene unify an image of humanity and an image of nature, but it also shows that humanity and nature do interact. In Wright's first poem, an element of nature, "Beads of Quicksilver," is reinforced by a human-made object, "a black umbrella." In "A Pale Winter Moon," the second line portrays the loneliness of a doll while a pale winter moon, a beauty of nature, is intensified by the presence of the doll, a human-made object. In contrast with Wright's and Basho's haiku given earlier in this chapter, the above three haiku by Wright and Kikaku lightly include human subjectivity in appreciating natural beauty, but the focus of their vision is on nature. In Wright's "Beads of Quicksilver" and "A Pale Winter Moon," the images of "a black umbrella," "a lonely doll," and in Kikaku's "The Bright Harvest," "the tatami mats," slightly reflect human sentiment and subjectivity since these objects are human-made. But the central image in each haiku represents a natural object: "moonlit April rain," "a pale winter moon," "the bright harvest moon," respectively.

Wright's collection includes a number of haiku that depict seasonal, climatic changes in nature as do those by classic Japanese haiku poets. Wright's "I Would Like a Bell" (haiku 13), for instance, is comparable to Buson's well-known "On the Hanging Bell" in their simple depiction of a spring scene:

13.   I would like a bell
        Tolling in this soft twilight
           Over willow trees.
                (Wright)

        On the hanging bell
        Has perched and is fast asleep,
        It's a butterfly.
                (Buson)[17]

Buson was well known in his time as an accomplished painter, and many of his haiku reflect his singular attention to color and its intensification. Wright's "A Butterfly Makes" (82), for example, is reminiscent of Buson's "Also Stepping On":

82.   A butterfly makes
        The sunshine even brighter
          With fluttering wings.
                (Wright)

> Also stepping on
> The mountain pheasant's tail is
> The spring setting sun.
>
> (Buson)[18]

For a seasonal reference to spring, Buson links an image of a bird with a spring sunset, because both are extremely colorful. As a painter he is also interested in an ambiguous impression the scene he has drawn gives him; it is not clear whether the setting sun is treading on the pheasant's tail or the tail on the setting sun. In any event, Buson has made both pictures beautiful to look at, just as Wright has drawn the pictures of a butterfly and the sunshine, themselves highly colorful and bright, which in turn intensify each other.

In another fine haiku, Wright portrays humanity's relationship with nature in terms of art:

> 571.   From across the lake,
>   Past the black winter trees,
>   Faint sounds of a flute.
>   (Wright)

Unlike "The Spring Lingers On" (47), discussed earlier, this haiku admits a human involvement in the scene: someone is playing the flute as the poet is listening from the other side of the lake. Through transference of the senses between the faint sounds of a flute and the black winter trees, an interaction of humanity and nature takes place. As the sound of a human through a musical instrument and the sight of nature affect each other, Wright has created delightful images of humankind as well as of nature. Wright's "From across the Lake" (571) has an affinity to Kikaku's "The Bright Harvest Moon," noted earlier, for both haiku are expressions of beauty as reified in objects, not in subjects, the poets themselves. As the image of beauty in Kikaku's haiku is intensified through the interaction of the moon and "the tatami mats," natural and human objects, so is Wright's image of beauty, "the sounds of a flute," appreciated through natural objects, "the lake" and "the black winter trees."

Wright's haiku in their portrayal of humankind's association with nature often conveys a kind of enlightenment, a new way of looking at human beings and nature. In some of the haiku, as the following examples show, Wright follows this tradition:

720.   A wilting jonquil
        Journeys to its destiny
            In a shut bedroom.
                (Wright)

722.   Lines of winter rain
        Gleam only as they flash past
            My lighted window.
                (Wright)

"A Wilting Jonquil" (720) teaches the poet the lesson that nature out of its environment cannot exhibit its beauty. In "Lines of Winter Rain" (722), the poet learns that only when an interaction between human beings and nature occurs can natural beauty be savored.

As these haiku by Wright show, Wright in his final years was much occupied with the intimate relationships of humanity to nature. In 1953, when he traveled to West Africa to write *Black Power,* he was deeply impressed with the African worldview that human beings are not at the center of the universe. Ashanti culture and belief, in particular, convinced him that the world of nature is pre-eminent over the scientific vision of that world, that intuition is pre-eminent over knowledge in the search for truth. In writing haiku Wright became aware that human subjectivity stands in the way of seeking truth. Not only do many of Wright's haiku thrive on poignant images of nature; they also admonish the reader that only by paying nature the utmost attention can human beings truly see themselves.

CHAPTER 10

Private Voice and Buddhist Enlightenment in Alice Walker's *The Color Purple*

Nineteenth-century American writers such as Emerson, Thoreau, and Whitman expressed their profound interest in Eastern philosophies and religions. When Emerson declared, "The Buddhist . . . is a Transcendentalist" (*Complete Essays* 91–92), he meant that Buddhism, unlike a religion, is a philosophy that emphasizes the primacy of the spiritual and transcendental over the material and empirical. Zen Buddhism in particular, unlike other sects in the same religion, teaches its believer how to achieve Buddhahood within the self, a precept that sounds much like the one given by Emerson, who urges the reader to think not for the sake of accomplishing things, but for the sake of realizing one's own world. The achievement of godhead within rather than its discovery elsewhere is echoed by Thoreau and Whitman as well. *Walden* shows the reader how to attain one's enlightenment through natural objects like trees, birds, and sands. In "Song of Myself" Whitman admonishes the reader: "Not I, not any one else can travel that road for you, / You must travel it for yourself" (64).[1]

In twentieth-century American literature, the influences of Eastern thought and poetics on Ezra Pound and William Carlos Williams in the 1910s and 1920s are well known,[2] as is the fascination of mid-century writers of the Beat Movement—such as Jack Kerouac, Allen Ginsberg, and Gary Snyder—with Zen Buddhism, as noted earlier. Since the late 1950s, not only have a number of African American writers, including Richard Wright, Charles Johnson, Ishmael Reed, Alice Walker, and Toni Morrison, all paid their homage to African philosophies and religions, but they have also expressed their strong interest in cross-culturalism. Among these writers, Wright, as shown in the previous chapter, was deeply influenced by Zen philosophy and aesthetics.

Although much contemporary African American literature focuses, as does Wright's later work, on African American cultural traditions, it is also drawn from, or meant to reflect on, cross-cultural and multicultural traditions and ideologies. *The Color Purple* (1982) serves as a prime example of such a text. While the novel reads distinctly contemporary because it concerns the gender conflicts and racial issues of African American tradition, as well as of more recent American cultural dialogue, it also reflects as strongly the philosophical and religious traditions of other cultures. In particular, I would like to demonstrate that, in establishing herself, the central character Celie acquires her own voice through Buddhist enlightenment. Walker has recently stated publicly that she considers herself a Buddhist, but it is unknown whether she had, in fact, an affinity with Buddhist thought when she wrote the novel over two decades ago. My primary aim is not to try to find the sources for Walker's interest in Buddhism but, through intertextuality, interauthoriality, and cross-culturalism, to show a reading of the Buddhist enlightenment behind Celie's self-creation, the novel's central theme.

1.

At the outset of her story, Celie is deprived of her own voice. Finding herself at a loss, she is unable to express herself. *The Color Purple* begins with a letter to God so that He may provide her with voice:

> Dear God,
>   I am fourteen years old. ~~I am~~ I have always been a good girl. Maybe you can give me a sign letting me know what is happening to me. (1)

Although she is able to hear the public voice that describes her pregnancy, for example, she does not understand what that description means; nor is she able to express her feelings about the traumatic event that has befallen her: "A girl at church say," Celie writes to God, "you git big if you bleed every month. I don't bleed no more" (6).

Despite her repeated appeal to God, He has failed to grant her a voice. As late as the midpoint of the story, when a series of other disasters have taken place, she continues to complain:

> Dear God,
> ....
> ....

But I feels daze.

My daddy lynch. My mama crazy. All my little half-brothers and sisters no kin to me. My children not my sister and brother. Pa not pa.
(183)

One of the difficulties Celie faces in her quest for voice is the concept of God
she has inherited from Christian doctrine: God and Christ are both male figures. To dramatize the dilemma of the gulf between His voice and hers,
Walker develops a dialectic discourse. Celie's sister Nettie, who works for a
Christian missionary stationed in the Olinka community in Africa, continues to communicate with Celie in the language Nettie has learned. Whereas
Nettie's language is stilted, wordy, and lengthy, Celie's is ungrammatical,
terse, and choppy. But Celie's language, like Huck Finn's, is vernacular and
sounds more natural than Nettie's. Just as Huck's language subverts Tom's, so
does Celie's "outsmart" Nettie's, which smacks of patriarchy, sexism, and
"political correctness."

The most important characteristic of Celie's language is poetry. Even at the
outset of the story, the reader is impressed that Celie has the potential to
become a poet: she is indeed endowed with poetic inspiration just as is the
young boy whose "tongue's use sleeping" in Whitman's "Out of the Cradle
Endlessly Rocking."[3] In *In Search of Our Mothers' Gardens* (1983) Walker discusses Celie's prototype: those ancestral "grand mothers and mothers of ours
. . . not Saints, but Artists; driven to a numb and bleeding madness by the
springs of creativity in them for which there was no release. . . . Perhaps she
sang . . . perhaps she wove the most stunning mats or told the most ingen-
ious stories of all the village storytellers. Perhaps she was herself a poet—
though only her daughter's name is signed to the poems we know" (233–43).
A young African American's potential to become a poet is also reminiscent of
the young Richard Wright's lyricism, vividly described in *Black Boy.* As mentioned earlier, one of Wright's haiku, "Don't they make you sad, / Those wild
geese winging southward, / O lonely scarecrow?" (*Haiku* 146) originates
from a passage in *Black Boy:* "There were the echoes of nostalgia I heard in
the crying strings of wild geese winging south against a bleak, autumn sky"
(*Black Boy* 14).[4]

The most serious obstacle that stands in the way of Celie's search for voice
is the fact that the public voice, the language of society, is dominated by
males. As the story begins, Celie is forced to identify the public voice with
the voice of Alphonso, who she supposes is her father but who turns out to
be her stepfather. Since God fails to answer her letters, she cannot help
accepting Alphonso's voice as the voice of powerful, earthly authority. She is

always at the mercy of Alphonso's language and action: during his first rape of Celie, Alphonso starts to choke her, "saying You better shut up and git used to it" (2). When her mother asks her who her newborn baby's father is, she gives an ambiguous reply: "I say God took it. He took it. He took it while I was sleeping. Kilt it out there in the woods. Kill this one too, if he can" (3). In Celie's voice, God and Alphonso, her baby's father, are merged into the almighty patriarchal figure.

As the story unfolds, however, Walker's use of patriarchal discourse becomes less direct and pervasive and at times reads as subtle. For example, Albert's family, and his father in particular, are portrayed as conventional and conservative. Albert's father tries to forbid Albert to marry the flamboyant blues singer Shug Avery for fear that her unknown paternity and her erotic behavior will ruin the family reputation. Albert's brother Tobias also tries to dissuade Albert from living with Shug, which would set up a rivalry between Celie and Shug, who is also known as "Queen Honeybee," a patriarchal, anti-feminist put-down. Such episodes suggest that even a man like Albert falls victim to the oppressive patriarchal family system as does Celie. Besides Shug, another blues singer, Mary Agnes, also challenges the patriarchal, racist convention. Mary creates her own songs:

> They calls me yellow
> like yellow be my name
>
> They calls me yellow
> like yellow be my name
>
> But if yellow is a name
> Why ain't black the same
>
> Well, if I say Hey black girl
> Lord, she try to ruin my game (104)

By denying her nickname and the categorization of color and sexual attraction made up by a racist society, Mary is able to express herself through her own voice.

Celie learns from Shug and Mary that the first step in creating her own voice is to make male language female. If Celie's "text, her creation of self-hood, is to proceed," Lindsay Tucker points out, "the male text of the deity must be overturned and rewritten in female terms" (84). All the male figures Celie is associated with in the beginning are called by their generic male titles:

her father by "Him," Albert by "Mr. ——," Samuel by the "Rev. Mr. ——."
It is little wonder that Nellie tries to make Celie acquainted with the deity of
the Olinka. In her letter to Celie, Nettie writes, "We know a roofleaf is not
Jesus Christ, but in its own humble way, is it not God? So there we sat, Celie,
face to face with the Olinka God. And Celie, I was so tired and sleepy and
full of chicken and groundnut stew, my ears ringing with song, that all that
Joseph said made perfect sense to me. I wonder what you will make of all
this?" (160).

This letter clearly indicates that Nettie understands the Olinka God to be
male. In this connection it would be significant to contrast the Olinka God
with the Akan God, the divinity of the Ashanti in West Africa, a central
theme of Wright's *Black Power*.[5] The Akan God, as Wright learned, is female,
and, as he reveals in expounding its history and doctrine, the religion has over
the centuries supported the survival of their life and culture. If Nettie's letter
about the Olinka intimates some forms of female oppression in that society,
Wright's observation vindicates the absence of such oppression in the
Ashanti.[6]

2.

Celie soon realizes that for her to acquire a voice of her own, her own body
must first be treated as a precious being. As Albert's wife, she is treated as if
she were a commodity like a cow, and her body is used like a toilet. She has
no pleasure but pain in their sexual relations, and Albert always demands that
she keep his house clean and take care of his unruly children. "He beat me
like he beat the children," Celie complains. "Cept he don't never hardly beat
them. He say, Celie, git the belt. The children be outside the room peeking
through the cracks. It all I can do not to cry. I make myself wood" (23).
Regarding her body as a piece of wood is equating a living being with a material thing. Buddhism teaches its believer that the soul exists not only in
human beings but all living beings. At this point of her self-creation and
search for voice, she says to herself, "Celie, you a tree. That's how come I
know trees fear man" (23).

A few scenes later Walker, through Celie's mouth, gives a parable of
Buddhist enlightenment with a pair of lucid signifiers, a living tree and a
table:

> Everybody say how good I is to Mr. —— children. I be good to them.
> But I don't feel nothing for them. Patting Harpo back not even like pat-

ting a dog. It more like patting another piece of wood. Not a living tree, but a table, a chifferobe. Anyhow, they don't love me neither, no matter how good I is. (31)

Her quest for voice and identity reaches its apogee when Shug Avery discusses with her the meaning of God. Shug says, "God is inside you and inside everybody else. You come into the world with God. But only them that search for it inside find it" (202). Upon hearing this definition of God, Celie applies it to her own life: "She say, My first step from the old white man was trees. Then air. Then birds. Then other people. But one day when I was sitting quiet and feeling like a motherless child, which I was, it come to me: that feeling of being part of everything, not separate at all. I knew that if I cut a tree, my arm would bleed" (203).

Shug's epiphany that God resides inside Celie and inside everybody else is akin to Emersonian and Whitmanesque transcendentalism. But Shug's further observation that only those who search for God inside them find it and Celie's knowledge that cutting a living tree is the same as cutting her arm suggest that Walker's belief bears a strong resemblance to Zen Buddhism. Zen teaches that divinity exists in nature only if the person is intuitively conscious of divinity in the self. To Emerson and Whitman, on the other hand, God exists in nature regardless of whether the person is capable of such intuition.

When Celie asks Shug whether God is male or female, Shug answers: "Yeah, It. God ain't a he or a she, but a It." To Celie's persistence, "But what do it look like?" Shug says, "Don't look like nothing. . . . It ain't a picture show. It ain't something you can look at apart from anything else, including yourself. . . . Everything that is or ever was or ever will be. And when you can feel that, and be happy to feel that, you've found It" (202–3). Shug's use of the word *nothing* is remindful of the Zen doctrine of *mu* and *satori*. This state of mind is absolutely free of materialistic and egotistic thought and emotion; it is so completely free that such a consciousness corresponds to that of nature. This state of mind is what postmodern psychoanalysts like Lacan call the unconscious and the real, the truth that is neither imaginary nor symbolizable.

Shug's and Celie's Zen-like enlightenment also has a striking affinity with what Wright calls in *Black Power* "his [the African's] primal outlook upon life" (266).[7] Just as enlightened Celie sees herself and trees, Wright saw in African life a closer relationship between human beings and nature than he did between human beings and their social and political environment. In his haiku, as well as in *Black Power*, Wright takes great pains to express a Zen-like enlightenment in which human beings must learn the conscious or unconscious truth of human existence from the spirit of nature.

A belief in the primacy of the spirit of nature over the strife of humanity is what Walker and Wright share. This primal vision of life, which has its genesis in *Black Boy* and its further pronouncement in much of Wright's later work, does underlie Walker's characterization of Celie and Shug in *The Color Purple*. In Wright's "Blueprint for Negro Writing" (1937), as pointed out earlier, one of the theoretical principles calls for the African American writer to explore universal humanism. Wright's explanation of the Ashanti convinced him that the defense of African culture meant renewal of Africans' faith in themselves. He realized that African culture was based upon universal human values—such as awe of nature, family kinship and love, faith in religion, and honor—that had made African survival possible.

Before discussing Ashanti culture in *Black Power*, Wright quotes a passage from Edmund Husserl's *Ideas* that suggests that the world of nature is pre-eminent over the scientific vision of that world, that intuition is pre-eminent over knowledge in the search for truth. Similarly, Wright's interpretation of African philosophy and Walker's demonstration of that philosophy in *The Color Purple* both recall a teaching in Zen Buddhism. Zen's emphasis on self-enlightenment is indeed reflected in Walker's characterization of Celie in *The Color Purple*. At the climactic moment of the novel Shug, like a Zen master, gives her disciple Celie an admonition on the doctrine of *mu:* "You can just relax, go with everything that's going" (203). With a *senryu*-like sense of humor, Shug continues her admonition: "I think it pisses God off if you walk by the color purple in a field somewhere and don't notice it" (203).[8] "The color purple," as a free signifier, may mean many things, but I would like to read it as Zen enlightenment.

3.

If Shug played the role of a Zen master, she would urge Celie to be self-reliant and find her own path in search of truth and happiness. And this is indeed what happens in the story after Shug gives Celie a lesson on the color purple. In the tradition of Zen instruction the attainment of *satori* is as practical as it is in actual human life, as noted earlier in my discussion of Ellison's *Invisible Man*. The young Bassui, a celebrated Zen priest in medieval Japan, asked his master, "What's the highway to self-elevation?" The master replied, "It's *never stop*." Bassui failed to understand what the master meant: the master told him, "It's just underneath your standpoint" (Ando 164). The master's point about *never stop* is reminiscent of the spirit's reply to Whitman in "Song of Myself":

This day before dawn I ascended a hill and look'd at the crowded heaven.
And I said to my spirit *When we become the enfolders of those orbs, and the
    pleasure and knowledge of every thing in them, shall we be fill'd and
    satisfied then?*
And my spirit said, *No, we but level that lift to pass and continue beyond.*
(64)

The Zen master's pronouncement also recalls the last passage in "Song of
Myself": "If you want me again look for me under your boot-soles. / . . . /
. . . / . . . . / Failing to fetch me at first keep encouraged, / Missing me one
place search another" (68).

Celie describes Shug's admonition of self-enlightenment and self-reliance
with sorrow and stoicism:

> Dearest Nettie,
>
> Sometimes I think Shug never loved me. I stand looking at my naked
> self in the looking glass. What would she love? I ast myself. My hair is
> short and kinky because I don't straighten it anymore. . . . Nothing young
> and fresh. My heart must be young and fresh though, it feel like it bloom-
> ing blood.
>
> I talk to myself a lot, standing in front the mirror. Celie, I say, hap-
> piness was just a trick in your case. Just cause you never had any before
> Shug, you thought it was time to have some, and that it was gon last.
> Even thought you had the trees with you. The whole earth. The stars. But
> look at you. When Shug left, happiness desert. (266)

This letter is remindful of Emerson's poem "Give All to Love," which is an
admonition that stoical self-reliance must be kept alive underneath one's passion: "Heartily know / When half-gods go, / The gods arrive" (*Poems* 65). As
long as one relies on others, "half-gods," one cannot attain enlightenment.

Celie's self-creation, inspired by self-enlightenment, depends upon annihilating the patriarchal and racist view of African American women and accepting her own body as beautiful and worthy of love and happiness. Although
Celie, perhaps mistakenly, thinks Shug's desertion of her is a sign of lack of
love, she feels her heart is still "young and fresh" and is "blooming blood"
(266). Earlier in the story Shug has taught Celie that when Celie felt beautiful and happy, that was exactly what God felt: "God love all them feelings.
That's some of the best stuff God did. And when you know God loves 'em
you enjoys 'em a lot more" (203). Such a revelation has also made Celie realize that a female body is a beautiful reflection of nature and divinity. She has

learned from Nettie that both the Olinka and Christians have a worldview just opposite to Celie's newly experienced outlook. Like the Ashanti, Celie is convinced that human beings are not the center of the universe. Nettie, on the other hand, writes: "I think Africans are very much like white people back home, in that they think they are the center of the universe and that everything that is done is done for them. The Olinka definitely hold this view. And so they naturally thought the road being built was for them" (174). *Black Power* demonstrated that the Ashanti were conscious of the unimportance of human beings in the universe.⁹ Celie thus shares her worldview with the Ashanti as Nettie does not.

Celie's change of heart about human life has now led to a more tolerant attitude toward others. Celie no longer hates Albert as she used to, for she now realizes that he is genuinely in love with Shug, who used to love him as well. Celie also observes that, like herself, he listens to her as if he were a disciple receiving admonition from a Zen master:

> Plus, look like he trying to make something out of himself. I don't mean just that he work and he clean up after himself and he appreciate some of the things God was playful enough to make. I mean when you talk to him now he really listen, and one time, out of nowhere in the conversation us was having, he said Celie, I'm satisfied this the first time I ever lived on Earth as a *natural* man. It feel like a *new* experience. (267; emphasis added)

Albert's recognition of himself being "a natural man" suggests that, like a true Buddhist, he adheres more to the spirit of nature than to the egotism of humanity. His life as "a new experience" suggests that it is based on Zen doctrine. Zen is not considered a religion which teaches the follower to have faith in a monolithic deity. Like Thoreauvian transcendentalism, Zen teaches one a way of life completely different from what one has been conditioned to lead.

As her worldview changes in the course of her story, Celie also learns under Shug's guidance that one must experience sexuality with the spirit of nature. The consummation of love she experiences with Shug is portrayed as a natural maternal experience of love: both make love not only without guilt and repression but without egotism and oppression. Indeed, annihilation of egotism and oppression is one of the cardinal principles of life taught in Buddhism. "Then," Celie says to God, "I feels something real soft and wet on my breast, feel like one of my little lost babies mouth. Way after while, I act like a little lost baby too" (118). Evoking "heaven," the supreme spirit of nature, or nirvana, Celie tells God, "I feel Shug's big tits sorta flop over my arms like suds. It feel like heaven is what it feel like, not like sleeping with Mr. —— at all" (119). Referring to the sexual relationship between Celie and Shug, Linda Abbandonato argues that sexuality is able to "resist the ideological laws that operate through its very terrain, to survive and flourish in 'aberrant' forms despite the cultural imposition of a norm." She also considers this kind of sexuality "highly disruptive potential" (1112). In the context of the novel, however, the sexuality of Celie and Shug seems far from "aberrant" and disruptive; rather it reads natural and peaceful.

Not only is this sexuality depicted as an innate maternal act of love, but it also reads as an ideal act of love between two individuals. It is concentric, as opposed to phallocentric: Shug and, in particular, Celie have both been victimized by patriarchal and racist conventions. Even Shug, a seemingly liberated woman, has fallen victim to the anti-feminist prejudice which Albert's family perpetuates. Most importantly, these two individuals' sexuality is consensual: their motive is an enactment of genuine, requited love. Their sexuality transcends all elements of materialistic desire in society that stand in the way of the search for love and happiness. Shug as a fictional character is not used for what Henry James calls *ficelle,* a functional character.[10] She appears in the story not merely as what Lindsey Tucker calls "an image, an objectification of the female to counter the victim-figures" (85).[11] Like Celie, whose heart "feel like it blooming blood" (266) and whose "arm would bleed" if she "cut a tree" (203), Shug also feels her heart pounding and feels her arm would bleed if she cut a live tree: both share the spirit of nature, upon which Buddhist doctrine is based.

In this novel Celie's and Shug's sexuality, drawn with Zen-like spontaneity and naturalness, is diametrically opposed to that fundamentally flawed human interaction: the rape of a woman by a man, which destroys love and tenderness, the most universal and precious human values. Some readers may call the two women's sexuality lesbian. Julia Kristeva has observed that "to believe that one 'is a woman' is almost as absurd and obscurantist as to believe that one 'is a man'" (qtd. in Abbandonato 1113). I agree with Kristeva and would like to say further that to call Celie and Shug lesbians is to grossly misread their sexual relationship. In *The Color Purple* they are *hito* or *ningen,* human beings, as they are called in Buddhist texts.

CHAPTER 11

Cross-Cultural Poetics:
Sonia Sanchez's *Like the Singing*
Coming Off the Drums

Some accomplished poets produced their work in isolation. Emily Dickinson is one of the world's best-known and widely admired poets, though at the time of her death in 1886, only eight of her more than seventeen hundred poems had been published. Richard Wright, as noted earlier, wrote in exile over four thousand haiku in his last year and half. But only twenty-four of them had posthumously appeared in print before the publication of *Haiku: This Other World* (1998), a collection of 817 haiku Wright himself had selected.

Time has changed not only for the poet but for the literary public. Readers of poetry over a century ago were not quite familiar with the style and vision of Dickinson, who wrote terse verses with the bold, startling imagery. Nor were readers as interested in cross-cultural visions as are today's readers. When Wright experimented with his massive collection of haiku in the late 1950s, he did so in isolation, just as Dickinson wrote her poems in isolation. Recovering from illness, Wright composed his haiku in bed at home as well as in the hospital, in cafés, in restaurants, and in Paris as well as in the French countryside.

Sonia Sanchez, by contrast, has appeared as a postmodern, postcolonial, and remarkably cross-cultural poet. Such an observation, however, does not suggest that Dickinson and Wright were less cross-cultural. Indeed, Dickinson's readers have long recognized in her poetry the Calvinist tendency to look inwardly, as well as the transcendental view of nature and humanity. Many of her poems also exhibit a dialogue she had with contemporary industrial culture. And Wright's later work, such as "The Man Who Lived Underground" and haiku, shows his interest in French existentialism as well as in Zen aesthetics.

While Sanchez is known as an activist poet, much of her poetic impulse in *Like the Singing Coming Off the Drums* (1998) derives from the tradition of Japanese haiku, in which a poet pays the utmost attention to the beauty inherent in nature. A great majority of Sanchez's latest collection of poems are entitled haiku, tanka, or sonku. These poems reveal that Sanchez, turning away from the moral, intellectual, social, and political problems dealt with in her other work, found her latent poetic sensibility in nature. Above all, her fine pieces of poetry show, as do classic Japanese haiku and tanka, the unity and harmony of all things, the sensibility that nature and human beings are one and inseparable. In this collection, much of her poetry poignantly expresses a desire to transcend social and racial differences and a need to find union and harmony with nature.

1.

Many of the haiku and tanka presented in the first section of Sanchez's collection, entitled "Naked in the Streets," reflect the poetic tradition in which human action emulates nature. As the section title suggests, Sanchez creates an image of nature out of a scene of streets. Today the poet as well as most of her readers lives in the streets, just as classic haiku poets and their readers lived and worked closely with nature. The first haiku in *Like the Singing Coming Off the Drums* conveys the delightful sensation one feels in contact with nature:

> you ask me to run
> naked in the streets with you
> i am holding your pulse. (4)

Much in the same spirit, Whitman writes in "Song of Myself":

> I will go to the bank by the wood and become undisguised and naked,
> I am mad for it to be in contact with me. (25)

While immersing herself in nature, Sanchez from time to time subtly expresses her aversion to artificiality and domesticity. The first song in "Naked in the Streets" reads:

> i cannot stay home
> on this sweet morning

i must run singing   laughing
through the streets of Philadelphia.
i don't need food or sleep or drink
on this wild scented day
i am bathing in the waves of your breath. (5)

The urge Sanchez feels to cleanse herself of the unnatural and the artificial also echoes in Whitman's "Song of Myself":

Houses and rooms are full of perfumes, the shelves are crowded with
    perfumes,
I breathe the fragrance myself and know it and like it,
The distillation would intoxicate me also, but I shall not let it. (25)

Both Sanchez and classic Japanese haiku poets are always inspired by the visual beauty in which nature presents itself. Buson was well known in his time as a professional painter, and many of his haiku reflect his singular attention to color and its intensification. One of Sanchez's haiku included in the middle section, "Shake Loose My Skin," and one of the longer poems, "A Poem for Ella Fitzgerald," both thrive on colorful imagery. The haiku reads:

i am you loving
my own shadow watching
this noontime butterfly. (61)

"A Poem for Ella Fitzgerald," the longest poem in this collection, is focused on these lines:

the moon turned red in the sky,
....
nightingales in her throat
....
an apollo stage amid high-stepping
yellow legs
....
i remember it was april
and the flowers ran yellow
the sun downpoured yellow butterflies (104–7)

Both poems are reminiscent of Buson's "Also Stepping On," a haiku compared to Wright's haiku in chapter 9:

Also stepping on
The mountain pheasant's tail is
The spring setting sun.[1]

For a seasonal reference to spring, Buson links an image of a bird with a spring sunset, because both are highly colored. As a painter he is also fascinated by an ambiguous impression the scene he has drawn gives him; it is not clear whether the setting sun is treading on the pheasant's tail or the tail on the setting sun. In any event, Buson has made both pictures beautiful to behold. In Sanchez's haiku "I Am You Loving," it is ambivalent whether the focus is on "my own shadow" or "this noontime butterfly"; both constitute beautiful images of nature. Likewise, "A Poem for Ella Fitzgerald" juxtaposes the image of the red moon with that of nightingales. Sanchez in these poems creates, as does Buson in his, a pair of counter-images, themselves highly colorful and bright, which in turn intensify each other.

In portraying nature, Sanchez is at times puzzled by its spontaneous imagery. Two of the poems in the collection—"I Collect" (sonku) and "In This Wet Season" (haiku)—have a thematic affinity with the famous haiku by Moritake (1472–1549):

Rakka eda ni	Fallen petals
Kaeru to mireba	Seemed to return to the branch,—
Kocho kana	A butterfly![2]

Both of Sanchez's poems "I Collect" and "In This Wet Season" create an illusion similar to that in Moritake's poem. "I Collect" begins with a query:

i collect
wings what are
you bird or
animal? (15)

In the other poem, Sanchez is reluctant to draw a distinction between children and birds, hands and rain:

in this wet season
of children raining hands
we catch birds in flight. (103)

As brought up in my reading of Wright's haiku in chapter 9, it is this haiku by Moritake that influenced Ezra Pound's composition of the famous metro poem, often regarded as the first published haiku written in English:

> The apparition of these faces in the crowd:
>   Petals, on a wet, black bough.
>   ("Vorticism" 467)

As pointed out earlier, Pound was influenced by Japanese poetry in general and by the art of haiku in particular. In the "Vorticism" essay, he quoted Moritake's haiku, just before discussing his "In a Station of the Metro."[3]

In emulating the spirit of nature, Japanese poets are often struck with awe and respect. A score of American poets, such as Emerson, Dickinson, Pound, and Wright, viewed nature from a similar vantage point. And Sanchez seems to have followed the same tradition. In keeping with this tradition, the haiku poet may aim not only at expressing sensation but also at generalizing and hence depersonalizing it. This characteristic can be shown even by one of Basho's lesser-known haiku:

> Hiya hiya to   How cool it is,
> Kabe wo fumaete   Putting the feet on the wall:
> Hirune kana[4]   An afternoon nap.

Basho was interested in expressing how his feet, anyone's feet, would feel when placed on the wall in the house on a warm summer afternoon. His subject was nothing other than this direct sensation. He did not want to convey any emotion, any thought, any beauty; there remained only poetry, only nature. In a similar vein Sanchez expresses, in two of the haiku included in "Naked in the Streets," the pure sensation nature offers for human perception:

> i count the morning
> stars the air so sweet i turn
> riverdark with sound. (8)

> i come from the same
> place i am going to my
> body speaks in tongues. (9)

The predilection to portray human life in close association with nature means that the poet is more interested in genuinely natural sentiments than in moral, ethical, or political problems. Looking at the wind as a primal signifier of nature, Sanchez composed two poems in "Naked in the Streets," one entitled "Haiku" and the other "Blues Haiku":

Haiku
how fast is the wind
sailing? how fast did i go
to become slow? (38)

Blues Haiku
let me be yo wil
derness let me be yo wind
blowing you all day. (39)

Traditionally, another singular, awe-inspiring signifier of nature in haiku is silence. Besides "The Old Pond," Basho is known for another haiku that concerns nature's silence, "It's Deadly Quiet," another well-known haiku that I compared to Wright's haiku in chapter 9:

It's deadly quiet
Piercing into the rocks
Is the shrill of cicada[5]
            (Basho)

In the middle section, "Shake Loose My Skin," Sanchez wrote this haiku:

how still the morning sea
how still this morning skin
anointing the day. (50)

Just as Basho was awed by the silence pervading the backdrop of the scene in contrast to "the shrill of cicada," Sanchez is struck by the equation of the stillness of both "the morning sea" and "this morning skin." As pointed out earlier, Richard Wright, perhaps influenced by Basho, composed the following pair of haiku in which he focused on nature's silence:

In the silent forest
A woodpecker hammers at
The sound of silence.
            (Wright)

> A thin waterfall
> Dribbles the whole autumn night,—
> How lonely it is.[6]
>   (Wright)

What is common in these haiku by the three poets is that the scene is drawn with little detail and the mood is provided by a simple, reserved description of fact. These haiku create the kind of beauty associated with the aesthetic sensibility of *sabi* that suggests loneliness and quietude as opposed to overexcitement and loudness.[7]

Traditionally as well, the haiku in its portrayal of human beings' association with nature expresses the poet's enlightenment, a new way of looking at humanity and nature. In some of her poems in *Like the Singing Coming Off the Drums,* Sanchez follows this tradition. The second stanza in "Love Poem [*for Tupac*]," the following lines suggest Sanchez's fascination with the Buddhistic worldview of reincarnation:

> the old ones
> say we don't
> die we are
> just passing
> through into
> another space. (111)

The Buddhist concept of reincarnation, as discussed in my reading of Wright's *Black Power,* has a striking affinity with the Akan concept of life and death. Buddhism and the Akan religion share the belief, as does Lacan, that death is not the opposite of life but that death is a continuation of life.[8]

The following haiku expresses not only the concept of reincarnation but also an enlightenment in Zen philosophy:

> what is done is done
> what is not done is not done
> let it go . . . like the wind. (27)

The last line, "let it go . . . like the wind," spontaneously expresses the truth about nature and humanity. Some of Sanchez's haiku like this one have an affinity with the Zen concept of *mu.* This state of nothingness, as discussed earlier, is devoid of all thoughts and emotions that are derived from human subjectivity and egotism and contrary to the conscious or unconscious truth represented by nature. An enlightened person is liberated from the self-centered worldview, convention, or received opinion that lacks fairness and justice. While Sanchez, in the first two lines of this haiku, describes facts in human life, she, in the last line, as a Zen master gives the admonition that one must emulate the principles of nature in molding one's conduct and action.

Another haiku by Sanchez, included at the end of "Naked in the Streets," also concerns the Zen-like discipline of thought:

> let us be one with
> the earth expelling anger
> spirit unbroken. (44)

In the middle section of "Shake Loose My Skin," Sanchez composed another Zen-inspired haiku:

> you are rock garden
> austere in your loving
> in exile from touch. (97)

In these haiku Sanchez tries to render the austerity of the human mind by viewing nature as a revelation.

Not only do many of Sanchez's haiku follow Zen doctrine; they also share the aesthetic principles that underlie classic haiku. One of the most delicate principles of Eastern art is called *yugen,* mentioned earlier. Originally *yugen* in Japanese art was an element of style pervasive in the language of *noh.* It was also a philosophical principle that originated in Zen metaphysics. In Zen, every individual possesses Buddhahood and must realize it. *Yugen,* as applied to art, designates the mysterious and dark, what underlies the surface. This mode of expression, as I have noted earlier, is subtle rather than obvious, suggestive rather than declarative.[9] *Yugen* functions in art as a means by which human beings can comprehend the course of nature. Although *yugen* seems allied with a sense of resignation, it has a far different effect upon the human psyche. The style of *yugen* can express either happiness or sorrow. Cherry blossoms, however beautiful they may be, must fade away; love between man and woman is inevitably followed by sorrow.

The sense of loss also underlies the principle of *yugen.* Sanchez's first tanka in "Naked in the Street" expresses such a sentiment:

> i thought about you
> the pain of not having

you cruising my bones.
no morning saliva smiles this
frantic fugue about no you. (18)

A pair of blues haiku, included in the same section, figure a brightened sense of *yugen:*

when we say good-bye
i want yo tongue inside my
mouth dancing hello. (16)

you too slippery
for me. can't hold you long or
hard. not enough nites. (17)

As aesthetic principles, *yugen* and the blues share the sentiments derived from private and personal feelings. As modes of expression, the blues stylistically differs from *yugen* since, as Amiri Baraka has observed, the blues "issued directly out of the shout and of course the spiritual" (62). Whereas *yugen* is characterized by reservation and modesty, the blues tradition calls for worldly excitement and love. Unlike *yugen,* the blues confine its attention solely to the immediate and celebrates the bodily expression: both "When We Say Good-Bye" and "You Too Slippery" convey direct, unreserved sexual manifestations. Most importantly, Sanchez tries to link the blues message with sexually charged language so as to liberate black bodies from the distorted images slavery inflicted.

That the blues tradition has a greater impact on Sanchez's poetry than does the aesthetics of *yugen* can be seen in the way Sanchez constructs her imagery. If imagery in classic haiku is regarded as indirect and suggestive, the imagery in Sanchez's poetry has the directness and clarity of good prose as opposed to the suggestiveness and vagueness of symbolist poetry. The first poem in "Naked in the Streets" has an extremely sensuous image: dancing is described in terms of "corpuscles sliding in blood" (3). In the second poem of the same section, a haiku quoted earlier, the central image of running "naked in the streets" does not suggest anything other than what it describes:

you ask me to run
naked in the streets with you
i am holding your pulse. (4)

In another poem, a blues haiku in "Shake Loose My Skin," a series of images consist of instantaneous actions:

> legs wrapped around you
> camera. action. tightshot.
> this is not a rerun. (68)

Both poems have an affinity with imagistic poems in the expression of love, such as Pound's "Alba":

> As cool as the pale wet leaves
>   of lily-of-the-valley
>   She lay beside me in the dawn.
>   (*Personae* 109)

In this haiku-like poem, what Pound expressed was not the personal feeling he had about the woman lying beside him at dawn but his spontaneous sensation of the coolness of "the pale wet leaves / of lily-of-the-valley." Likewise, the actions themselves of running "naked in the streets" and "legs wrapped around you" were Sanchez's subjects in the poems.

Such poems as "You Ask Me to Run" and "Legs Wrapped around You" bear a structural resemblance as well to Pound's famous imagistic haiku, "In a Station of the Metro," quoted earlier. Unlike Sanchez's haiku, Pound's "In a Station of the Metro" is constructed in two lines simply because Pound had in mind "a form of super-position" in which the poem was to be composed. "In a poem of this sort," he explained, "one is trying to record the precise instant when a thing outward and objective transforms itself, or darts into a thing inward and subjective" ("Vorticism" 467). Compared to Pound's "In a Station of the Metro," Sanchez's "You Ask Me to Run" has a similar structure in imagery. Just as in the other haiku, "Legs Wrapped around You," Sanchez in this poem is trying to record the precise instant when a thing outward and objective, that is, running "naked in the streets," transforms itself or darts into a thing inward and subjective, that is, the image of "i am holding your pulse." The image of running "naked in the streets" is based in immediate experience, whether real or imagined since Sanchez lived in Philadelphia. Not only did she see the "thing," but it must have generated such a sensation that she could not shake it from her mind.

Most discussions about the genesis of the imagist movement are speculative at best. Pound's insistence that an image in poetry must be active rather than passive suggests that a modernist poem such as Pound's and

Sanchez's is not a description of something, but, as Aristotle said of tragedy, an action. Pound approaches Aristotelianism in his insistence that the image of the faces in the crowd in his metro poem was not simply a description of his sensation at the station but an active entity capable of dynamic development. According to his experience, this particular image instantly transformed itself into another image, the image of the petals on a wet, black bough. To Pound the success of this poem resulted from his instantaneous perception of the relatedness between the two entirely different objects. Although in Sanchez's poems the two related objects are not entirely different, as in Pound's "In a Station of the Metro," Sanchez's images, like Pound's, are strikingly active and instantaneous rather than symbolic and suggestive.

2.

Although most of the short poems collected in *Like the Singing Coming Off the Drums* are stylistically influenced by the poetics of haiku as well as by the aesthetics of modernist poetry, much of Sanchez's ideological concern is postmodern, postcolonial, and African American. Many of her poems aim at teaching African Americans to achieve individualism and value their heritage. Even such a haiku as

> mixed with day and sun
> i crouched in the earth carry
> you like a dark river. (36)

succinctly expresses what Langston Hughes does in "The Negro Speaks of Rivers":

> I've known rivers:
> I've known rivers ancient as the world and older than the flow of human
>   blood in human veins.
>
> My soul has grown deep like the rivers.
>
> I bathed in the Euphrates when dawns were young.
> I built my hut near the Congo and it lulled me to sleep.
> I looked upon the Nile and raised the pyramids above it.
> I heard the singing of the Mississippi when Abe Lincoln went down to

New Orleans, and
I've seen its muddy bosom turn all golden in the sunset.
I've known rivers:
Ancient, dusky rivers.

My soul has grown deep like the rivers.

(*Selected Poems* 4)

Sanchez and Hughes are both portraying how the African American soul, a symbol of humanity, is deeply embedded in the earth. The soul, as Hughes sees, "has grown deep like the rivers"; anyone endowed with it, like Sanchez, carries anyone else "like a dark river."

Hughes's signifying thrives on a chain of signs, signifiers, and signifieds. While "the Euphrates," "the Congo," "the Nile," and "the Mississippi" are all signs of great rivers, they also signify different human histories. All of the signifieds in turn signify yet other historical events. For African Americans, "the Mississippi" signifies its "singing . . . when Abe Lincoln / went down to New Orleans"; not only does it signify "its muddy bosom," but its signified in turn signifies a beautiful image, the golden river under sunset. Sanchez's haiku, on the other hand, consists of fewer but nonetheless equally powerful signs, signifiers, and signifieds: the words "mixed," "day," "sun," "i," "crouched," "earth," "carry," "you," "dark," and "river." These words express natural, spontaneous human sentiments, as do those in classic haiku, rather than emotional, personal feelings. In fact, an epiphany given in Sanchez's haiku, "Mixed with Day and Sun," bears a strong resemblance to a cross-cultural vision captured in Hughes's "The Negro Speaks of Rivers."

Sanchez's most important thematic concern is love of humanity, an act of faith that must begin with self-love. The last poem in the collection, dedicated to Gwendolyn Brooks, is a response and rejoinder to such a poem as Brooks's "The Mother." Not only is Brooks portrayed as "a holy one," but she has also become a universal symbol of the mother with enduring love and humanity:

for she is a holy one
restringing her words
from city to city
so that we live and
breathe and smile and
breathe and love and
breath her . . .
this Gwensister called life. (133)

The sign that Sanchez's "For Sister Gwen Brooks" shares with Brooks's "The Mother" signifies the universal vision that love emanates from mother. Sanchez's refrain "for she is a holy one" further signifies the goddess worshiped among the Ashanti and the female king who owns her children, as described in Richard Wright's *Black Power*. In *Pagan Spain,* as Wright speculates, universal motherhood has derived from the Virgin Mary, "Maya, the mother of Buddha," and "Isis, mother of Horus." As Wright remarks, "Egyptians worshiped Isis . . . and she was called Our Lady, the Queen of Heaven, Mother of God" (*Pagan Spain* 65).

In "The Mother," Brooks, referring to the issue of abortion as a sign, makes it signify the universal issue of love. The opening lines graphically describe the lifeless fetuses:

> Abortions will not let you forget.
> You remember the children you got that you did not get,
> The damp small pulps with a little or with no hair,

"The damp small pulps," a signified, in turn signifies "[the] singers and workers," the objects of motherly love, who would have flourished if their unborn bodies had not been aborted:

> The singers and workers that never handled the air.
> You will never neglect or beat
> Them, or silence or buy with a sweet.
> You will never wind up the sucking-thumb
> Or scuttle off ghosts that come.
> You will never leave them, controlling your luscious sigh,
> Return for a snack of them, with gobbling mother-eye.

Brooks as a mother expresses her remorse for aborting her children as if she committed a crime:

> I have heard in the voices of the wind the voices of my dim killed
>   children.
> I have contracted. I have eased
> My dim dears at the breasts they could never suck.
> I have said, Sweets, if I sinned, if I seized
> Your luck
> And your lives from your unfinished reach,
> If I stole your births and your names,

Your straight baby tears and your games,
Your stilted or lovely loves, your tumults, your marriages, aches, and your
    deaths,

Toward the end of the poem, however, the issue of abortion signifies that of nurture. Millions of children the world over, born of poverty and neglect, are Brooks's ultimate issue and concern. While the poem, on the surface, depicts the abortion of a fetus, Brooks appeals to the moral conscience of adults with profound love and compassion for children. The poem is also a social protest in allusion to the issue of nurturing children instead of a debate on the issue of abortion in itself:

If I poisoned the beginnings of your breaths,
Believe that even in my deliberateness I was not deliberate.
Though why should I whine,
Whine that the crime was other than mine?—
....
You were born, you had body, you died.
It is just that you never giggled or planned or cried.
                                        (*Selected Poems* 4–5)

Brooks agonizes over the callousness of society, which stunted and killed children, who would have become "singers and workers." "The Mother," then, reads as an admonition that neglect of children is the fault of society, not that of mother. It is only natural and universal that mother should love child; it is unnatural and immoral that society should refuse to nurture children.

The penultimate poem in *Like the Singing Coming Off the Drums* is dedicated to Cornel West. In contrast to the rest of the poems, it is a prose poem like Whitman's "Song of Myself." Cornel West, a Harvard professor, is not presented as a spokesman of the academia but is characterized as a cultural activist like Whitman, Hughes, and Brooks, each of whom in a unique way sought to apotheosize the humanity of the land. Sanchez sees West as a foremost individual at the dawn of the twenty-first century, a spokesperson always "questioning a country that denies the sanctity, the holiness of children, people, rivers, sky, trees, earth" (130). Sanchez urges the reader to "look at the father in him. The husband in him. The activist in him. The teacher in him. The lover in him. The truth seeker in him. The James Brown dancer in him. The reformer in him. The defender of people in him. The intellectual in him" (130–31). West is

This man. Born into history. This humanist. This twenty-first-century traveler pulling us screaming against our will towards a future that will hold all of humankind in an embrace. He acknowledges us all. The poor. Blacks and whites. Asians and Native Americans. Jews and Muslims. Latinos and Africans. Gays and Lesbians. (131)[10]

Rather than dwelling on the racial conflict and oppression the country has suffered, Sanchez admonishes the reader to see cross-pollination in the various cultures brought together to the land.

Whether *Like the Singing Coming Off the Drums* is Sanchez's best work remains to be seen in the generations to come, but her effort to use diverse principles of aesthetics in molding her poetry has few precedents in American literature. Thematically, nineteenth-century American poets such as Emerson, Poe, Dickinson, and Whitman were partly influenced by various cultural and religious thoughts, just as twentieth-century American poets such as Ezra Pound, Wallace Stevens, Richard Wright, Allen Ginsberg, and Gary Snyder at some points in their careers emulated Eastern poetics. Sanchez, on the other hand, remains one of the accomplished contemporary American poets writing from the perspective of cross-cultural visions in shaping the form and content of her poetry.

CHAPTER 12

James Emanuel's Jazz Haiku and African American Individualism

While haiku is a traditional Japanese poetic form, jazz has its origin in African American music. Despite technical differences in composition, haiku and jazz have been known for their powerful expressions of human sentiments by celebrated artists in both genres. *Jazz from the Haiku King* (1999) is the latest collection of James Emanuel's work, in which a contemporary African American poet has presented a series of literary experiments he calls "jazz haiku."[1] Just as jazz has crossed cultural boundaries the world over in modern times, Emanuel's intention is to translate the musical expressions of African American life, its pain and joy, into the 5–7–5 syllabic measures of haiku. In so doing, he has also attempted to expand the imagery of the traditional haiku beyond its single impression by including narrative and rhyme.

In Japanese culture, as pointed out earlier, haiku has served as an expression of the unity and harmony of all things, a sensibility that humanity and nature are one and inseparable. Haiku poets are attracted to such objects as flowers, trees, birds, sunsets, the moon, and genuine love. The seventeen-syllable verse form had been preserved by poets for nearly three centuries until the late seventeenth century. As mentioned earlier, by the time Basho in the late seventeenth century composed the first version of his celebrated poem on a frog jumping into the old pond, haiku had become a highly stylized expression of poetic vision.[2]

Even on the surface jazz and haiku have much in common. As jazz performance thrives on an endless improvisation which the composer fashions from traditional materials, so does haiku composition thrive on an infinite improvisation upon beautiful objects in nature and humanity. Because of improvisation, the composer in both genres must efface his or her identity. In jazz, play changes on ideas as well as on sounds to create unexpected sensations. In haiku, the poet spares no pains to capture unexpected sensations. In both genres, the composer and the composed, subject and object, coalesce as the identity of the composer disappears in the wake of creation.

Jazz also shares many of the philosophical principles that underlie haiku. As noted in the introduction to this book, haiku since Basho has been traditionally associated with Zen philosophy. Zen teaches the follower to attain enlightenment, a new way of looking at humanity and nature. Just as Zen stresses self-reliance, not egotism, and nature, not materialism, so does jazz. Like haiku, jazz—characterized by innovation—seeks a new way of looking at ourselves and the world around us. Just as jazz challenges us to hear sounds and rhythms we have not heard before, so haiku challenges us to see images of humanity and nature we have not seen before. Jazz and haiku enable us to open our minds and imagine ways of reaching a higher ground in our present lives.

1.

Unlike those of haiku, the origin and development of jazz are well known by African American writers. Although jazz originated in the South from the blues and spirituals, it evolved into city music, flourishing with the Harlem Renaissance in the 1920s and with the Chicago Renaissance in the late 1930s and the early 1940s. As African Americans migrated to northern cities, they bore with them what Ralph Ellison called "the painful details and episodes of a brutal experience alive in one's aching consciousness, to finger its jagged grain, and to transcend it, not by the consolation of philosophy but by squeezing from it a near-tragic, near comic lyricism" ("Wright's Blues" 202).[3] To Richard Wright, jazz or spirituals convey "bitter rebellion" that "simmers" behind them. When hearing such music, Wright stressed, one must not erase the fact that hatred was what constituted African American life, "the hatred of the disinherited from which no black man can isolate himself" (*Conversations* 108).

Not only did Wright and Ellison agree that African American music is a poignant expression of painful experience, but they also observed that it is a most effective means by which to battle racism. African American music, as a cultural critique, is to deconstruct the power of authority. Music decenters the outdated authority and creates in its place a new authority, what Alan Nadel calls "one composed of subversive strategies drawing from African-American traditions of 'call & response,' 'signifyin',' and 'loud talking'" (Werner, *Playing* xix).

As African music, the blues has served as an artistic, metaphoric ideal of freedom and individualism. Langston Hughes, a central figure of the Harlem Renaissance in the 1920s, wrote a series of poems collected in *The Weary Blues* (1926). These poems celebrated African American experience and inspired African Americans to achieve individualism and self-reliance despite their adversity and loneliness. In "The Weary Blues" he provides a portrayal of a blues singer:

> In a deep song voice with a melancholy tone
> I heard that Negro sing, that old piano moan—
> "Ain't got nobody in all this world,
> Ain't got nobody but ma self.
> I's gwine to quit ma frownin'
> And put ma troubles on the shelf."
>
> (*Selected Poems* 33)

To Hughes, the blues was a response to an unjust, unnatural racist system of power that had consistently degraded and denied African American experience.

Unlike Hughes, Wright believed that the blues represents a simplistic form of African American vernacular aesthetics. In his foreword to Paul Oliver's *Blues Fell This Morning,* Wright characterizes the blues as having "a vocabulary terser than Basic English, shorn of all hyperbole, purged of metaphysical implications, wedded to a frankly atheistic vision of life, and excluding almost all references to *nature* and her various moods" (viii; emphasis added). In *12 Million Black Voices* Wright describes the blues as a passive form of musical expression: "The ridiculousness and sublimity of love are captured in our blues, those sad-happy songs that laugh and weep all in one breath, those mockingly tender utterances of a folk imprisoned in steel and stone" (128).

At the opening scene in *Native Son,* Bigger's mother sings:

> *Life is like a mountain railroad*
> *With an engineer that's brave*
> *We must make the run successful*
> *From the cradle to the grave. . . .*
> (*Native Son* 14)

"The song," Wright remarks, "irked him [Bigger] and he was glad when she stopped and came into the room with a pot of coffee and a plate of crinkled bacon" (14). Later in the story, Jan argues that a Communist revolution needs African Americans, who have "spirit," and says, "And their songs—the spirituals! Aren't they marvelous?" Bigger says that he can't sing, but Mary Dalton, closing her eyes, sings:

> *"Swing low, sweet chariot,*
> *Coming fer to carry me home. . . ."*

Although Jan joins in, Bigger, Wright comments, "smiled derisively. Hell, that ain't the tune, he thought" (76–77).

As the migration from the South to Chicago and other Great Lakes cities continued in the early decades of the twentieth century, the sacred traditions of the southern black church developed into the gospel music of Clara Ward, Roberta Martin, and Mahalia Jackson. This gospel music "in turn contributed to the vocal styles fundamental to fifties rhythm and blues and sixties soul music" (Werner, *Playing* 244). Along with the musical developments, Wright organized a series of meetings for African American writers and artists, establishing the South Side Writers' Group in 1936. In such meetings he submitted for discussions his essays and his drafts of "Down by the Riverside," "Long Black Song," and "Bright and Morning Star" (Fabre, *Quest* 128).

In contrast to the blues and the spirituals, jazz is well known for improvisation and syncopation. Individualism, which also distinguishes jazz, aside, another salient feature of jazz is the anonymity of jazz artists, as Ellison observes:

> Some of the most brilliant of jazzmen made no records; their names appeared in print only in announcements of some local dance or remote "battles of music" against equally uncelebrated bands. Being devoted to an art which traditionally thrives on improvisation, these unrecorded artists very often have their most original ideas enter the public domain almost as rapidly as they are conceived to be quickly absorbed into the thought and technique of their fellows. Thus the riffs which swung the dancers and the band on some transcendent evening, and which inspired others to competitive flights of invention, become all too swiftly a part of the general style, leaving the originator as anonymous as the creators of the architecture called Gothic. (*Shadow* 234)

The anonymity of jazz musicians has an affinity with that of *noh* dramatists. W. B. Yeats, inspired by *noh* drama, wrote such plays as *At the Hawk's Well*. In the performance of the play, he used masks to present anonymous, time-honored expressions, just as the Roman theater used masks instead of makeup (Noguchi, *Spirit* 60). Yeats clearly implied in his letter to Yone Noguchi that contemporary arts in the West were infected with egotism while classical works of art in Japan were created as if anonymously (Noguchi, *Selected Writings* 2: 14).

What seemed to have inspired Yeats was the "simplicity" of the artists, an ancient form of beauty that transcended time, place, and personality. Irked by modern ingenuity and science, he was adamantly opposed to realism in art and literature. For him realism failed to uncover the deeply ingrained human spirit and character. He later discovered that noble spirits and profound emotions are expressed with simplicity in the *noh* play. Noguchi observed: "It was the time when nobody asked who wrote them, if the plays themselves were worthy. What a difference from this day of advertisement and personal ambition! . . . I mean that they are not the creation of one time or one age; it is not far wrong to say that they wrote themselves, as if flowers or trees rising from the rich soil of tradition and Buddhistic faith" (*Spirit* 63). In its simplicity and appeal, jazz has much in common with *noh* drama.

Unlike the blues, jazz is characterized by its flexibility and creativity. Just as the blues emphasizes individuality and personality, so does jazz emphasize anonymity and impersonality. While both individuality and communal affirmation are central to the blues, their relationship and their importance to jazz differ from those to the blues. "Seen in relation to the blues impulse," Craig Werner observes, "the jazz impulse provides a way of exploring implications of realizing the relational possibilities of the (blues) self, and of expanding the consciousness of self and community through a process of continual improvisation" (*Playing* xxii). Involving both self-expression and community affirmation, jazz is a genre of ambivalence, of what Ellison calls "a cruel contradiction." He remarks:

> For true jazz is an art of individual assertion within and against the group. Each true jazz moment (as distinct from the uninspired commercial performance) springs from a contest in which each artist challenges all the rest; each solo flight, or improvisation, represents (like the successive canvasses of a painter) a definition of his identity: as individual, as member of the collectivity and as a link in the chain of tradition. (*Shadow* 234)

In light of the relation of self and community, jazz also bears a strong resemblance to *renga,* fifteenth-century Japanese linked verse, from which haiku evolved. *Renga,* which flourished in the beginnings as comic poetry was a continuous chain of fourteen (7–7) and seventeen (5–7–5) syllable verses, each independently composed, but connected as one poem, a communal composition.[4]

In practice, however, jazz in the early 1950s emphasized individuality, in technical virtuosity and theoretical knowledge, rather than community and its involvement with jazz. "In response," Werner notes, "jazz musicians such as Miles Davis, Ornett Coleman, and John Coltrane established the contours of the multifaceted 'free jazz' movement, which includes most AACM [the Association for the Advancement of Creative Musicians] work" (*Playing* 247). As Gayl Jones has also remarked, jazz—rendered through nonchronological syncopation and tempo—thrives on the essence of jazz, "the jam session," that "emerges from an interplay of voices improvising on the basic themes or motifs of the text in keywords and phrases." This interplay of self and other and self and community, what Jones calls "seemingly nonlogical and associational," makes the jazz text more complex, flexible, and fluid than the blues text (*Liberating* 200). Jazz, as Louis Armstrong said, is a genre of music that should never be played in the same way as before.[5]

While jazz has served African Americans as an artistic medium for conveying pain and suffering, it has also expressed natural human desire. Toni Morrison's *Jazz,* as I have earlier argued, is intended not only as a battle against racism but more importantly as a blueprint for fulfillment of desire by African Americans. The novel demonstrates that only when "the village within" is established in the city will African Americans be able to fulfill their desire. Morrison's attempt to equate desire with sexuality through jazz is corroborated by Wright's view of jazz. As noted earlier, Wright was familiarly known as "Dick" in Harlem. He told Frank Tenot, an interviewer: "The black bourgeoisie don't like either [gospel or jazz], because in their anxiety to imitate whites, they consider both to be 'primitive' art forms, incapable of expressing lofty, 'civilized' sentiments." Wright believed that the African American bourgeoisie's taste for music was corrupted by Hollywood music and American musicals, the type of music he called "[v]ery bad music." In sum, he told Tenot: "Not to be a black bourgeois and to understand that the main gift that jazz has to offer the world today is an affirmation of *desire*" (*Conversations* 242–43).

Wright's emphasis on jazz as an expression of desire notwithstanding, jazz has a strong affinity with haiku. Not only are jazz and haiku well-established art forms; they both stand in sharp antithesis to materialism and commercialism. There is little wonder, then, that Wright regarded Hollywood music and American musicals as vulgar representations of materialism and capitalism, to which he was averse all his life. The four thousand haiku he wrote in his final eighteen months, as discussed earlier, poignantly express his conviction that materialism and its corollary, greed, were the twin culprits of racial conflict.

Jazz has also been a catalyst for African Americans to attain their individualism, but Ellison and Wright clearly differ in their views of how to achieve this individualism. Ellison defines jazz as a means of expressing individualism in relation to collectivity and tradition. Wright, on the other hand, defines writing as a means of expressing individuality independent of collectivity and tradition. In "Blueprint for Negro Writing," as pointed out earlier, Wright envisions African American individualism as buttressed by the twin pillars of "perspective" and "intellectual space" which must not be influenced by any traditions or world movements. "At its best," he stresses, "perspective is a preconscious assumption, something which a writer takes for granted, something which he wins through his living" (45–46). The reason for his defection from the Communist Party was that Communists deprived him of his individuality. In defining African American narrative of "ascent" and "immersion," Robert Stepto shows that ascent narrative, diverting from familial or communal postures, develops into "a new posture in the least oppressive environment—at best one of solitude; at worst, one of alienation" (167).

In Toni Morrison's *Jazz,* African American individualism finds expression and representation in the various events the author explores in the novel. At first she focuses on the courtship of Violet and Joe. For them, individualism does not simply mean freedom from racial oppression in American life; it is a sign of creation and progression, the twin actions which urban mood and urban music are urging upon them. Paradoxically, lack of space in the city creates more action and generates more desire: "Her hip bones rubbed his thigh as they stood in the aisle unable to stop smiling." The rhythm of jazz represents an undulating movement that urges the listener into individuality rather than conformity. Just as Hollywood music and American musicals conform to materialistic and commercial impulses, African American jazz, in its freely improvised and syncopated sounds and rhythms, expresses subjective and individualistic sentiments. "However they came, when or why," Morrison writes in *Jazz,* "the minute the leather of their soles hit the pavement—there was no turning around" (32). Likewise, the sound of drums has the effect of urging on a mature, middle-aged African American woman like Alice Manfred to seek liberty and happiness, but more importantly it inspires her with a sense of individuality and responsibility.

2.

Just as many modern African American writers have been inspired by jazz, so also has James Emanuel. His poetry, moreover, as the title of this book indicates, seeks a means of expression shared by jazz and haiku. Jazz and haiku both convey spontaneously created expressions that are free from any economic, social, or political impulses. "Jazz," he writes in his preface, "I knew—like the Caruso I heard on the same phonograph—had no boundaries; but its immense international magnetism seemed inadequately explored in poetry" (iv–v). In haiku, despite its brevity, he found much of the height and depth of vision that he did in jazz.

In the haiku entitled "Dizzy Gillespie (News of His Death)," placed in the middle of the collection, Emanuel hears Gillespie's music reverberate in the sky and on earth:

> Dizzy's bellows pumps.
> Jazz balloon inflates, floats high.
> Earth listens, stands by. (44)

Traditionally haiku express and celebrate the unity of humanity and nature: the opening line of a haiku usually has a *kigo* (seasonal word). Even though Emanuel's "Dizzy Gillespie" lacks a seasonal reference, it displays the nexus of humanity and nature: Gillespie and sky and earth. This haiku is an elegy for Gillespie, just as Whitman's "When Lilacs Last in the Dooryard Bloom'd" is an elegy for Lincoln. In celebrating the lives of the great men, both poems express the immortality of their spirits. Just as Lincoln will return with lilacs in the spring and the North Star at night, Gillespie will be remembered for his jazz.

Emanuel's haiku on Gillespie is also remindful of Zen philosophy, which emphasizes the fusion of humanity and nature. Zen teaches its followers to transcend the dualism of life and death. Zen master Dogen, mentioned earlier, observed that life and death are not separated as they seem and that there is no need to avoid death. Similarly, Emanuel and Whitman both sought a reconciliation of life and death. Whitman's feat of turning the national bereavement in the elegy into a celebration of death is well known, but less known is his idea of death given in "A Sight in Camp in the Daybreak Gray and Dim." To Whitman, the dead soldier in this poem appears no less divine than the savior Christ; they both represent the living godhead. In a similar vein, as Gillespie's jazz balloon floats high in the sky and the earth stands by and listens, this jazz master is vividly alive.

Emanuel captures the affinity of jazz and haiku in many of the poems in the collection. The first chapter, "Page One," features various types of jazz haiku with translations into other languages: "The Haiku King," "Jazzanatomy," "Jazzroads," "Jazzactions," "Bojangles and Jo." The first of the four poems under the group title "Jazzanatomy" reads:

> EVERYTHING is jazz:
> snails, jails, rails, tails, males, females,
> snow-white   cotton bales. (2)

To Emanuel, jazz represents all walks of life, human and nonhuman alike. Human life is represented by males and females, animal life by snails and tails, and inanimate life by "snow-white cotton bales" "My haiku," Emanuel remarks in his preface, "added the toughness of poverty and racial injustice" (iv). The images of "jails" and "cotton bales," signifying the unjustified imprisonment of African Americans and their immoral slave labor, represent the twin evils in American life: racism and poverty. "Song of Myself," a narrative and autobiographical poem, also concerns all walks of American life. Focusing on human life, Whitman declares: "I am the poet of the Body and I am the poet of the Soul," and "I am the poet of the woman the same as the man." About the problems of good and evil, he writes: "The pleasures of heaven are with me and the pains of hell are with me" (39).

Emanuel's view of humanity and nature is shared by his American predecessors, such as Whitman, Countee Cullen, and Wright. The opening pages of Wright's *Black Power* have a passage addressed "To the Unknown African" and two quotations from Cullen and Whitman. "To the Unknown African" records an observation derived from Wright's view that the African was victimized by slave trades because of the African's primal outlook on human existence. The quotations from both Cullen and Whitman suggest that Africans, the inheritors and products of nature, have been exploited by a materialistic civilization. Before Europeans appeared with their machines, the continent had thrived on its pastoral idylls. Now it exists at the services of Western traders who exploit African products. Whitman's line *Not till the sun excludes you do I exclude you* expresses not merely his compassion for African Americans but strongly, as do Cullen's lines, their natural and divine heritage.[6]

Emanuel's attempt to unify human and natural spirits can be seen in many of his jazz haiku. What underlies his experimentation is a Jeffersonian belief that those who live and work intimately with the earth deserve divine protection.[7] In the haiku "Farmer," Emanuel depicts the affinity of a farmer with jazz:

> Good-grip Jazz, farmer:
> ploughed music like fields, worked late,
> kept all furrows   straight. (64)

Inspirational jazz is like a God-chosen farmer who cultivates the earth to attain the spirit of nature. The earth to Jefferson is "the focus in which he [God] keeps alive that sacred fire, which otherwise might escape from the face of the earth" (Jefferson 165). To Emanuel, jazz inspires genuine spirits just as the farmer keeps "all furrows straight." The word *straight* has a moral implication if this haiku is remindful of Jefferson's notes on farmers. "Corruption of morals in the mass of cultivators," Jefferson maintains, "is a phænomenon of which no age nor nation has furnished an example" (Jefferson 165). Unlike the traditional haiku with a single image or a juxtaposition of two separate images, Emanuel's "Farmer" portrays a pair of related actions in farming. Not only does a good farmer, like a good jazz musician, work "late"; he also keeps "all furrows straight."

The confluence of haiku and jazz in Emanuel's poems is based on the expression of natural, spontaneous responses to human life. This sensibility is distinguished from that of negotiation and ambivalence characteristic of social and political discourse. The first group of poems, "Jazzanatomy," presents—besides "EVERYTHING Is Jazz" discussed above—three other jazz haiku:

> Knee-bone, thigh, hip-bone.
> Jazz slips you percussion bone
> classified "unknown."

> Sleek lizard rhythms,
> cigar-smoke tunes, straight-gin sky
> laced with double moons.

> Second-chance rhythms,
> don't-give-up riffs: jazz gets HIGH
> off can'ts, buts, and ifs. (2)

The first haiku features the explosive sound produced by a percussion instrument, while the last two focus on the uniqueness of jazz rhythms. The second one, "Sleek Lizard Rhythms," characterizes the jazz rhythms not only as smooth like lizards but as capable of making thin tunes rise high as "straight-gin sky." In the third haiku, "Second-Chance Rhythms," Emanuel hears the rhythms getting "HIGH" by not giving up riffs. The height such rhythms attain enables the composer to rise above "can'ts, buts, and ifs." "Second-Chance Rhythms" bears a resemblance to Basho's "The Old Pond," mentioned earlier. Emanuel describes the ways in which the sound of jazz, transcending social and political interests and conflicts, enables him to attain peace of mind, just as Basho intimates the enlightenment he achieved by hearing the sound of the water bursting out of the tranquility of the world.

"Second-Chance Rhythms" is also reminiscent of Emily Dickinson's poem "The Soul Selects Her Own Society" in its rhythm:

> The Soul selects her own Society—
> Then—shuts the Door—
> To her divine Majority—
> Present no more—
>
> Unmoved—she notes the Chariots—pausing—
> At her low Gate—
> Unmoved—an Emperor be kneeling
> Upon her Mat—
>
> I've known her—from an ample nation—
> Choose One—
> Then—close the Valves of her attention—
> Like Stone—
>
> (Dickinson 1: 225)

Emanuel suggests the attitude of flexibility by describing jazz rhythms as having riffs, two or four or more refrains, in them. But he also stresses the decisiveness of jazz by capitalizing the word "HIGH." In Dickinson's poem, the flexibility in a woman's character is described by longer lines with four beats, such as the opening line of each stanza: "The Soul selects her own Society," "Unmoved—an Emperor be kneeling," and "I've known her—from an ample nation—." By contrast, the decisiveness in the woman's character is expressed by shorter staccato lines with two beats, such as the concluding line of each stanza: "Present no more—," "Upon her Mat—," and "Like Stone—."

Traditionally, haiku—seeking enlightenment on the spirit of nature—depicts the setting sun and the moon, mountains and seas, flowers and trees, but it does not concern human sexuality. Some contemporary haiku in America and Japan, however, are natural, spontaneous expressions of sexual desire, just as some forms of jazz are conducive to expressing sexuality. Rich Youmans, a contemporary American haiku poet, for example, includes such a haiku in his *haibun* (haiku essay) entitled "For My Wife on Our First Anniversary." Youmans describes scenes of nature in early spring, when he wakes at dawn and gazes at his sleeping wife. Such a passage, with its

Christian allusions, makes this *haibun* an aubade, a kind of morning love lyric. What this haiku poet experiences is an epiphany from the spirit of nature, the essential meaning of his life, his wife being both eros and agape. Her waking voice is related to an allusion to the Resurrection dogwood petals which are described as "cruciform." Youmans evokes the spirit of nature by the morning light transformed into prisms through the window glass, a figurative spiritualization of the physical world. The *haibun* ends with a haiku:

> prisms in
> early light:
> we make love
> (Youmans 15)

Just as Youmans seeks enlightenment on sexual love through a Christian revelation, so does Emanuel through jazz music. The first chapter, "Page One," ends with four jazz haiku under the title "Bojangles and Jo":

> Stairstep music: ups,
> downs, Bill Robinson smiling,
> jazzdancing the rounds.
>
> She raised champagne lips,
> danced inside banana hips.
> All Paris wooed   Jo.
>
> Banana panties,
> perfumed belt, JAZZ tattooing
> lush ecstasies felt.
>
> Josephine, royal,
> jeweling her dance, flushing
> the bosom of France. (8)

The stairstep music with "ups" and "downs" induces Bill Robinson to smile and jazzdance "the rounds." His smiling and jazzdancing, in turn, leads to Josephine's raising "champagne lips" and dancing "inside banana hips": "All Paris" woos her. "Banana panties," "perfumed belt," "JAZZ tattooing" each throw the listeners into "lush ecstasies." All in all, this jazz music makes Josephine "royal": she reigns as a goddess of love, "the bosom of France." Not only does Emanuel cast "Bojangles and Jo" in a narrative style, but this group of jazz haiku also bears some resemblance to *renku,* Japanese linked verse in the haiku manner.[8]

Emanuel's other unlinked, independently composed haiku are also jazz-like expressions of robust, natural human sexuality:

Duke Ellington
"I love you madly,"
Duke said.   Beauty his mistress,
jazz hammock their bed. (14)

Fashion Show
When you rock those hips
and turn like that, JAZZ, baby!
I know where it's at. (32)

In "Duke Ellington," their "jazz hammock," endlessly rocking, inspires them with love. In "Fashion Show," rocking "those hips" and turning "like that" instantly generate male desire.

Another group of haiku, entitled "'I'm a Jazz Singer,' She Replied," consists of an introductory haiku followed by four haiku, each beginning with "Jazz":

He dug what she said:
bright jellies, smooth marmalade
spread on warm brown bread.

"Jazz" from drowsy lips
orchids lift to honeybees
floating on long sips.

"Jazz": quick fingerpops
pancake on a griddle-top
of memories.   Stop.

"Jazz": mysterious
as nutmeg, missing fingers,
gold.   Less serious.

"Jazz": cool bannister.
Don't need no stair.   Ways to climb
when the sax is there. (83)

In contrast to the linked haiku in "Bojangles and Joe," each of the haiku in "'I'm a Jazz Singer,' She Replied" is independently composed. Whereas those linked haiku capture the interactions between the jazz musicians in depicting the generation of sexual desire, each of these haiku about a certain female jazz singer features a specific image characteristic of the singer: "drowsy lips," "long sips," "quick fingerpops," and "mysterious / . . . missing fingers." Focusing on such sensuous images and actions, each of the haiku inspires the audience to generate desire and love.

3.

From a philosophical perspective, Emanuel's jazz haiku has an affinity with the Zen concept of *mu*. A series of ten haiku in the chapter "Jazz Meets the Abstract (Engravings)," for example, describe various human actions in which Emanuel is in search of space, a Zen-like state of nothingness. This space is devoid of egotism and artificiality: it transcends human reasoning and personal vision. The first haiku follows:

> Space moves, contours grow
> as wood, web, damp, dust.   Points turn,
> Corners follow. JAZZ! (87)

In this haiku, jazz creates a space that moves as its contours ". . . grow / as wood, web, damp, dust," their points "turn," and their corners "follow." Neither intellectuality nor emotion such as hatred or anger is able to occupy such a space.

Emanuel further shows in his haiku the state of nothingness which jazz is able to achieve:

> No meaning at birth:
> just screams, squirms, frowns without sight,
> fists clenched against light. (88)

> Abstract, I try you
> (walk, sit, stretch).   You say nothing.
> Good fit; to wit: JAZZ. (90)

> No dust, rust, no guilt
> in home JAZZ built; it cheers, STANDS,
> charms guests from ALL lands. (93)

Jazz is like a newborn child with its "fists clenched against light." The child just "screams, squirms, frowns without sight"; all this has "No meaning at birth," a state of nothingness. Emanuel tries jazz, as he does an infant: "(walk, sit, stretch)." Like the infant, jazz says "nothing," *mu*, but is a good fit. Such a space has "No dust, rust," and such a state of mind has "no guilt." Whereas jazz was born and reared in America, it has attracted "guests from ALL lands." To Emanuel, jazz and Zen, characteristic of their respective cultures, have a common, universal appeal.

In other jazz haiku, Emanuel also envisions a world in which the state of *mu* can be attained. In this haiku, for example, height and intensity define jazz:

Soars, leapfrogs, yells: JAZZ!
But don't expect no tantrums,
no crazyman spells. (6)

Jazz "Soars, leapfrogs, yells." Emanuel cautions, however, that soaring sounds and "yells" do not signal "tantrums" and "crazyman spells." The sound of jazz, like the sound of the water made by a leaping frog in Basho's haiku, signifies enlightenment, the state of *mu*. Just as Basho is impressed with the depth and silence of the universe, so is Emanuel with the height and intensity of jazz. This state of consciousness jazz creates has the effect of cleansing the human mind of impurity. "Haiku on Louis Armstrong" captures Armstrong's ability to create his utopia, a "wonderworld," purified of social ills and racial conflicts:

Jazz-rainbow: skywash
his trumpet blew, cleansing air,
his wonderworld there. (56)

Armstrong's utopia is, in turn, buttressed by individualism. The last four haiku under the title "Steppin' Out on the Promise" in Chapter V, "Jazzmix," impress on African Americans the imperative of individualism:

Step out, Brother.   Blow.
Just pretend you plantin' corn,
gold seeds from your horn.

Step out, Sister.   Blow.
Must be Lord told you to play,
gifted you that way.

> Step out, Daughter.   Shine.
> Make 'em switch their lights on, chile.
> Make 'em jazzophile.
>
> Step out, Sonny.   Blow.
> Tell 'em all they need to know.
> Lay it on 'em.   GO! (84)

Emanuel impels each of the African Americans, brothers and sisters, sons and daughters, to be individualistic, self-reliant in their efforts to realize the Promised Land. He tells his brother to blow his horn and plant "gold seeds" from it; he tells his sister to blow her horn and play the way God told her. He urges his daughter to shine in her performance and make her audience "jazzophile," and he tells his son to blow his horn and enlighten his audience with "all they need to know." Emanuel's command "Step out," which begins each of the jazz haiku, emphasizes the principles of subjectivity and individuality in jazz performance. Each of the jazz haiku above, unlike a classic haiku, is united in its rhythm and meaning by a rhyme between the last two lines: "corn" and "horn," "play" and "way," "chile" and "jazzophile," "know " and "GO!"

Adding rhyme to haiku, much like deleting seasonal reference, is an innovation Emanuel has made in his haiku. He has attempted to widen the sensory impact of haiku beyond the effect of the single impression given in a traditional haiku. Jazz is not only an expression of African American individualism; it also inspires African Americans into cooperation and dialogue. A series of haiku under the title "Jazz as Chopsticks" feature the unity and cooperation of two individuals:

> If Twin's the arrow,
> Chops plays bow.   No JAZZ fallin'
> if they both don't go.
>
> Chops makes drum sounds SPIN.
> Twin coaxes them, herds them in,
> JAZZ their next of kin.
> ....
> When stuck on his lick,
> Chops runs the scale.   Twin slides loose,
> then   harpoons the whale.
>
> "Chops, whatcha doin'?"
> "Waitin' for Twin.   It's my bass
> his melody's in." (82)

The four haiku quoted above describe jazz performance in terms of a pair of chopsticks. In his notes Emanuel remarks: "Chops and Twin are names given to the chopsticks (Chops the slower, sturdier one, Twin the roaming, more imaginative one)" (82). The pair play the roles of bow and arrow: if they do not work together, they fall and fail to capture what they desire. The pair are in unison with the music, Chops making "drum sounds SPIN" and Twin coaxing them, herding them in. Jazz would not be inspirational if only one individual played the music: Chops's role is as important as Twin's. Jazz captures life as though the pair "harpoons the whale": while "Chops runs the scale," "Twin slides loose." And jazz music intensifies with a coordination of bass and melody, a pair of chopsticks.

Emanuel's admonition for African Americans to be individualistic in their lives is remindful of Zen doctrine. The concept of subjectivity in Zen, however, goes a step further, for it calls for a severe critique of self. The doctrine of *satori* calls for the follower to annihilate self to reach the higher state of *mu* so as to liberate self from the habitual way of life. In Zen, one must destroy not only self-centeredness and intellectualism but also God, Buddha, Christ, any prophet, or any idol because it is only the self, no one else, that can deliver the individual to the state of *mu*. Emanuel urges the liberation of self and the destruction of injustice in such jazz haiku as "Jackhammer," "Ammunition," and "Impressionist":

Jackhammer
Jackhammer Jazz POUNDS—
just breathes—on your door.   Message:
don't lock it no more.

Ammunition
Weapons ready-y-y.   JAZZ!
People fall, rise   hypnotized,
maybe   civilized.

Impressionist
Impressionist pipe
puffs JAZZ   where   pigments solo,
brightsoapbubbling air.
(70)

Each poem focuses on the sound of jazz that inspires the liberation of self from the ways one has been conditioned to lead. Jazz pounds away the door of racism. Jazz is an ammunition to destroy barbarism: people will "fall, rise hypnotized, / maybe civilized." Through its impressionist pipe, jazz creates "brightsoapbubbling air," a colorful, exciting new world.

The liberation of self which jazz inspires is akin to the concept of liberation in Zen. Zen teaches its followers to liberate themselves from human laws, rules, and authorities. For jazz, as for Zen, liberation results from one's desire to adhere to the law and spirit of nature. The haiku "The Rabbit Capers" resembles a *senryu:*[9]

> White Bugsy Rabbit
> went scratch-scratch-scratch: jailed for theft
> from The Old Jazz Patch. (78)

The jazz caper is portrayed as a work of art that is created for its own sake: the jazzrabbit, in another haiku, "aims his gun, shoots / . . . just for fun" (78). For Emanuel, jazz inspires one, as does Zen, with a new way of life: jazz and Zen admonish one to purge one's mind and heart of any materialistic thoughts and feelings and appreciate the wonder of life here and now.

4.

In portraying the union of humanity and nature, the haiku poet must achieve its effect by expressing the feeling of unity and harmony. Based on Zen philosophy, such feelings are motivated by a desire to perceive the harmony of nature and human life, an intuition that nothing is alone, nothing is out of the ordinary. The famous haiku by Basho below expresses the unity and relatedness in human life:

> Autumn is deepening:
> What does the neighbor do
> For a living?[10]

While traveling, Basho rested in a lodge where he saw another traveler, a stranger, staying overnight. As he was reminded of an autumnal self, he was also concerned about the other person. Because he did not come from a well-to-do family, his life as an artist was that of a wandering bard who was enormously interested in the commonplace and in the common people.

Like this haiku, many of Emanuel's haiku also express genuine feelings about his fellow human beings. Like Whitman's "Song of Myself," the dominant voice recorded in Emanuel's jazz haiku, "John Coltrane," for example, is that of the common people:

> "Love Supreme," JA-A-Z train,
> tops. Prompt lightning-express,   but
> made ALL   local   stops. (24)

The three jazz haiku under the title "The Middle Passage" depict the pain and suffering of fellow human beings as poignantly as does the prose of Toni Morrison's *Beloved* and Charles Johnson's *The Middle Passage:*

> Tight-bellied ships, gorged
> to the core, JAZZ claiming berths
> where breath soured no more.

> Chains, whips, ship-to-shore.
> JAZZ   don't talk about   these things
> It   can't do without?

> Chainmates, black, vomit
> for breath, sang LIFE into JAZZ
> while leaping to death. (74)

In emphasizing "the toughness of poverty and racial injustice" in African American life, Emanuel at times uses narrative style and rhyme. Not only do these haiku on the Middle Passage capture the epitome of racial injustice, but Emanuel is also able to intensify his vision in a painful narrative as he is not in a single haiku. All the same, his narrative haiku are endowed with natural, universal sentiments, as they are not motivated by social or political protests. The feelings expressed in Emanuel's haiku transcend those of the individual or society; they are nature-centered sentiments, not even human-centered emotions. Limiting each of the haiku to a single impression, as he has attempted to do, he is able to avoid overly intellectualized or moralized reasoning.

One of the poetic sensibilities that characterize haiku is called *wabi*. Some poets are inspired by the sentiment that human beings desire beauty more than food, a sensibility animals do not possess. The expression of *wabi* in classic haiku is characterized by feelings of agedness, leanness, and coldness, as well as poverty. Richard Wright, too, as mentioned earlier, composed some of his haiku that reflect the sensibility of *wabi:*

Merciful autumn
Tones down the shabby curtains
        Of my rented room. (*Haiku* 44)

Wright, while describing his poverty and isolation, intimates the transcendence of materialism and the creation of beauty. Wright captures the beauties of nature represented by various images, such as the setting sun in "That abandoned house, / With its yard of fallen leaves, / In the setting sun" (*Haiku* 10); one more winter in "In this rented room / One more winter stands outside / My dirty window pane" (*Haiku* 103); one buzzing fly in "This tenement room / In which I sweat this August / Has one buzzing fly" (*Haiku* 106); the moonlight in "I am paying rent / For the lice in my cold room / And the moonlight too" (*Haiku* 115); and the autumn sun in "My decrepit barn / Sags full of self-consciousness / In this autumn sun" (*Haiku* 174). Such beauties of nature compensate for the poet's plight of existence and fulfill his goals as an artist.

As Emanuel's haiku on the blues show, the sensibility of *wabi* also underlies his poetics:

I

Woman's gone.   BLUES knocks
my door, says "Hello, honey.
Who-o-o you waitin' for?"

II

No use cryin' 'bout
what she did   after she found
where my heart was hid.

III

Been ridin' the rails.
Butt's dusty.   When I last ate?
My mem'ry's rusty. (98)

The images of a woman gone, a man crying, and a man riding on a freight train, all convey the sensibility of *wabi,* the feelings of loneliness, but the beauty of the blues compensates for such feelings. "Been ridin' the rails," as Emanuel writes in a footnote, refers to "riding freight trains, like a hobo, looking for work in distant towns" (98). He further depicts the toughness of poverty in a long narrative poem, "Sittin'—Log Blues." Despite his unemployment and homelessness, an African American man named Log raises his hopes with toughness and austerity: "I'm standin' kinda crooked, Lord," Log says, / "but standin' up is hard to beat" (103).

This perspective in viewing pain, poverty, and loneliness in light of their compensation creates paradox. Emily Dickinson's view of failure is paradoxical, for she shows that success is best appreciated by failure:

> Success is counted sweetest
> By those who ne'er succeed.
> To comprehend a nectar
> Requires sorest need.

> Not one of all the purple Host
> Who took the Flag to-day
> Can tell the definition,
> So clear of Victory

> As he defeated—dying—
> On whose forbidden ear
> The distant strains of triumph
> Burst agonized and clear!
> (Dickinson 1: 53)

Emanuel's narrative poem "The Knockout Blues" also expresses paradox. An African American finds his poverty compensated for by the strength of his character in winning the battle of life: "Willin' to work for a wage less than fair, / I couldn't find nothin' but a knockout stare" (104). Despite the racial prejudice rampant in American society, the hero of the poem is proud to say:

> If my arms and legs is wobbly,
> if my neck is leanin' in,
> I been fightin' what I couldn't see
> in places wasn't worth bein' in. (105)

"The Downhill Blue" also resounds with paradox. The poet-narrator is least afraid of going downhill because "They say I'm tough with steerin' wheels / and mighty sharp with brakes" (106). "But whatever's below's," he observes, is too deep for a spineless man to fathom. Endowed with character and discipline that have guided his life, he is now prepared to meet the challenge. With a bit of humor, he imagines that as he digs deeper, he will end up on the other side of the earth: "when I break through I'll be a Chinese man. / If the earth be's round the way they say, / when I come up it'll be a OPPOSITE day. / Downhill's a long, long way to go, / but I can dig it if I dig it slow. / I'll turn up talkin' in a Chinese way: / servin' up the blues on a thank-you tray" (107).[11] "The Downhill Blues" also suggests that Emanuel's poetic experiment is an attempt to gauge African American life from a non-western, cross-cultural point of view.

Such ideas of compensation and paradox enable Emanuel to focus on the creation of beauty in his jazz haiku. A haiku on Billie Holiday celebrates a state of mind similar to *wabi:*

> Hurt, always hurt.   Wounds
> bled, wounds,   scarred stand-up power:
> this worn, sad flower. (46)

Despite, and because of, the wounds, "this worn, sad flower" is strengthened by its "stand-up power." This haiku not only expresses a poetic enlightenment but also delineates the beauty of a flower, a symbol of nature. The focus in the rest of the haiku on Billie Holiday is on the beauty of nature:

> Wrong arms to sleep on,
> bruises to wear, long white gloves,
> one rose in her hair.

> Domino lovers,
> Strange Fruit men, Ill-Wind hustlers,
> then the frost set in. (46)

While such images as "one rose" and "the frost set in" brighten up the feelings of pain and hardship, they also remain beautiful by themselves. In the haiku "Sonny Rollins (Under the Williamsburg Bridge)," Emanuel depicts a lone-wolf in flight as a thing of beauty:

> Worldwaif: lone-wolf notes,
> blown in pain with all his might,
> heal themselves in flight. (54)

For an African American artist, not only does nature heal the artist's wounds; it also creates a powerful image of beauty.

Jazz, as Emanuel remarks in his preface, "has crossed oceans and continents to spread its gospel of survival through job and artistic imagination" (v). Throughout *Jazz from the Haiku King* he is intent upon composing haiku on the basis of its well-established philosophical and aesthetic principles. Philosophically, his finely wrought haiku enlighten the reader just as inspiring jazz does the listener. Aesthetically as well, Emanuel's haiku, sharing the devices of both haiku and jazz by which to seize the moments of revelation, express natural, spontaneous sentiments. His haiku, with sharp, compressed images, strongly reflect the syncopated sounds and rhythms of African American jazz.

Notes

The Chicago Renaissance, Theodore Dreiser, and
Richard Wright's Spatial Narrative

1. Among African American works, perhaps the most successful effort to fictionalize that memory was made by Toni Morrison in *Beloved* (1987).

2. Dreiser, a son of a poor immigrant, spoke only German in his early childhood. Farrell, who grew up in the Irish-American neighborhoods of Chicago, drew on his early experience in *Studs Lonigan;* both Farrell and Wright were influenced by Dreiser as they influenced each other. Algren, who was also closely associated with Wright, wrote *Never Come Morning,* which Wright said, "deals with Polish life": praising Algren's work, Wright called it "as hard hitting a realistic piece of writing as you will ever read." Bellow, born of Russian immigrant parents in Canada, was raised in Chicago in a multicultural (English, French, and Jewish) household. See Wright, *Conversations with Richard Wright,* ed. Keneth Kinnamon and Michel Fabre, 46. Subsequent references will parenthetically appear in the text as *Conversations.*

3. Wright, "Blueprint for Negro Writing," rpt. in *Richard Wright Reader,* ed. Ellen Wright and Michel Fabre, 45. The essay was originally published in *New Challenge* 2 (Fall 1935): 53–65. Further references to the essay are to *Richard Wright Reader* and are given in the text as "Blueprint."

4. In ranking modern novelists writing in English—compared with the three Britons, Meredith, Hardy, and the early H. G. Wells—Allen Tate wrote in 1948: "I am convinced that among American novelists who have had large publics since the last war, only Dreiser, Faulkner, and Hemingway are of major importance" (86).

5. In response to a question of the influence of American novelists on French novelists, Wright said, "Sartre and Camus show that. French writers realized that action was lacking in their novels, at least in the raw, rapid, sure form that characterizes the good American writers (Hemingway, Caldwell, Lewis, and others). We should make clear that this only concerns the focus of some chapters in which the fiction is presented in vivid terms, without apparent style, to lay out a very intense impression. Now, in philosophical and conceptual matters, the influence is null" (*Conversations* 137).

6. Because Sister Carrie is not a portrait of a suffering woman, Wright must have meant *Jennie Gerhardt,* a story of an enduring woman who fights against the prejudices of class and gender.

7. In a *New York Post* interview in 1938, Wright stated: "I wanted to show exactly

what Negro life in the South means today. . . . I think the importance of any writing lies
in how much felt life is in it." The interviewer stated: "From reading Mencken in
Memphis, Richard Wright branched out in Chicago to Henry James and Dostoievsky, to
Hemingway, Malraux, Faulkner, Sherwood Anderson and Dreiser, writers of 'the more or
less naturalistic school,' although he lays no claims to being, or even wanting to be, a 'naturalistic' writer" (*Conversations* 4).

8. Stephen Crane, *Great Short Works of Stephen Crane,* 183. Textual references to
Jennie Gerhardt are to *Jennie Gerhardt,* 1911, ed. James L. W. West III (Philadelphia:
University of Pennsylvania Press, 1992), and are subsequently given in parentheses.

9. Page references to Wright's "Big Boy Leaves Home" are to *Uncle Tom's Children*
(1965).

10. Blyden Jackson, "Richard Wright in a Moment of Truth," 172. Jackson's essay
originally appeared in *Southern Literary Journal* 3 (Spring 1971): 3–17.

11. See Michael Atkinson, "Richard Wright's 'Big Boy Leaves Home' and a Tale from
Ovid: A Metamorphosis Transformed."

12. Page references to "Nigger Jeff" are to *Free and Other Stories* and are parenthetically given in the text as *Free.*

13. See James Baldwin, "Many Thousands Gone," in *Notes of a Native Son,* 33. The
essay first appeared in *Partisan Review* 18 (November–December 1951): 665–80.

14. Although Brooks recognized in Twain a genius and a "tortured conscience," he
thought that Twain's dedication to humor, "[the] spirit of the artist in him," diluted his philosophy of humankind. See Van Wyck Brooks, "From *The Ordeal of Mark Twain,*" 295–300.

15. In a letter of July 10, 1945, to Yvette Eastman, one of Dreiser's young mistresses
who had a literary ambition, Dreiser wrote:

> Yvette Dear:
>   Such a poetic, Lovely letter from you this morning July 10*th.* You are off
> on a hill somewhere—up near Brewster, and you fairly sing of the heavens
> and the earth which considering all you have to do and your unchanging
> sense of duty always impresses me. I marvel that you dont [*sic*] at least ver-
> bally rebel against the conditions that have almost always made you earn
> your own way. So often I feel that it might be a relief to you if you were to
> write an honest forth right book like *Black Boy* and in it have your say con-
> cerning all the things you have had to endure and so what you think of life.
> It would be colorful and more dramatic and I feel it would sell, yet not only
> the data but because of the beauty of your prose. Why not.

See Yvette Eastman, *Dearest Wilding: A Memoir with Love Letters from Theodore Dreiser,*
211.

NOTES TO CHAPTER 2:
The Cross-Cultural Vision of Ralph Ellison's *Invisible Man*

1. In his essay "Remembering Richard Wright," included in *Going to the Territory,*
Ellison expresses his indebtedness to the encouragement and advice Wright offered the
young Ellison. Ellison, however, is somewhat critical of *Native Son*: "I feel that *Native Son*

was one of the major literary events in the history of American literature. And I can say this even though at this point I have certain reservations concerning its view of reality" (*Going* 210–11). But, among Wright's works, Ellison was most impressed by *12 Million Black Voices,* which he viewed Wright's "most lyrical work." While Ellison thought that this compelling work of literature "could move [Wright's] white readers to tears," he also realized that Wright forged "such hard, mechanical images and actions that no white reading them could afford the luxury of tears" (*Going* 211).

2. Wright similarly refers to the Irish tradition in *12 Million Black Voices:* "We lose ourselves in violent forms of dances in our ballrooms. The faces of the white world, looking on in wonder and curiosity, declare: '*Only* the negro can play!' But they are wrong. They misread us. We are able to play in this fashion because we have been excluded, left behind; we play in this manner because all excluded folk play. The English say of the Irish, just as America says of us, that only the Irish can play, that they laugh through their tears. But every powerful nation says this of the folk whom it oppresses in justification of that oppression" (128)

3. For a study of Malraux's influence on Ellison, see Savery.

4. *Conversations with Richard Wright* also is witness to Ellison's alliance with modern European literatures and traditions. In an interview for *American Weekend,* published in Paris on 24 January 1959, Wright said: "Negro literature . . . is a good barometer of Negro reaction. As fields open up to Negroes, it will be reflected in Negro literature. There is a large group of Negro writers in Europe—Demby and Ellison in Rome, for instance. All of them are broadening their experiences in a European context" (*Conversations* 185).

5. Kun Jong Lee demonstrates that while Ellison appropriates Emerson's condescending attitude toward the black race, he redirects this negative aspect of Emersonian self-reliance. Ellison, Lee argues, "both accepts and rejects Emersonianism" (342).

6. Robert Butler reads as a trope the veteran in *Invisible Man,* whose words admonish the protagonist to "learn to look beneath the surface" (*Invisible Man* 153) and subvert the materialistic values of the Horatio Alger myth ("City as Psychological Frontier" 127).

7. For recent discussions of Zen philosophy and aesthetics, see Hakutani, "Emerson" and "Ezra Pound."

8. For a discussion of the relationship between Zen and Lacan, see Samuels.

9. Most modern works on Zen stress the importance of genderlessness in their discussions of Zen. See, for example, Kurebayashi, 142–49.

10. The Zen master's pronouncement "*never stop*" recalls Whitman's last passage in "Song of Myself": "Failing to fetch me at first keep encouraged, / Missing me one place search another" (68), or the last lines in "Passage to India": "O my brave soul! / O farther farther sail! / O daring joy, but safe! are they not all the seas of God? / O farther, farther, farther sail!" (294). Whitman's final statement in "Song of Myself"—"If you want me again look for me under your boot-soles" (68)—echoes the Zen master's: "It's just underneath your standpoint."

11. In the chapter "The Whiteness of the Whale" in *Moby-Dick,* Melville writes: "Is it that by its indefiniteness it shadows forth the heartless voids and immensities of the universe, and thus stabs us from behind with the thought of annihilation, when beholding the white depths of the milky way? Or is it, that as in essence whiteness is not so much a color as the visible absence of color, and at the same time the concrete of all colors; is it for these reasons that there is such a dumb blankness, full of meaning, in a wide landscape of snows—a colorless all-color of atheism from which we shrink?" (169).

NOTES TO CHAPTER 3:
No Name in the Street: James Baldwin's Exploration of
American Urban Culture

1. Baldwin writes: "If we—and now I mean the relatively conscious whites and the relatively conscious blacks, who must, like lovers, insist on, or create, the consciousness of the others—do not falter in our duty now, we may be able, handful that we are, to end the racial nightmare, and achieve our country, and change the history of the world" (*Fire* 141).

2. In his last volume of essays Baldwin makes a similar assertion about African Americans' somber realization of themselves: "This is why blacks can be heard to say, *I ain't got to be nothing but stay black, and die!:* which is, after all, a far more affirmative apprehension than *I'm free, white, and twenty-one*" (*Devil* 115).

3. Karin Moller, noting "Baldwin's mood of sombre, retrospective lucidity," writes: "The author's disillusionment with America persists throughout . . ." (131). Nick Aaron Ford writes: "It is a more hardboiled, pessimistic, disillusioned view of his country and its people" (O'Daniel, *Baldwin* 101).

4. In 1961 Baldwin wrote in his essay "In Search of a Majority": "Whether I like it or not, or whether you like it or not, we are bound together forever. We are part of each other. What is happening to every Negro in the country at any time is also happening to you. There is no way around this. I am suggesting that these walls—these artificial walls—which have been up so long to protect us from something we fear, must come down" (*Nobody* 114). In 1963 he wrote in "My Dungeon Shook": "Well, the black man has functioned in the white man's world as a fixed star, as an immovable pillar: and as he moves out of his place, heaven and earth are shaken to their foundations. . . . But these men are your brothers—your lost, younger brothers. And if the word *integration* means anything, this is what it means: that we, with love, shall force our brothers to see themselves as they are, to cease fleeing from reality and begin to change it" (*Fire* 20–21).

5. Baldwin argues that although Wright's authorial voice records the black anger as no black writer before him has ever done, it is also, unhappily, the overwhelming limitation of *Native Son.* What is sacrificed, according to Baldwin, is a necessary dimension to the novel: "the relationship that Negroes bear to one another, that depth of involvement and unspoken recognition of shared experience which creates a way of life" (*Notes* 27).

6. Benjamin DeMott regards Tony Maynard as an undeveloped character despite much space given for that purpose, but one might argue that *No Name in the Street* is not a collection of biographical portraits like Dreiser's *Twelve Men* and *A Gallery of Women,* but rather an autobiographical narrative centering on its protagonist Baldwin. See DeMott, 158. The same argument applies to Baldwin's characterization of the black postal worker described earlier. Cf. Gitlin, 469–70.

7. Moller observes that Baldwin's various episodes are fragmentary and that his style in *No Name in the Street* is pretentiously casual (129).

NOTES TO CHAPTER 4:
If Beale Street Could Talk: Baldwin's Search for Love and Identity

1. I agree with Kichung Kim, who advances the theory that the difference between

Wright and Baldwin arises from the two different concepts of human beings. Kim argues that the weakness Baldwin sees in Wright and other protest writers "is not so much that they had failed to give a faithful account of the actual conditions of man but rather that they had failed to be steadfast in their devotion . . . to what man might and ought to be. Such a man . . . will not only survive oppression but will be strengthened by it." See Kim, "Wright, the Protest Novel, and Baldwin's Faith."

2. See Saul Bellow, *Seize the Day*, 25. Tish in *If Beale Street Could Talk* often wonders if their expecting baby has inherited Fonny's narrow, slanted eyes like those of Chinese people.

3. Saunders Redding observed that Wright, who paid homage to Africa, failed to find home in Africa. See Redding, "Reflections on Richard Wright," 204. Like Wright, John A. Williams, who hailed from Mississippi, has said, "I have been to Africa and know that it is not my home. America is." See Williams, *This Is My Country Too*, 169.

4. I agree with Benjamin DeMott, who regards Tony Maynard as an undeveloped and unimpressive character, but the weakness of Baldwin's characterization results from his use of a sterile man in the context of creation and rebirth (DeMott 158).

5. See Baldwin's interview by Kalamu ya Salaam, "James Baldwin: Looking towards the Eighties" (Salaam 40).

6. Sandra A. O'Neile observes in her essay, "Fathers, Gods, and Religion: Perceptions of Christianity and Ethnic Faith in James Baldwin," that "more than the heritage of any other Black American writer, Baldwin's works illustrate the schizophrenia of the Black American experience with Christianity." Black people, she argues, needed a distinction "between Christianity as they knew it to be and Christianity as it was practiced in the white world" (O'Neile 125–43).

NOTES TO CHAPTER 5:
Jazz and Toni Morrison's Urban Imagination of Desire and Subjectivity

1. Morrison's village within the city is similar to Richard Wright's black church in the city. While Wright dismissed Christianity as useless for African Americans' freedom and subjectivity, he valued the black church in the city because it enhanced their community life. In *12 Million Black Voices*, he observes: "Despite our new worldliness, despite our rhythms, our colorful speech, and our songs, we keep our churches alive. . . . Our churches are centers of social and community life, for we have virtually no other mode of communication and we are usually forbidden to worship God in the temples of the Bosses of the Buildings. The church is the door through which we first walked into Western civilization" (130–31).

2. Morrison defines Harlem as "a Black city" which "held this village quality for Black people—although on a grand scale and necessarily parochial . . . but the relationships were clannish because there was joy and protection in the clan" ("City Limits" 38).

3. What impressed Wright when he arrived in Chicago from the Deep South was the relative absence of discrimination. "It was strange," he wrote in *American Hunger*, "to pause before a crowded newsstand and buy a newspaper without having to wait until a white man was served" (1–2). Although he was allowed to sit beside white men and women on a streetcar, as are Jake Jackson and his companions in *Lawd Today*, he began to

feel "a different sort of tension than I had known before. I knew that this machine-city was governed by strange laws" (2). *American Hunger* also describes an episode which suggests that some white citizens were not so much obsessed with the problems of race as were Southerners and that a black man was often treated by white citizens as an equal.

4. Similarly, Dreiser in *Jennie Gerhardt,* as pointed out earlier, describes the city as a site of freedom in thought and action. Although Lester is characterized as an animalistic man, he is also seen as an erudite man who is keenly aware of his religious, cultural, and social environment.

5. Wright's "primal outlook upon life" derives from Edmund Husserl's *Ideas,* from which Wright quotes a passage. Husserl is suggesting the preeminence of the physical world over the scientific vision of that world and a reliance on intuition rather than on history in the search for truth. Morrison's concept of life, which is also based on awe of nature as is Husserl's and Wright's, is closely allied with her concept of society, which, much like Wright's African primal outlook, emphasizes kinship and love in the family.

6. Joe Trace's concern over the plight of African American children to be born in racist society recalls Sethe's willingness to kill their children in *Beloved* so as to spare them the pain and suffering of slavery, and of Roxy's desire to switch her own infant with a white one in the cradle in Mark Twain's *Pudd'nhead Wilson.*

7. While James is known for generating desire impressionistically, Dreiser depicts desire as if he were a romantic transcendentalist. In portraying Hurstwood's desire, Dreiser draws on the mood of spring: "Meanwhile, he accepted his present situation with Carrie, getting what joy out of it he could. Out came the sun by noon, and poured a golden flood through their open windows. Sparrows were twittering. There were laughter and song in the air. Hurstwood could not keep his eyes from Carrie. She seemed the one ray of sunshine in all his trouble. Oh, if she would only love him wholly—only throw her arms around him . . ." (*Sister Carrie* 316).

8. In his "Vorticism" essay Pound considered an image not as a decorative emblem or symbol but as a seed capable of germinating and developing into another organism.

9. In an interesting analysis of Morrison's use of figurative language in *Jazz,* Jocelyn Chadwick-Joshua notes: "Alice unsuccessfully attempts to navigate her niece away from people represented by Violet and Joe Trace, the synecdochal representations of '[the] embarrassing kind' (*Jazz* 79). More specifically, to Alice, Joe and Violet become a metonymy for impending danger and their actions synecdochal proof" (Chadwick-Joshua 175).

10. Chadwick-Joshua remarks that Morrison introduces Felice synecdochically and "elects to allow the city to reveal her piece-meal—a slowly-evolving synecdoche. Interestingly, the girl is referred to by name as friend and companion to Alice's niece, Dorcas, even on the night Joe shoots Dorcas. But the real connection and the substantive characterization of Felice, or the girl with the Okeh record, evidences itself only the final third of the novel" (179).

11. Elizabeth M. Cannon observes that the significance of soloists in jazz is indicative of individualism. "Jazz," Cannon notes, "is also the perfect vehicle for suggesting that the object of desire is subjectivity: Jazz wouldn't be jazz without the improvisation of soloists" (237).

12. In an interpretation of Morrison's paradoxical expression, Chadwick-Joshua notes that *Jazz's* voice "possesses a womanist voice that is itself a womanist voice of paradox—a

voice that entices and seduces to one's regret yet a voice that nurtures and omnisciently *knows* what an individual will need and set about appropriate preparations" (179).

13. In search of his mother, Joe Trace confronts what he had imagined to be the woman named "Wild," a signifier of nature, and utters: "Give me a sign, then. You don't have to say nothing. Let me see your hand. Just stick it out someplace and I'll go; I promise. A sign. . . . You my mother?" The narrator observes by saying, "Yes. No. Both. Either. But not this nothing" (178). "The small children," the narrator observes, "believed she was a witch, but they were wrong. This creature hadn't the intelligence to be a witch. She was powerless, invisible, wastefully draft. Everywhere and nowhere" (179). Morrison's use of the word *nothing* as a trope for one's inability to see truth is similar to Melville's metaphysics in "The Whiteness of the Whale" in *Moby-Dick:* Melville questions whether whiteness, the absence of color, signifies "the heartless voids" of the universe and a state of nothingness (169). If the ubiquity of nothingness is a representation of the absence of God, this concept has some affinity with the Zen enlightenment, the state of nothingness, which enables a Zen follower to attain self-reliance by annihilating Buddha.

NOTES TO CHAPTER 6:
Wright's *The Outsider* and French Existentialism

1. See Charles I. Glicksberg, "Existentialism in *The Outsider*" and "The God of Fiction." Michel Fabre specifically indicates that Wright's composition of *The Outsider* was influenced by Camus's *The Stranger.* See Fabre, "Richard Wright, French Existentialism, and *The Outsider*," 191.

2. See James N. Rhea, *Providence Sunday Journal,* 22 March 1953.

3. See Saunders Redding, *Baltimore Afro-American,* 19 May 1953; Lloyd Brown, "Outside and Low."

4. See Glicksberg, "Existentialism in *The Outsider*"; "The God of Fiction."

5. See Albert Camus, *Lyrical and Critical Essays* 335–37.

6. See, for instance, Robert de Luppe, *Albert Camus* 46–47.

7. The most precise analysis of Camus's concept of time is presented in Ignace Feuerlicht, "Camus's *L'Étranger* Reconsidered."

8. See Redding's review in *Baltimore Afro-American,* in Reilly, *Reception* 225–27; and Melvin Altschuler, "An Important, but Exasperating Book," in *Washington Post,* in Reilly, *Reception* 203–4.

NOTES TO CHAPTER 7:
Pagan Spain: Wright's Discourse on Religion and Culture

1. Paul Gilroy, in *The Black Atlantic,* has defended Wright's later works, such as *Black Power, Pagan Spain,* and *The Color Curtain,* against "those tendencies in African-American literary criticism which argue that the work he produced while living in Europe was worthless when compared to his supposedly authentic earlier writings" (x).

2. See Mary Ellen Stephenson, 307.

3. See Wright, "Interview with Richard Wright," *L'Express,* in *Conversations with Richard Wright,* 203.

4. See "No Castles in Spain," *Charlotte News,* rpt. Reilly, *Critical Reception,* 290.

5. See Redding, *Baltimore Afro-American,* rpt. Reilly, *Critical Reception,* 299.

6. The supreme, pantheistic divinity in Shintoism, the Japanese state religion, is the goddess *Ama-Terasu Ohmi Kami,* literally translated as "Heaven-Shining Great God."

7. See Francis E. McMahon, S. J., "Spain Through Secularist Spectacles," *America,* rpt. Reilly, *Critical Reception,* 300.

8. Instead of emphasizing sexuality as the cause of repression, Carl Jung theorized that the primal, universal, collective unconsciousness has a sexual as well as nonsexual component. According to Jungian psychology, personality consists of the *persona,* which is consciously presented to the world, and the *anima,* which is unconsciously repressed. When Wright explored the Black Virgin at Montserrat, he seemed to be more impressed by the collective, racial unconsciousness akin to Jungianism than by the sexual repression in Freudianism. To his Spanish companion Wright said, "Pardo, don't you see that conglomeration of erect stone penises? Open your eyes, man. You can't miss. I'm not preaching the doctrines of Freud. Let the facts you see speak to you—" (*Pagan Spain* 66).

9. The paradox of bullfighting is also apparent in the expression of "*Ole!*" when the matador incites the bull. The expression means "For God's sake," the pagan religious phrases of the Moors, but the audience, as Wright points out, were not aware of the pagan origin of the expression. It is seemingly contradictory that the matador and the audience were invoking the name of God in keeping with Christian as well as pagan tradition. Wright makes a reference in the footnote to Américo Castro's *The Structure of Spanish History* (*Pagan Spain* 90).

10. Big Boy, hiding in a kiln, watches Bobo being lynched and burned:

> "LES GIT SOURVINEERS!"
> . . .
> "Everybody git back!"
> "Look! Hes gotta finger!"
> . . .
> "He's got one of his ears, see?"
> . . .
> "HURRY UP N BURN THE NIGGER FO IT RAINS!"
> . . . .

> Bobo was struggling, twisting; they were binding his arms and legs. . . . The flames leaped tall as the trees. The scream came again. Big Boy trembled and looked. The mob was running down the slopes, leaving the fire clear. Then he saw a writhing white mass cradled in yellow flame, and heard screams, one on top of the other, each shriller and shorter than the last. The mob was quiet now, standing still, looking up the slopes at the writhing white mass gradually growing black, growing black in a cradle of yellow flame. (*Uncle Tom's Children* 49)

11. Wright describes the scene where a black physician examined Chris's body: "He rolled the corpse upon its back and carefully parted the thighs. 'The *genitalia* are gone,' the doctor intoned. Fishbelly saw a dark, coagulated blot in a gaping hole between the

thighs and, with defensive reflex, he lowered his hands nervously to his groin. 'I'd say that the genitals were pulled out by a pair of pliers or some like instrument,' the doctor inferred. 'Killing him wasn't enough. They had to *mutilate* 'im. You'd think that disgust would've made them leave *that* part of the boy alone. . . . No! To get a chance to *mutilate* 'im was part of why they killed 'im. And you can bet a lot of white women were watching eagerly when they did it. Perhaps they knew that that was the only opportunity they'd ever get to see a Negro's genitals—'" (*Long Dream* 78).

Notes to Chapter 8:
The African "Primal Outlook upon Life": Wright and Morrison

1. Discussing Wright's impressions of a colonial city like Accra, which looked sordid and decaying, Jack B. Moore remarks: "True, the Old Slave Market in Christianborg is crumbling, its walls rotting and columns broken into rubble . . . but that is made to seem not a symbol of the old life's death, but of the constant decay of matter in the city where Ghana's new life will soon be constructed and centered" (71).

2. Commenting on African American novelists' use of a journey motif, Trudier Harris observes: "Paule Marshall has consciously tried to reconnect African-American and African traditions by exploring those in the Caribbean; her *Praisesong for the Window* (1983) also incorporates a journey motif with a quest for ancestors through legends told about them and ceremonies performed for them" (191).

3. Iyunolu Osagie, also intrigued by Beloved's appearance and disappearance, argues that "the stories about Beloved's identity, her appearance, and her leave-taking are actually left to the reader's imagination." Osagie further notes that the "multiple readings of *Beloved* echo the elusive nature of psychoanalysis and its tendency to recover itself constantly; this tendency makes psychoanalysis an uncanny representation of literature" (435).

4. Dogen's teaching is a refutation of the assumption that life and death are entirely separate entities as are seasons (Kurebayashi 121–29).

5. Interviewed by *L'Express* in 1955 shortly after the publication of *Black Power,* Wright responded to the question, "*Why do you write?*": "The accident of race and color has placed me on both sides: the Western World and its enemies. If my writing has any aim, it is to try to reveal that which is human on both sides, to affirm the essential unity of man on earth" (*Conversations* 163).

6. Baby Suggs's celebration of love and kinship bears a resemblance to the opening lines of Whitman's "Song of Myself":

> I celebrate myself, and sing myself,
> And what I assume you shall assume,
> For every atom belonging to me as good belongs to you.

> I loafe and invite my soul,
> I lean and loafe at my ease observing a spear of summer grass. (25)

Later in the story, Morrison, in describing Baby Suggs's self-creation, refers to "the roots of her tongue" (141), with which Baby Suggs tries to fill "the desolated center where the self that was no self made its home" (140). Whitman's lines quoted above are followed by these lines:

> My tongue, every atom of my blood, form'd from this soil, this air,
> Born here of parents born here from parents the same, and their parents the
>   same, (25)

7. Trudier Harris reads Sethe's infanticide in light of the love theme: "If, on the other hand, we understand, accept, and perhaps even approve of the dynamics that allowed a slave mother to kill rather than have her children remanded to slavery, would not the dominant theme be love?" (159–60).

8. While Wright was emotionally attracted to tribal life, he was critical of its mysterious elements. Although he was convinced of the inevitable industrialization capitalism would bring about in Africa, he was extremely apprehensive of the exploitation of human power, a new form of slavery, that industrialism would introduce into Africa. Whether his argument is concerned with people or politics, his emphasis is placed on self-creation, the generation of confidence in Africans themselves individually and as a culture.

9. Sethe's paradox is remindful of the action of Roxy, a slave mother in Mark Twain's *Pudd'nhead Wilson*. What Roxy does in switching the babies is deemed morally just because her action comes from her heart, from a mother's genuine love for her child.

10. Osagie's observation seems to reflect Wright's: "Freudian psychoanalysis," Osagie argues, "has its foundation in the oedipus complex. African psychoanalysis has its roots in the social and cultural setting of its peoples—in their beliefs in concepts such as nature, the supernatural realm, reincarnation, and retribution" (424).

11. Wright also maintains that the Freudian approach does not apply to paganism, which characterizes Spanish culture. In discussing the symbolism of the Black Virgin, he tells his Spanish companion: "I'm not preaching the doctrine of Freud. Let the facts you see speak to you" (*Pagan Spain* 66). Later in the book Wright observes that "to have attempted a psychological approach in a Freudian sense would have implied a much more intimate acquaintance with the daily family lives of the people than I had—an access to case histories and clinical material even. Otherwise my facts would have been forever wide of the theories. In the end I resolved to accept the brute facts and let the theories go" (195).

NOTES TO CHAPTER 9:
The Poetics of Nature: Wright's Haiku, Zen, and Lacan

1. According to Toru Kiuchi, this South African poet, identified as Sinclair Beiles in Michel Fabre's *Richard Wright: Books and Writers* (14), was "one of the Beat poets and . . . his and the Beat poets' interest in Zen led Wright to the knowledge of haiku." Kiuchi further notes: "Because the Beat Hotel was in the Latin Quarter and Wright lived very close to the hotel, Wright must have haunted the hotel bar. I assume that Wright took an interest in Zen, an Asian religious philosophy, which some of the Beat poets brought up as one of the important topics, and that Wright then must have known haiku through his conversations with Beiles" (Kiuchi 1).

2. In 1960 Wright selected, under the title *This Other World: Projections in the Haiku*

Manner, 817 of the 4,000 haiku he had written in the last eighteen months of his life. This collection was published as *Haiku: This Other World*, ed. Yoshinobu Hakutani and Robert L. Tener, in 1998, and was reprinted in 2000. In this edition each of the haiku is numbered consecutively 1 through 817. The haiku quoted in the chapter are from this edition and identified by number.

3. To Melville, if you unscrew your navel, your backside falls off. See the scene of the doubloon in *Moby-Dick* at the end of chapter 99 (363): Melville's navel symbolizes the limit of intersubjectivity. Beyond the navel, the backside of the navel, lies the absolute real—unknown and unconscious to the subject.

4. For a further discussion of Lacan as the master of psychoanalysis, see Samuels and Borch-Jacobsen.

5. Barthes found an empty center in signs of traditional Japanese culture, such as its food, its landscapes, and its quintessential poetic form, haiku (3–37).

6. The original and the translation are quoted from Blyth, *History of Haiku*, 2: 56.

7. A literal translation of the first two lines, "Rakka eda ni / Kaeru to mireba," reads, "A fallen flower appears to come back to its branch."

8. See Pound, "Vorticism." For the influence of haiku on Pound's imagism, see Hakutani, "Ezra Pound."

9. See the cover of *Haiku: This Other World.*

10. In *Richard Wright: Daemonic Genius*, a biographical and critical study, Margaret Walker remarks: "He absolutely worshipped the art of poetry. He felt a close affinity to all modern poets and their poetry and read poetry with a passion—Shakespeare, Hart Crane, T. S. Eliot, Yeats, Ezra Pound, Dylan Thomas, and Walt Whitman. . . . In the last years of his life, Wright discovered the Japanese form of poetry known as Haiku and became more than a little interested in what was not just a strange and foreign stanza but an exercise in conciseness—getting so much meaning or philosophy in so few words" (313–14).

11. *Hokku* is an older term for haiku. Basho and other haiku poets in the seventeenth and eighteenth centuries called haiku *hokku.*

12. Traditionally, the principle of instantaneity and spontaneity is as fundamental to the composition of haiku as the same principle is when applied to Zen-inspired painting and calligraphy. One must efface subjectivity: the longer it takes one to compose the work, the more likely it is for subjectivity to take over the composition.

13. The original of the haiku is in Henderson, 40. The translation is by Hakutani.

14. The original of the haiku is in Henderson, 18. The translation is quoted from Blyth, *History of Haiku* 2, xxix.

15. For a definition of *sabi* and other terms in Eastern and Japanese aesthetics, see Hakutani, *Richard Wright*, 275–82.

16. The original of the haiku is in Henderson, 58. The translation is by Hakutani.

17. The original of the haiku is in Henderson, 104. The translation is by Hakutani.

18. The original of the haiku is in Henderson, 102. The translation is by Hakutani.

Notes to Chapter 10:
Private Voice and Buddhist Enlightenment in Alice Walker's
The Color Purple

1. For comparative studies of American transcendentalism and Zen, see, for example,

Ando, *Zen and American Transcendentalism,* and Hakutani, "Emerson, Whitman, and Zen Buddhism."

2. For recent studies of the influences of Eastern poetics on Ezra Pound and William Carlos Williams, see, for example, Hakutani, "Ezra Pound," and Tomlinson.

3. Whitman in "Out of the Cradle Endlessly Rocking," endowing a young boy with a poetic inspiration, celebrates the birth of a poet:

> Demon or bird! (said the boy's soul,)
> Is it indeed toward your mate you sing? or is it really to me?
> For I, that was a child, my tongue's use sleeping, now I have heard you,
> Now in a moment I know what I am for, I awake,
> And already a thousand singers, a thousand songs, clearer, louder and more
>   sorrowful than yours,
> A thousand warbling echoes have started to life within me, never to die.
> (183)

4. Wright's lyricism is evident in the early section of *Black Boy* in which a young African American seeks a harmony between nature and society.

5. As discussed earlier, after his journey into Africa to write *Black Power,* Wright traveled to Spain to write *Pagan Spain.* Even compared with some parts of Africa, and most of Asia, Spain to him lagged behind in its progress toward modernism. "The African," Wright notes in *Pagan Spain,* "though thrashing about in a void, was free to create a future, but the pagan traditions of Spain had sustained no such mortal wound" (193). Such a critical view of Spain notwithstanding, Wright was nevertheless sympathetic toward the energetic maternal instinct of the Spanish woman without which Spanish culture would not have survived after World War II. Wright discovered, as noted earlier, a strong affinity between the indigenous matriarchalism in the Ashanti and the stalwart womanhood in Spain.

6. In his review of *The Color Purple,* Mel Watkins commented: "While Netti[e]'s letters broaden and reinforce the theme of female oppression by describing customs of the Olinka tribe that parallel some found in the American South, they are often mere monologues on African history. Appearing, as they do, after Celie's intensely subjective voice has been established, they seem lackluster and intrusive" (7).

7. Wright defines the African primal view of life in terms of the cultural differences between a person of African heritage and that of a European immigrant: "There is no reason why an African or a person of African descent—in America, England, or France—should abandon his primal outlook upon life if he finds that no other way of life is available, or if he is intimidated in his attempt to grasp the new way. . . . There is nothing mystical or biological about it. When one realizes that one is dealing with two distinct and separate worlds of psychological being, two conceptions of time even, the problem becomes clear; it is a clash between two systems of culture" (*Black Power* 266).

8. During the eighteenth century a satirical form of haiku called *senryu* was developed by Karai Senryu (1718–90) as a kind of "mock haiku" with humor, moralizing nuances, and a philosophical tone, expressing "the incongruity of things" more than their oneness, dealing more often with distortions and failures, not just with the harmonious beauty of nature.

9. Wright writes about the Ashanti's worldview: "The pre-Christian African was impressed with the littleness of himself and he walked the earth warily, lest he disturb the presence of invisible gods. When he wanted to disrupt the terrible majesty of the ocean in order to fish, he first made sacrifices to its crashing and rolling waves; he dared not cut down a tree without first propitiating its spirit so that it would not haunt him; he loved his fragile life and he was convinced that the tree loved its life also" (*Black Power* 261–62).

10. In his preface to *The Ambassadors,* James accounts for the function of a minor character like Maria Gostrey in his rendition of a major character, Lambert Strether: "The *'ficelle'* character of the subordinate party is as artfully dissimulated, throughout, as may be, and to that extent that, with the seams or joints of Maria Gostrey's ostensible connectedness taken particular care of, duly smoothed over, that is, and anxiously kept from showing as 'pieced on'; this figure doubtless achieves, after a fashion, something of the dignity of a prime idea" (13).

11. Shug plays the role of a functional character, Tucker maintains, so that Celie is able to "'write herself' . . . to counter the victim-figures like her mother, and the dominant male figures of Albert and her father" (85).

Notes to Chapter 11:
Cross-Cultural Poetics: Sonia Sanchez's
Like the Singing Coming Off the Drums

1. The original in Japanese reads "Yama-dori-no / o / wo / fumu / haru no / iri-hi / kana." The English translation is by Hakutani.

2. The original and the translation are quoted from Blyth, *History of Haiku* 2: 56. A literal translation of Moritake's first two lines would be, "A fallen flower appears to come back to its branch," as noted in chapter 9 on Wright's haiku.

3. For the influence of haiku on Pound's imagism, see Hakutani, "Ezra Pound."

4. The original is quoted from Henderson. The translation of this haiku is by Hakutani.

5. The translation of this haiku is by Hakutani.

6. See *Haiku: This Other World* by Richard Wright. The 817 haiku are numbered consecutively, as noted earlier: "In the Silent Forest" is number 316, and "A Thin Waterfall" 569.

7. The word *sabi* in Japanese, a noun, derives from the verb *sabiru,* to rust, implying that what is described is aged. Buddha's portrait hung in Zen temples, the old man with a thin body, is nearer to his soul just as the old tree with its skin and leaves fallen is nearer to the very origin and essence of nature. For a further discussion of Buddha's portrait, see Loehr, 216.

8. As discussed earlier, while Freud defines death as the opposite of life, meaning that death reduces all animate things to the inanimate, Lacan defines death as "human experience, human interchanges, intersubjectivity," suggesting that death is part of life (*Seminar II* 80). To Lacan, the death instinct is not "an admission of impotence, it isn't a coming to a halt before an irreducible, an ineffable last thing, it is a concept" (*Seminar II* 70).

9. In reference to the works of Zeami, the author of many of the extant *noh* plays, Arthur Waley, perhaps one of the best-known scholars of Eastern literature, expounds on this difficult term:

It is applied to the natural graces of a boy's movements, to the gentle restraint of a nobleman's speech and bearing. "When notes fall sweetly and flutter delicately to the ear," that is the *yugen* of music. The symbol of *yugen* is "a white bird with a flower in its beak." "To watch the sun sink behind a flower-clad hill, to wander on and on in a huge forest with no thought of return, to stand upon the shore and gaze after a boat that goes hid [*sic*] by far-off islands, to ponder on the journey of wild-geese seen and lost among the clouds"—such are the gates to *yugen*. (Waley 21–22)

10. This stanza, filled with rather superficial racial and cultural labels, is reminiscent of the least inspiring stanza in Whitman's "Song of Myself":

> Magnifying and applying come I,
> Outbidding at the start the old cautious hucksters,
> Taking myself the exact dimensions of Jehovah,
> Lithographing Kronos, Zeus his son, and Hercules his grandson,
> Buying drafts of Osiris, Isis, Belus, Brahma, Buddha,
> In my portfolio placing Manito loose, Allah on a leaf, the crucifix engraved,
> With Odin and the hedeous-faced Mexitli and every idol and image, (58)

NOTES TO CHAPTER 12:
James Emanuel's Jazz Haiku and African American Individualism

1. See "Author's Preface" in *Jazz from the Haiku King* (iv). Page references to Emanuel's poems discussed in this chapter are to this edition, hereafter cited parenthetically.

2. See Donald Keene's detailed historical account of *haikai* poetry, from which haiku evolved (337–55).

3. Ellison's essay originally appeared in *Antioch Review* 5 (June 1945): 198–211.

4. The first collection of *renga*—*Chikuba Kyogin Shu* (*Comic Song Collection*, 1499)—includes over two hundred *tsukeku* (adding verses) linked with the first verses of another poet. As the title of the collection suggests, the salient characteristic of *renga* was a display of ingenuity and coarse humor. This volume also collected twenty *hokku* (starting verses). Because *hokku*, an earlier term for haiku, was considered the most important verse of a *renga*, it was usually composed by the senior poet attending a *renga* session. On the origin and development of *renga* and haiku, see Keene, 11–55.

5. Craig Werner has provided an incisive account of the jazz impulse: "Jazz, observed Louis Armstrong, is music that's never played the same way once. The world changes, the music changes. Jazz imagines the transitions, distills the deepest meanings of the moment we're in, how it developed from the ones that came before, how it opens up into the multiple possibilities of the ones to come" (*Change* 132).

6. In "A Sight in Camp in the Daybreak Gray and Dim" (219), an elegy for dead soldiers, Whitman celebrates their death and alludes to their natural and divine heritage. Even though he finds them physically dead, he senses that their bodies, united with the earth, are spiritually alive.

7. Thomas Jefferson's *Notes on the State of Virginia* (1785) has a passage revealing his basic attitude toward nature and humanity: "Those who labour in the earth are the chosen people of God, if ever he had a chosen people, whose breasts he has made his peculiar deposit for substantial and genuine virtue" (164–65).

8. On the origin and development of this verse form, see Keene, 109–15.

9. *Senryu,* as noted earlier, is a humorous haiku with moralizing nuances and a philosophical tone that expresses the incongruity of things rather than their oneness. Because *senryu* tend to appeal more to one's sense of the logical than to intuition, this jazz haiku can be read as a *senryu.*

10. The original of "Autumn Is Deepening" is quoted from Imoto, *Basho: Sono Jinsei to Geijitsu* [*Basho: His Life and Art*] (231). The translation is by Hakutani.

11. Emanuel's humorous imagination, in which he is dreaming of digging the earth deeper to reach the other side of the world, is reminiscent of Mark Twain's. In *Adventures of Huckleberry Finn,* Tom Sawyer talks about his outrageous, farfetched imagination, in which Jim, imprisoned in the dungeon of the Castle Deep and given a couple of case-knives, would be able to dig himself out through the earth for thirty-seven years and come out in China. Despite Huck's rebuke of Tom for entertaining such an idea, Twain's conjuring up visions of Jim's freedom from slavery to a slaveless society is akin to Emanuel's wish for jazz to cross cultural borders in disseminating the African American suffering and joy. See *Adventures of Huckleberry Finn,* 191–92.

Works Cited

Abbandonato, Linda. "A View from 'Elsewhere': Subversive Sexuality and the Rewriting of the Heroine's Story in *The Color Purple*." *PMLA* 106 (October 1991): 1106–15.

Adams, Donald J. "Speaking of Books." *New York Times Book Review* 16 February and 6 April 1958.

Aldridge, John. "The Fire Next Time?" *Saturday Review* (15 June 1974): 24–25.

Altschuler, Melvin. "An Important, but Exasperating Book." *Washington Post* 22 March 1953.

Ando, Shoei. *Zen and American Transcendentalism*. Tokyo: Hokusei Press, 1970.

Atkinson, Michael. "Richard Wright's 'Big Boy Leaves Home' and a Tale from Ovid: A Metamorphosis Transformed." *Studies in Short Fiction* 24 (Summer 1987): 251–61.

Bakhtin, Mikhail M. *The Dialogic Imagination*. Ed. Michael Holquist. Trans. Caryl Emerson and Michael Holquist. Austin: University of Texas Press, 1981.

Baldwin, James. *Blues for Mister Charlie*. London: Michael Joseph, 1965.

———. *The Devil Finds Work*. New York: Dial, 1976.

———. "Everybody's Protest Novel." *Partisan Review* 16 (1949): 578–85.

———. *The Fire Next Time*. New York: Dell, 1963.

———. *If Beale Street Could Talk*. New York: Dial, 1974.

———. "Many Thousands Gone." *Partisan Review* 18 (November–December 1951): 665–80.

———. *No Name in the Street*. New York: Dell, 1972.

———. *Nobody Knows My Name*. New York: Dell, 1961.

———. *Notes of a Native Son*. 1955. New York: Bantam, 1964.

Baraka, Amiri. *Blues People*. New York: William Morrow, 1963.

Barthes, Roland. *Empire of Signs*. Trans. Richard Howard. New York: Hill and Wang, 1982.

Bellow, Saul. *Seize the Day*. New York: Viking, 1956.

Blyth, R. H. *Haiku: Eastern Culture*. 1949. Tokyo: Hokuseido, 1981.

———. *A History of Haiku*. 2 vols. Tokyo: Hokuseido, 1963, 1964.

Bontemps, Arna. "Review of Richard Wright, *The Outsider*." *Saturday Review* 36 (28 March 1953): 15–16.

Borch-Jacobsen, Mikkel. *Lacan: The Absoloute Master*. Trans. Douglas Brick. Stanford: Stanford University Press, 1991.

Brooks, Gwendolyn. *Selected Poems*. New York: Harper and Row, 1963.

Brooks, Van Wyck. "From *The Ordeal of Mark Twain*." *Adventures of Huckleberry Finn*. Ed. Schully Bradley et al. New York: Norton, 1977. 295–300.

Brown, Lloyd. "Outside and Low." *Masses and Mainstream* 6 (May 1953): 62–64.

Brown, Sterling A. "Review of *Native Son.*" *Opportunity* 18 (1940): 185–86. Rpt. Reilly, *Reception,* 95–98.

Butler, Robert. "The City as Psychological Frontier in Ralph Ellison's *Invisible Man* and Charles Johnson's *Faith and the Good Thing.*" *The City in African-American Literature.* Ed. Yoshinobu Hakutani and Robert Butler. Madison, NJ: Farleigh Dickinson University Press, 1995. 123–37.

———. *Native Son: The Emergence of a New Black Hero.* Boston: Twayne, 1991.

Camus, Albert. *Lyrical and Critical Essays.* Ed. Philip Thody. Trans. Ellen C. Kennedy. New York: Knopf, 1968.

———. *The Stranger.* 1942. Trans. Stuart Gilbert. New York: Vintage, 1946.

Cannon, Elizabeth M. "Following the Traces of Female Desire in Toni Morrison's *Jazz.*" *African American Review* 31 (Summer 1997): 235–47.

Carpenter, Frederic I. *Emerson and Asia.* Cambridge: Harvard University Press, 1930.

Castro, Américo. *The Structure of Spanish History.* Princeton: Princeton University Press, 1954.

Chadwick-Joshua, Jocelyn. "Metonymy and Synecdoche: The Rhetoric of the City in Toni Morrison's *Jazz.*" *The City in African-American Literature.* Ed. Yoshinobu Hakutani and Robert Butler. Madison, NJ: Fairleigh Dickinson University Press, 1995. 168–80.

Chase, Richard. *The American Novel and Its Tradition.* New York: Doubleday, 1957.

Crane, Stephen. *Great Short Works of Stephen Crane.* Ed. James B. Colvert. New York: Harper and Row, 1965.

Danquah, J. B. *The Akan Doctrine of God: A Fragment of Gold Coast Ethics and Religion.* London: Frank Cass, 1944.

de Luppe, Robert. *Albert Camus.* Paris: Temps Present, 1951.

DeMott, Benjamin. "James Baldwin on the Sixties: Acts and Revelations." *James Baldwin: A Collection of Critical Essays.* Ed. Keneth Kinammon. Englewood Cliffs, NJ: Prentice-Hall, 1974. 155–62.

Dickinson, Emily. *The Poems of Emily Dickinson.* 3 vols. 1951. Ed. Thomas H. Johnson. Cambridge: Harvard University Press, 1963.

Dreiser, Helen. *My Life with Dreiser.* Cleveland: World, 1951.

Dreiser, Theodore. *An American Tragedy.* 1925. New York: New American Library, 1964.

———. *A Book about Myself.* New York: Boni and Liveright, 1923.

———. *Jennie Gerhardt.* Ed. James L. W. West III. Philadelphia: University of Pennsylvania Press, 1992.

———. "Mark the Double Twain." *English Journal* 24 (October 1935): 615–27.

———. "Nigger Jeff." *Free and Other Stories.* New York: Boni and Liveright, 1918. 76–111.

———. *Selected Magazine Articles of Theodore Dreiser: Life and Art in the American 1890s.* 2 vols. Ed. Yoshinobu Hakutani. London and Toronto: Associated University Presses, 1985–87.

———. *Sister Carrie.* New York: Doubleday, 1900.

———. "Some Aspects of Our National Character." *Hey Rub-A-Dub Dub.* New York: Boni Liveright, 1920. 24–59.

Eastman, Yvette. *Dearest Wilding: A Memoir with Love Letters from Theodore Dreiser.* Ed. Thomas P. Riggio. Philadelphia: University of Pennsylvania Press, 1995

Eliot, T. S. *The Complete Poems and Plays 1909–1950*. New York: Harcourt, Brace, 1952.

Ellison, Ralph. *Going to the Territory*. New York: Random House, 1986.

———. *Invisible Man*. 1952. New York: Vintage, 1995.

———. "The Negro and the Second World War." *Negro Quarterly* (1943). Rpt. *Cultural Contexts for Ralph Ellison's Invisible Man*. Ed. Eric J. Sundquist. Boston: Bedford, 1995. 233–40.

———. "Richard Wright's Blues." *Critical Essays on Richard Wright*. Ed. Yoshinobu Hakutani. Boston: G. K. Hall, 1980. 201–12.

———. *Shadow and Act*. New York: Random, 1964.

Emanuel, James A. *Jazz from the Haiku King*. Detroit: Broadside Press, 1999.

Emerson, Ralph Waldo. *The Complete Essays and Other Writings of Ralph Waldo Emerson*. Ed. Brooks Atkinson. New York: Modern Library, 1940.

———. *Journals of Ralph Waldo Emerson, 1820–1872*. Vol. 6. Ed. E. W. Emerson and W. E. Forbes. Boston: Houghton Mifflin, 1911.

———. *The Poems of Ralph Waldo Emerson*. Ed. Louis Untermeyer. New York: Heritage Press, 1945.

———. *Selected Writings of Ralph Waldo Emerson*. Ed. William H. Gilman. New York: New American Library, 1965.

Fabre, Michel. *Richard Wright: Books and Writers*. Jackson: University Press of Mississippi, 1990.

———. "Richard Wright, French Existentialism, and *The Outsider*." *Critical Essays on Richard Wright*. Ed. Yoshinobu Hakutani. Boston: G. K. Hall, 1982. 182–98.

———. *The Unfinished Quest of Richard Wright*. New York: William Morrow, 1973.

Farrell, James T. "Lynch Patterns." *Partisan Review* 4 (May 1938): 57–58.

Feuerlicht, Ignace. "Camus's *L'Étranger* Reconsidered." *PMLA* 78 (December 1963): 606–21.

Fullington, James F., ed. *Prose and Poetry from the Old Testament*. New York: Appleton, 1950.

Gilroy, Paul. *The Black Atlantic: Modernity and Double Consciousness*. Cambridge: Harvard University Press, 1993.

Gitlin, Todd. "Yet Will I Maintain Mine Own Ways Before Him." *Nation* (10 April 1972): 469–70.

Glicksberg, Charles I. "Existentialism in *The Outsider*." *Four Quarters* 7 (January 1958): 17–26.

———. "The God of Fiction." *Colorado Quarterly* 7 (Autumn 1958): 207–20.

Hakutani, Yoshinobu. "Emerson, Whitman, and Zen Buddhism." *Midwest Quarterly* 31 (Summer 1990): 433–48.

———. "Ezra Pound, Yone Noguchi, and Imagism." *Modern Philology* 90 (August 1992): 46–69.

———. "Nature, Haiku, and 'This Other World.'" *Richard Wright and Racial Discourse*. Columbia: University of Missouri Press, 1996.

Harris, Trudier. *Fiction and Folklore: The Novels of Toni Morrison*. Knoxville: University of Tennessee Press, 1991.

Hemingway, Ernest. *The Sun Also Rises*. New York: Charles Scribner's Sons, 1926.

Henderson, Harold G. *An Introduction to Haiku: An Anthology of Poems and Poets from Basho to Shiki*. New York: Doubleday, 1958.

Hicks, Granville. "Outcasts in a Caldron of Hate." *Saturday Review* 45 (1962): 21.

Howe, Irving. "James Baldwin: At Ease in Apocalypse." *Harper's Magazine* 237 (1968): 92, 95–100.

Hughes, Langston. "Harlem." *Selected Poems of Langston Hughes.* New York: Vintage, 1990.

———. "My Early Days in Harlem." *Harlem USA.* Ed. John Henrik Clark. New York: Collier, 1964. 57–61.

Hurston, Zora Neale. "Stories of Conflict." *Saturday Review of Literature* 17 (2 April 1938): 32.

Jackson, Blyden. "Richard Wright in a Moment of Truth." *Modern American Fiction: Form and Function.* Ed. Thomas Daniel. Baton Rouge: Louisiana State University Press, 1989. 170–83.

James, Henry. "Preface to *The Ambassadors.*" *The Ambassadors.* Ed. S. P. Rosenbaum. New York: Norton, 1964. 1–15.

Jefferson, Thomas. *Notes on the State of Virginia.* Ed. William Peden. Chapel Hill: University of North Carolina Press, 1955.

Jones, Gayl. *Liberating Voices: Oral Tradition in African-American Literature.* Cambridge: Harvard University Press, 1991.

Jones, LeRoi. *Home: Social Essays.* New York: Apollo, 1966.

Joyce, Ann Joyce. *Richard Wright's Art of Tragedy.* Iowa City: University of Iowa Press, 1986.

Kearns, Edward. The 'Fate' Section of *Native Son.*" *Contemporary Literature* 12 (1971): 146–55.

Keene, Donald. *World within Walls: Japanese Literature of the Pre-Modern Era, 1600–1867.* New York: Grove, 1976.

Kim, Kichung. "Wright, the Protest Novel, and Baldwin's Faith." *CLA Journal* 17 (March 1974): 387–96.

Kinnamon, Keneth. *The Emergence of Richard Wright.* Urbana: University of Illinois Press, 1972.

Kinnamon, Keneth and Michel Fabre. "Jazz and Desire: Frank Tenot/1961." *Conversations with Richard Wright.* Ed. Keneth Kinnamon and Michel Fabre. Jackson: University Press of Mississippi, 1993. 242–43.

Kiuchi, Toru. "The Identity of the South African Poet." Letter to Yoshinobu Hakutani 7 August 2005.

Kurebayashi, Kodo. *Introduction to Dogen Zen.* Tokyo: Taiho Rinkaku, 1984.

Lacan, Jacques. *The Four Fundamental Concepts of Psychoanalysis.* Ed. Jacques-Alain Miller. Trans. Alan Sheridan. New York: Norton, 1981.

———. *The Seminar of Jacques Lacan, Book I: Freud's Papers on Technique 1953–1954.* Trans. John Forrester. New York: Norton, 1988.

———. *The Seminar of Jacques Lacan, Book II: The Ego in Freud's Theory and in the Technique of Psychoanalysis 1954–1955.* Ed. Jacques-Alain Miller. Trans. Sylvana Tomaselli. New York: Norton, 1988.

Learned, Barry. "U.S. Lets Negro Explain Race Ills, Wright Declares." *Conversations with Richard Wright.* Ed. Keneth Kinnamon and Michel Fabre. Jackson: University Press of Mississippi, 1993. 184–86.

Lee, Kun Jong. "Ellison's *Invisible Man:* Emersonianism Revised." *PMLA* 107 (March 1992): 331–44.

McKay, Nelie. "An Interview with Toni Morrison." *Contemporary Literature* 24 (Winter 1983): 413–29.

McMahon, Francis E., S. J. "Spain through Secularist Spectacles." *America* 96 (9 March 1957): 648, 653. Rpt. in Reilly, *Reception,* 300.

Margolies, Edward. *The Art of Richard Wright.* Carbondale: Southern Illinois University Press, 1969.

Matthiessen, F. O. *Dreiser.* New York: William Sloane, 1951.

Melville, Herman. *Moby-Dick.* Ed. Harrison Hayford and Hershel Parker. New York: Norton, 1967.

Moller, Karin. *The Theme of Identity in the Essays of James Baldwin.* Gotenborg, Sweden: Acta Universitatis Gothoburgensis, 1975.

Moore, Jack B. "No Street Numbers in Accra." *The City in African-American Literature.* Ed. Yoshinobu Hakutani and Robert Butler. Madison, NJ: Fairleigh Dickinson University Press, 1995. 64–78.

Morrison, Toni. *Beloved.* New York: Knopf, 1987.

———. "City Limits, Village Values: Concepts of the Neighborhood in Black Fiction." *Literature and the Urban Experience: Essays on the City and Literature.* Ed. Michael C. Jaye and Ann Chalmers Watts. New Brunswick: Rutgers University Press, 1981. 37–38.

———. *Conversations with Toni Morrison.* Ed. Danielle Taylor-Guthrie. Jackson: University Press of Mississippi, 1994.

———. *Jazz.* New York: Plume, 1993.

———. "Memory, Creation, and Writing." *Thought* 59 (1984): 385–90.

———. *Playing in the Dark: Whiteness and the Literary Imagination.* New York: Vintage, 1993.

———. "Rootedness: The Ancestor as Foundation." *Black Women Writers (1950–1980): A Critical Evaluation.* Ed. Mari Evans. Garden City: Doubleday, 1984. 339–45.

Myrdal, Gunnar. *An American Dilemma: The Negro Problems and American Democracy.* 2 vols. 1944. New York: McGraw Hill, 1962.

Noguchi, Yone. *Selected English Writings of Yone Noguchi: An East-West Literary Assimilation.* Ed. Yoshinobu Hakutani. 2 vols. London and Toronto: Associated University Presses, 1990, 1992.

———. *The Spirit of Japanese Poetry.* New York: Dutton, 1914.

———. *The Story of Yone Noguchi.* London: Chatto and Windus, 1914.

Oates, Joyce Carol. "A Quite Moving and Very Traditional Celebration of Love." *New York Times Book Review* (26 May 1974): 1–2.

O'Daniel, Thomas B., ed. *James Baldwin: A Critical Evaluation.* Washington, DC: Howard University Press, 1977.

O'Neile, Sandra A. "Fathers, Gods, and Religion: Perceptions of Christianity and Ethnic Faith in James Baldwin." *Critical Essays on James Baldwin.* Ed. Fred L. Standley and Nancy V. Burt. Boston: G. K. Hall, 1988. 125–43.

Orwell, George. *Selected Essays.* London: Harmondsworth, 1951.

Osagie, Iyunolu. "Is Morrison Also among the Prophets?: 'Psychoanalytic' Strategies in *Beloved.*" *African American Review* 28 (Fall 1994): 423–40.

Pockett, Leslie, ed. "Tomorrow's Classics: Forty Well-Known Creators, Critics, and Connoisseurs of High and Pop Art Speculate on Which Modern Works Will Endure." *Avant Garde* 6 (January 1969): 28–31.

Pound, Ezra. "As for Imagisme." *New Age* 14 (1915).

———. *Literary Essays of Ezra Pound.* Ed. and intro. T. S. Eliot. Nofolk, CT: New Directions, 1954.

———. *Personae.* New York: New Directions, 1926.

———. "Vorticism." *Fortnightly Review* n.s. no. 573 (1 September 1914): 461–71.

Prescott, Orville. Review of Richard Wright, *The Outsider. New York Times* 10 March 1953.

Purdy, Stropher B. "*An American Tradgedy* and *L'Étranger.*" *Comparative Literature* 19 (Summer 1967): 252–68.

Redding, Saunders. "Reflections on Richard Wright: A Symposium on an Exiled Native Son." *Anger and Beyond: The Negro Writer in the United States.* Ed. Herbert Hill. New York: Harper, 1966.

———. Review of *The Outsider. Baltimore Afro-American* (19 May 1953): 15–16.

Reilly, John M., ed. *Richard Wright: The Critical Reception.* New York: Franklin, 1978.

Rhea, James N. *Providence Sunday Journal.* 22 March 1953.

Salaam, Kalamu ya. "James Baldwin: Looking towards the Eighties." *Critical Essays on James Baldwin.* Ed. Fred L. Standley and Nancy V. Burt. Boston: G. K. Hall, 1988. 35–42.

Samuels, Robert. "Emerson, Lacan, and Zen: Transcendental and Postmodern Conceptions of the Eastern Subject." *Postmodernity in East-West Cross-Culturalism.* Ed. Yoshinobu Hakutani. London and Toronto: Associated University Presses, 2002. 157–67.

Sanchez, Sonia. *Like the Singing Coming Off the Drums.* Boston: Beacon Press, 1998.

Savery, Pancho. "'Not like an arrow, but a boomerang': Ellison's Existential Blues." *Approaches to Teaching Ellison's* Invisible Man. Ed. Susan Resneck Parr and Pancho Savery. New York: MLA, 1986. 65–74.

Standley, Fred L. and Nancy V. Burt, eds. *Critical Essays on James Baldwin.* Boston: G. K. Hall, 1988.

Stephenson, Mary Ellen. "Spain Gets Bitter Barks from Visitor." *Richard Wright: The Critical Reception.* Ed. John M. Reilly. New York: Burt Franklin, 1978. 307.

Stepto, Robert. *From behind the Veil: A Study of Afro-American Narrative.* Urbana: University of Illinois Press, 1979.

Tate, Allen. "Techniques of Fiction." *Visions and Revisions in Modern American Literary Criticism.* Ed. Bernard S. Oldsey and Arthur O. Lewis, Jr. New York: E. P. Dutton, 1962. 81–96.

Tener, Robert. "The Where, the When, the What: A Study of Richard Wright's Haiku." *Critical Essays on Richard Wright.* Ed. Yoshinobu Hakutani. Boston: G. K. Hall, 1982. 273–98.

Tomlinson, Charles. "Introduction to *Selected Poems* by William Carlos Williams." *William Carlos Williams and Charles Tomlinson: A Transatlantic Connection.* Ed. Barry Magid and Hugh Whitemeyer. New York: Peter Lang, 1999. 89–102.

Tucker, Lindsey. "Alice Walker's *The Color Purple:* Emergent Woman, Emergent Text." *Black American Literature Forum* 22 (Spring 1988): 81–95.

Twain, Mark. *Adventures of Huckleberry Finn.* Ed. Sculley Bradley et al. New York: Norton, 1977.

———. *Pudd'nhead Wilson* and *Those Extraordinary Twins.* Ed. Sidney E. Berger. New York: Norton, 1980.

Waley, Arthur. *The No Plays of Japan.* New York: Grove, 1920.

Walker, Alice. *The Color Purple.* 1982. New York: Pocket Books, 1985.

———. *In Search of Our Mothers' Gardens.* New York: Harcourt, 1983.

Walker, Margaret. *Richard Wright: Daemonic Genius.* New York: Warner Books, 1988.

Watkins, Mel. "Review." *The New York Times Book Review.* 25 July 1982.

Werner, Craig. *A Change Is Gonna Come: Music, Race & the Soul of America.* New York: Plume, 1999.

———. *Playing the Changes: From Afro-Modernism to the Jazz Impulse.* Urbana: University of Illinois Press, 1994.

Whitman, Walt. *Complete Poetry and Selected Prose.* Ed. James E. Miller, Jr. Boston: Houghton Mifflin, 1959.

Williams, John A. *This Is My Country Too.* New York: New American Library, 1965.

Wintz, Cary D. *Black Culture and the Harlem Renaissance.* Houston: Rice University Press, 1988.

Wright, Richard. *American Hunger.* 1977. New York: Harper and Row, 1979.

———. *Black Boy: A Record of Childhood and Youth.* 1945. New York: Harper and Row, 1966.

———. *Black Power: A Record of Reactions in a Land of Pathos.* New York: Harper and Brothers. 1954.

———. "Blueprint for Negro Writing." *Richard Wright Reader.* Ed. Ellen Wright and Michel Fabre. New York: Harper and Row, 1978. 36–49.

———. *The Color Curtain: A Report on the Bandung Conference.* Cleveland: World, 1956.

———. *Conversations with Richard Wright.* Ed. Keneth Kinnamon and Michel Fabre. Jackson: University Press of Mississippi, 1993.

———. *Early Works.* Ed. Arnold Rampersad. New York: Library of America, 1991.

———. *Eight Men.* Cleveland: World, 1961.

———. Foreword to *Blues Fell This Morning* by Paul Oliver. London: Horizon Press, 1960.

———. *Haiku: This Other World.* Ed. Yoshinobu Hakutani and Robert L. Tener. New York: Arcade, 1998. Rpt. New York: Random House, 2000.

———. "How 'Bigger' Was Born." *Native Son.* 1940. New York: Harper and Row, 1966. vii–xxxiv.

———. "An Interview with Richard Wright by Peter Schmid / 1946." *Conversations with Richard Wright.* Ed. Keneth Kinnamon and Michel Fabre. Jackson: University Press of Mississippi, 1993. 106–10.

———. "Jazz and Desire: An Interview with Richard Wright by Frank Tenot / 1960." From *Cahiers du Jazz* 4 (April 1961): 53–54. Trans. John DuVal. *Conversations with Richard Wright.* Ed. Keneth Kinnamon and Michel Fabre. Jackson: University Press of Mississippi, 1993. 242–43.

———. *Later Works.* Ed. Arnold Rampersad. New York: Library of America, 1991.

———. *The Long Dream.* 1958. New York: Harper and Row, 1987.

———. "The Man Who Lived Underground." *Eight Men.* Cleveland: World, 1961.

———. *Native Son.* 1940. New York: Harper and Row, 1966.

———. *The Outsider.* 1953. New York: Harper and Row, 1965.

———. *Pagan Spain.* New York: Harper and Brothers, 1957.

———. "This Other World: Projections in the Haiku Manner." Ms. New Haven: Beinecke Rare Book and Manuscript Library, 1960.

————. *12 Million Black Voices: A Folk History of the Negro in the United States.* New York: Viking, 1941.

————. *Uncle Tom's Children.* 1940. New York: Harper and Row, 1965.

Youmans, Rich. "For My Wife on Our First Anniversary." *Brussels Sprout* 11, no. 3 (1994): 15.

Zola, Emile. "The Experimental Novel." *Documents of Modern Literary Realism.* Ed. George J. Becker. Princeton: Princeton University Press, 1963. 162–96.

Index

Abbandonato, Linda, 17
Adams, Donald J., 38
Adventures of Huckleberry Finn (Twain), 42, 44, 233n11
"After the Sermon" (Wright), 162
Akan Doctrine of God, The (Danquah), 143
"Alba" (Pound), 189
Albert Camus (de Luppe), 225n6
Aldridge, John, 77
Alger, Horatio, 221n6
Algren, Nelson, 21, 219n2
"Also Stepping On" (Buson), 167, 182
Altschuler, Melvin, 225n8
Ambassadors, The (James), 90, 231n10
American Dilemma: The Negro Problem and American Democracy, An (Myrdal), 4
American Hunger (Wright), 22, 48, 223n3, 224n3
American Tragedy, An (Dreiser), 34–41, 115
"Ammunition" (Emanuel), 211
Anderson, Sherwood, 220n7
Ando, Shoei, 59, 176, 230n1
Another Country (Baldwin), 7, 75–76, 79
Aristotle, 190
Armstrong, Louis, 56, 95, 200, 209, 232n5
"As for Imagisme" (Pound), 164
Aswell, Edward, 26
Atkinson, Michael, 28–29, 220n11
At the Hawk's Well (Yeats), 198
Autobiography, The (Franklin), 5

"Autumn Is Deepening" (Basho), 233n10

Bakhtin, Mikhail, vii, 5–6, 43
"Baldwin: At Ease in Apocalypse" (Howe), 60
Baldwin, James, vii, 2, 7–9, 21, 60–82, 140, 220n13, 222nn1–7, 223nn1, 4–6
Baraka, Amiri, viii, 9, 188. *See also* Jones, LeRoi
Barthes, Roland, 11, 158, 229n5
Basho, 156, 158–59, 161, 163, 165–67, 184–85, 195–96, 204–5, 212, 229n11
Basho: His Life and Art (Imoto), 233n10
Bassui, 59, 176
"Beads of Quicksilver" (Wright), 167
Beauvoir, Simone de, 101, 109
Beiles, Sinclair, 154, 228n1
Bellow, Saul, 21, 74–75, 219n2, 223n2
Belmonte, Juan, 133–34
Beloved (Morrison), 15, 44, 139–44, 146–48, 150, 213, 219n1, 224n6, 227n3
"Big Boy Leaves Home" (Wright), 27–30, 33, 132, 154, 220nn9, 11
Big Sea, The (Hughes), 3, 86
Black Atlantic: Modernity and Double Consciousness, The (Gilroy), 225n1
Black Boy: A Record of Childhood and Youth (Wright), vii, 1–2, 5–8, 24–25, 30–31, 34, 43, 47–48, 60, 153–54, 172, 176, 220n15, 230n4

*Black Power: A Record of Reactions in a
    Land of Pathos* (Wright), 11, 14–15,
    85, 120–21, 124, 132, 137, 139–41,
    143–44, 147–48, 150, 160, 169,
    174–76, 178, 186, 192, 203, 225n1,
    227n5, 230nn5, 7, 231n9
"Blueprint for Negro Writing"
    (Wright), 2–3, 21–23, 46, 153, 176,
    201, 219n3
Blues Fell This Morning (Oliver), 197
Blues for Mister Charlie (Baldwin), 78
"Blues Haiku" (Sanchez), 185
Blyth, R. H., 13, 144, 154–56, 163,
    229nn6, 14, 231n2
"Bojangles and Jo" (Emanuel), 202,
    206, 208
Bontemps, Arna, 118
Book about Myself, A (Dreiser), 30
Borch-Jacobsen, Mikkel, 229n4
"Bright and Morning Star" (Wright),
    198
"Bright Harvest Moon, The" (Kikaku),
    166–68
Brooks, Gwendolyn, 21, 164, 191–93
Brooks, Van Wyck, 42–43, 220n14
Brown, James, 193
Brown, Lloyd, 225n3
Buddha, 13, 58, 97, 125, 143, 192,
    211, 225n13, 231n7
Burroughs, William, 154
Buson, 156, 163, 167–68, 182–83
Butler, Robert, 221n6
"Butterfly Makes, A" (Wright), 167

Caldwell, Erskine, 219n5
Calmer, Alan, 21
Camus, Albert, vii, 6, 13, 23, 55, 101,
    103, 105–10, 113–16, 118–19,
    219n5, 225nn1, 5, 7
"Camus's *L'Étranger* Reconsidered"
    (Feuerlicht), 225n7
Cannon, Elizabeth M., 224n11
Caruso, Enrico, 202
Castro, Américo, 226n8
Cayton, Horace, 5
Chadwick-Joshua, Jocelyn, 224nn9–10,
    12
*Change Is Gonna Come: Music, Race &
    the Soul of America, A* (Werner),
    232n5
Charles, Ray, 79, 89
Chesnutt, Charles W., 1
Christ, 58, 174, 202, 211
"City as Psychological Frontier"
    (Butler), 221n6
"City Limits, Village Values: Concepts
    of the Neighborhood in Black
    Fiction" (Morrison), 82, 223n2
Coleman, Ornett, 200
Color Curtain, The (Wright), 10,
    120–21, 225n1
Color Purple, The (Alice Walker), 11,
    44, 170–79, 230n6
Coltrane, John, 200
Columbus, Christopher, 129
Comic Song Collection, 232n4
*Complete Essays and Other Writings of
    Ralph Waldo Emerson, The*
    (Emerson), 170
Conrad, Joseph, 121
Conversations with Richard Wright
    (Kinnamon and Fabre), 22–24,
    89–122, 196, 200, 219nn2, 5,
    220n7, 221n4, 225n3, 227n5
Conversations with Toni Morrison
    (Taylor-Guthrie), 85
Cooper, James Fenimore, 19–20
Cortés, Hermán, 122
Crane, Hart, 229n10
Crane, Stephen, 24–26, 47, 68, 76, 87,
    107–8, 220n8
Crime and Punishment (Dostoevski),
    103, 110
"Crow, A" (Basho), 165
Cullen, Countee, 203

Danquah, J. B., 143
Davis, Miles, 200
Dawn (Dreiser), 5, 34, 60
*Dearest Wilding: A Memoir with Love
    Letters from Theodore Dreiser*
    (Eastman), 220n15

DeMott, Benjamin, 61, 222n6, 223n4
Derrida, Jacques, 10–11
Devil Finds Work, The (Baldwin), 222n2
Dickens, Charles, 24
Dickinson, Emily, 160–61, 180, 184, 194, 205, 215
"Dizzy Gillespie (News of His Death)" (Emanuel), 202
Dogen, 14–15, 143, 159, 202, 227n4
Dostoevski, Fedor M., vii, 7, 101, 103, 220n7
"Down by the Riverside" (Wright), 198
"Downhill Blue, The" (Emanuel), 215–16
Drake, St. Clair, 5
Dreiser, Helen, 36
Dreiser, Theodore, vii, 1–2, 5, 19, 21, 23–26, 30–43, 60, 76, 90, 107–8, 115, 219nn2, 4, 220nn7, 15, 222n6, 224nn4, 7
Du Bois, W. E. B., 1, 6, 78
"Duke Ellington" (Emanuel), 207

Eastman, Yvett, 220n15
Eight Men (Dreiser), 53–54
Eliot, T. S., 8–9, 47, 90, 229n11
Ellington, Duke, 207
Ellison, Ralph, vii, 2–9, 44–54, 56–59, 62, 176, 196, 198–99, 201, 220n1, 221nn1, 3–5, 232n3
Emanuel, James, viii, 12, 195–217, 232n1, 233n11
Emerson, Ralph Waldo, 6, 13–14, 48–50, 55, 57–58, 88, 143, 170, 175, 177, 184, 194, 221nn5, 7
"Emerson, Whitman, and Zen Buddhism" (Hakutani), 221n7, 230n1
Empire of Signs (Barthes), 158
"Existentialism in *The Outsider*" (Gliksberg), 106, 225nn1, 4
"Experiment in Misery, An" (Stephen Crane), 68
"Ezra Pound, Yone Noguchi, and Imagism" (Hakutani), 221n7, 229n8, 230n2, 231n3

Fabre, Michel, 27, 88, 106, 109, 154, 198, 219nn2–3, 225n1, 228n1
"Farmer" (Emanuel), 203–4
Farrell, James T., 21, 76, 219n2
"Fashion Show" (Emanuel), 207
"Fathers, Gods, and Religions: Perceptions of Christianity and Ethnic Faith in James Baldwin" (O'Neile), 223n6
Faulkner, William, 8–9, 23, 47, 219n4, 220n7
Feuerlicht, Ignace, 225n7
Fire Next Time, The (Baldwin), 60, 66, 222nn1, 4
"For My Wife on Our First Anniversary" (Youmans), 205
"For Sister Gwen Brooks" (Sanchez), 192
For Whom the Bell Tolls (Hemingway), 121
Ford, Nick Aaron, 222n3
Four Fundamental Concepts of Psychoanalysis, The (Lacan), 142, 156
Franco, Francisco, 121–22, 127, 136–37
Franklin, Benjamin, 5
Free and Other Stories (Dreiser), 31–33, 220n12
Freneau, Philip, 15
Freud, Sigmund, 15, 125, 159, 226n8, 231n8
"From across the Lake" (Wright), 168
From behind the Veil: A Study of Afro-American Narrative (Stepto), 201
Frost, Robert, 57
Fullington, James F., 63

Gallery of Women, A (Dreiser), 222n6
Gillespie, Dizzy, 202
Gilroy, Paul, 121, 225n1
Ginsberg, Allen, 154, 170, 194
Giovanni's Room (Baldwin), 7
Gitlin, Todd, 222n6
"Give All to Love" (Emerson), 177
Glicksberg, Charles I., 106, 225nn1, 4
Go Tell It on the Mountain (Baldwin), 7

"God of Fiction, The" (Glicksberg),
106, 225nn1, 4
Going to the Territory (Ellison), 47,
220n1, 221n1
Great Short Works of Stephen Crane,
220n8
Gulliver's Travels (Swift), 62

Haas, Robert, 12
Hagel, Geog Wilhelm Friedrich, 101
"Haiku" (Sanchez), 185
"Haiku King, The" (Emanuel), 202
"Haiku on Louis Armstrong"
(Emanuel), 209
Haiku: This Other World (Wright),
12–13, 55, 155, 160, 172, 180, 214,
229nn2, 9, 231n6
Hakutani, Yoshinobu, 221n7, 229nn2,
8, 13, 15–18, 230nn1–2, 231nn1,
3–5, 233n10
Hardy, Thomas, 219n4
Harris, Trudier, 227n2, 228n7
Hawthorne, Nathaniel, 42, 88
Heidegger, Martin, 9, 118
Hemingway, Ernest, 9, 23, 47, 121,
134–15, 219nn4–5, 220n7
Henderson, Harold G., 229nn13–14,
16–18, 231n4
Hicks, Granville, 21, 76
History of Haiku, A (Blyth), 156,
229nn6, 14, 231n2
Hitler, Adolf, 35
Holiday, Billie, 216
"How 'Bigger' Was Born" (Wright), 6,
20, 36, 38, 43, 74
Howe, Irving, 1–2, 60
"Hugh Selwyn Mauberley" (Pound), 10
Hughes, Langston, 3–4, 8–9, 47,
82–83, 86, 190–91, 193, 197
Hurston, Zora Neale, 21
Husserl, Edmund, 176, 224n5

"I Am You Loving" (Sanchez), 183
"I Collect" (Sanchez), 183
"I, Too" (Hughes), 4
"I Would Like a Bell" (Wright), 167

Ideas (Husserl), 176, 224n5
If Beale Street Could Talk (Baldwin), 8,
72–81, 223n1
"'I'm a Jazz Singer,' She Replied"
(Emanuel), 207–8
Imoto, Noichi, 233n10
"Important, but Exasperating Book,
An" (Altschuler), 225n8
"Impressionist" (Emanuel), 211
"In a Station of the Metro" (Pound),
163–64, 184, 189–90
"In Search of a Majority" (Baldwin),
222n4
In Search of Our Mothers' Gardens (Alice
Walker), 172
"In the Silent Forest" (Wright), 165,
231n6
"In the Winter Dusk" (Wright), 162
"In This Wet Season" (Sanchez), 183
"Indian Burying Ground, The"
(Freneau), 15
"Interview with Richard Wright by
Peter Schmid, An" (Wright), 225n3
Invisible Man (Ellison), 3, 6–7, 44–45,
47–48, 50–54, 56, 58, 176, 221n6
Isis, 192
Issa, 156, 163
"It Is September" (Wright), 56
"It's Deadly Quiet" (Basho), 165, 185

"Jackhammer" (Emanuel), 211
Jackson, Blyden, 27, 220n10
Jackson, Mahalia, 198
James, Henry, vii, 7, 9, 42, 47, 90, 179,
220n7, 224n7, 231n10
James Baldwin: A Critical Evaluation
(O'Daniel), 222n3
"James Baldwin: Looking towards the
Eighties," 223n5
Jazz (Morrison), 82–98, 200–201,
224nn9, 12
"Jazz as Chopsticks" (Emanuel), 210
Jazz from the Haiku King (Emanuel),
195, 232n1
"Jazz Meets the Abstract (Engravings)"
(Emanuel), 208

"Jazzactions" (Emanuel), 202
"Jazzanatomy" (Emanuel), 202, 204
"Jazzmix" (Emanuel), 209
"Jazzroads" 202
Jefferson, Thomas, 82, 204, 233n7
Jennie Gerhardt (Dreiser), vii, 1, 19,
    24–26, 43, 219n6, 220n8, 224n4
"John Coltrane" (Emanuel), 213
Johnson, Charles, viii, 170, 213
Jones, Gayl, 200
Jones, LeRoi, 82. *See also* Baraka, Amiri
Joyce, James, 9, 47
Jung, Carl, 128, 226n8

Keene, Donald, 232nn2, 4, 233n8
Kerouac, Jack, 154, 170
Kierkegaard, Sören Aabye, 101, 118
Kikaku, 163, 166–68
Kim, Kichung, 222n1, 223n1
King, Martin Luther, Jr., 69–70
Kinnamon, Keneth 38, 88, 219n2
Kipling, Rudyard, 11
Kiuchi, Toru, 228n1
"Knockout Blues, The" (Emanuel), 215
Kristeva, Julia, 12, 179
Kurebayashi, Kodo, 159, 221n9, 227n4

Lacan, Jacques, vii, 6, 15, 58, 142,
    156–59, 161, 221n8, 229n4, 231n8
Lao Zse, 56
Later Works (Wright), 102–5
Lawd Today (Wright), 117, 223n3
Lawrence, D. H., 121
"Leaf Chases Wind, A" (Wright), 163
Learned, Barry, 120
Lee, Kun Jong, 221n5
"Legs Wrapped around You" (Sanchez),
    189
L'Étranger, 115, 225n1. See also
    Stranger, The
Lewis, Sinclair, 219n5
*Liberating Voices: Oral Tradition in African-
    American Literature* (Jones), 200
"Ligeia" (Poe), 141
Like the Singing Coming Off the Drums
    (Sanchez), 180–94

Lincoln, Abraham, 191, 202
"Lines of Winter Rain" (Wright), 169
Literary Essays of Ezra Pound (Pound),
    161
Loehr, Max, 231n7
"Long Black Song" (Wright), 112, 148,
    198, 227n1
Long Dream, The (Wright), 132
"Love Poem [for Tupac]" (Sanchez),
    186
Luppe, Robert de, 225n6
"Lynch Patterns" (Farrell), 21
Lyrical and Critical Essays (Camus),
    225n5

McKay, Nelie, 89, 140
McMahon, Francis E., S. J., 226n7
Maggie: A Girl of the Streets (Stephen
    Crane), 24, 26
Malraux, André, 23, 47, 51, 220n7,
    221n3
"Man Who Lived Underground, The"
    (Wright), 52, 56, 180
"Man Who Went to Chicago, The"
    (Wright), 38
Man's Fate (Malraux), 47
"Many Thousands Gone" (Baldwin),
    76, 220n13
Margolies, Edward, 107, 116
"Mark Double Twain" (Dreiser), 43
Marshall, Paule, 227n2
Martin, Roberta, 198
Matthiessen, F. O., 36–37
Maya, 125, 192
Maynard, Tony, 70, 80, 222n6, 223n4
Melville, Herman, 20, 47, 59, 88,
    221n11, 225n13, 229n3
"Memory, Creation, and Writing"
    (Morrison), 139, 142
Mencken, H. L., 220n7
Meredith, George, 219n4
Metamorphoses (Ovid), 28
"Middle Passage, The" (Emanuel), 213
Middle Passage, The (Johnson), 213
"Mixed with Day and Sun" (Sanchez),
    191

Moby-Dick (Melville), 19, 84–85,
    221n11, 225n13, 229n3
Moller, Karin, 222nn3, 7
Moore, Jack B., 227n1
Moore, Lenard D, viii
Moritake, 163, 183–84, 231n2
Morrison, Toni, viii, 9, 15, 44, 47,
    82–98, 139–50, 170, 200–201, 213,
    219n1, 223nn1–2, 224nn5, 9, 10,
    12, 225n13, 227n6
"Mother, The" (Brooks), 191–93
Mussolini, Benito, 35
"My Dungeon Shook" (Baldwin),
    222n4
"My Early Days in Harlem" (Hughes),
    82
Myrdal, Alva, 121
Myrdal, Gunnar, 4–5, 121

Nadel, Alan, 196
"Naked in the Streets" (Sanchez), 181,
    184–85, 187–88
Native Son (Wright), 1–2, 5, 21, 34–42,
    44, 67, 73–74, 153, 197, 220n1,
    222n5
"Nature" (Emerson), 14
"Negro and the Second World War,
    The" (Ellison), 48–49
"Negro Speaks of Rivers, The"
    (Hughes), 4, 190–91
Never Come Morning (Algren), 219n2
Nietzsche, Friedrich Wilhelm, 101,
    118, 136
"Nigger Jeff" (Dreiser), 30–34,
    220n12
Nkrumah, Kwame, 148–49
"No Castle in Spain" (Anon), 226n4
No Name in the Street (Baldwin),
    60–72, 75–76, 78–81, 222nn6–7
Nobody Knows My Name (Baldwin), 60,
    62, 73, 140, 222n4
Noguchi, Yone, 56, 158–59, 199
Notes of a Native Son (Baldwin), 7, 60,
    62–63, 76, 220n13, 222n5
Notes on the State of Virginia (Jefferson),
    233n7

Oates, Joyce Carol, 73
O'Casey, Sean, 47
O'Daniel, Thomas B., 222n3
"Off the Cherry Tree" (Wright), 163
"Old Pond, The" (Basho), 158, 185,
    204
Oliver, Paul, 197
"On the Hanging Bell" (Buson), 167
O'Neile, Sandra A., 223n6
"Open Boat, The" (Stephen Crane), 87,
    107
Ordeal of Mark Twain, The (Brooks),
    220n14
Orwell, George, 8
Osagie, Iyunolu, 227n3, 228n10
"Our National Character" (Dreiser), 39
"Out of the Cradle Endlessly Rocking"
    (Whitman), 172, 230n3
"Outside and Low" (Brown), 225n3
Outsider, The (Wright), vii, 6–7, 55, 73,
    75, 80, 101–19, 225nn1, 4
"Over-Soul, The" (Emerson), 13
Ovid, 28, 220n11

Pagan Spain (Wright), 11–12, 120–39,
    150, 192, 225n1, 226n8, 228n11,
    230n5
"Page One" (Emanuel), 202, 206
"Pale Winter Moon, A" (Wright), 167
Perón, Juan Domingo, 121
Perrone, Juan S. J., 123
Personae (Pound), 189
*Playing in the Dark: Whiteness and the
    Literary Imagination* (Morrison), 47,
    83–84, 93, 95
*Playing the Changes: From Afro-
    Modernism to the Jazz Impulse*
    (Werner), 196, 198–200
Poe, Edgar Allan, 117, 141, 194
"Poem for Ella Fitzgerald, A" (Sanchez),
    182–83
Pound, Ezra, vii–viii, 9–10, 92, 161,
    163–65, 170, 184, 189–90, 194,
    221n7, 224n8, 229nn8, 10, 230n2,
    231n3
Praisesong for the Window (Marshall),

227n2
Prescott, Orville, 118
"Problem of Theme, The" (Wright),
    153
Pudd'nhead Wilson and *Those
    Extraordinary Twins* (Twain), 42, 81,
    224n6, 228n9
Purdy, Stropher B., 115

"Rabbit Capers, The" (Emanuel), 212
Rampersad, Arnold, 101
Redding, Saunders, 118, 124, 223n3,
    225nn3, 8, 226n5
Reed, Ishmael, viii, 9, 170
"Reflections on Richard Wright: A
    Symposium on an Exiled Native
    Son" (Redding), 223n3
Reilly, John M., 225n8, 226nn4–5, 7
"Remembering Richard Wright"
    (Ellison), 220n1
Rhea, James N., 225n2
Richard Wright and Racial Discourse
    (Hakutani), 229n15
Richard Wright: Books and Writers
    (Fabre), 228n1
Richard Wright: Daemonic Genius
    (Margaret Walker), 229n10
"Richard Wright, French Existentialism,
    and *The Outsider*" (Fabre), 106, 109,
    225n1
"Richard Wright in a Moment of Truth"
    (Jackson), 220n10
Richard Wright Reader (Ellen Wright
    and Fabre), 219n3
Richard Wright: The Critical Reception
    (Reilly), 225n8, 226nn4–5, 7
"Richard Wright's 'Big Boy Leaves
    Home' and a Tale from Ovid: A
    Metamorphosis Transformed"
    (Atkinson), 220n11
"Richard Wright's Blues" (Ellison), 196
"Road Not Taken, The" (Frost), 57
Robinson, Bill, 206
"Rootedness: The Ancestor as
    Foundation" (Morrison), 140, 148
Rousseau, Jean Jacques, 127

Rushdie, Salman, 10

Salaam, Kalamu ya, 223n5
Samuels, Robert, 221n8, 229n4
Sanchez, Sonia, viii, 12, 180–94
Sandburg, Carl, 135
Sartre, Jean-Paul, 6, 23, 101, 105, 109,
    118, 219n5
Satanic Verses, The (Rushdie), 10
Savery, Pancho, 221n3
Seaver, Edwin, 22
"Second-Chance Rhythms" (Emanuel),
    204–5
"Seen from a Hilltop" (Wright), 162
Seize the Day (Bellow), 74, 223n2
*Selected English Writings of Yone Noguchi:
    An East-West Literary Assimilation*
    (Noguchi), 159, 199
Selected Poems (Brooks), 193
Selected Poems of Langston Hughes
    (Hughes), 83, 191, 197
Selected Writings of Ralph Waldo Emerson
    (Emerson), 49–50, 55
*Seminar of Jacques Lacan, Book I: Freud's
    Papers on Technique 1953–1954, The*
    (Lacan), 58, 158
*Seminar of Jacques Lacan, Book II: The
    Ego in Freud's Theory and in the
    Technique of Psychoanalysis, The*
    (Lacan), 157–59, 231n8
Senryu, Karai, 230n8
Shadow and Act (Ellison), 45, 47, 51,
    198–99
"Shake Loose My Skin" (Sanchez), 182,
    185, 187,189
Shakespeare, William, 229n10
Shobogenzo (Dogen), 14, 159
"Sight in Camp in the Daybreak Gray
    and Dim, A" (Whitman), 202,
    232n6
Sister Carrie (Dreiser), 1, 24, 40, 91,
    108, 224n7
"Sittin'-Log Blues" (Emanuel), 214
"Sleek Lizard Rhythms" (Emanuel), 204
Snyder, Gary, 154, 170, 194
"Song of Myself" (Whitman), 146,

170, 176–77, 181–82, 193, 203, 212, 221n10, 227n6, 232n10
"Sonny Rollins (Under the Williamsburg Bridge)" (Emanuel), 216
"Soul Selects Her Own Society, The" (Dickinson), 205
"Spain through Secularist Spectacles" (McMahon), 226n7
Spirit of Japanese Poetry, The (Noguchi), 56, 199
"Spring Lingers On, The" (Wright), 168
Stein, Gertrude, 121
Stephenson, Mary Ellen, 225n2
"Steppin' Out on the Promise" (Emanuel), 209
Stepto, Robert, 201
Stevens, Wallace, 194
"Stories of Conflict" (Hurston), 21
"Stormy Weather" (Ellison), 3
Story of Yone Noguchi, The (Noguchi), 56
Stowe, Harriet Beecher, 7
Stranger, The (Camus), 55, 103, 106–8, 110–11, 113, 115, 117–19. See also L'Étranger
Structure of Spanish History, The (Castro), 226n8
Studs Lonigan (Farrell), 219n2
Sun Also Rises, The (Hemingway), 23, 121, 134
Swift, Jonathan, 62

"Take Me to the Water" (Baldwin), 66, 68, 70, 79
Tate, Allen, 219n4
Tell Me How Long the Train's Been Gone (Baldwin), 8
Tener, Robert L., 229n2
Tenot, Frank, 89, 200
Their Eyes Were Watching God (Hurston), 21
Theme of Identity in the Essays of James Baldwin (Moller), 222nn3, 7
These Low Grounds (Turpin), 3

"Thin Waterfall, A" (Wright), 165, 231n6
This Is My Country Too (Williams), 223n3
"This Other World: Projections in the Haiku Manner" (Wright), 154, 163, 165, 228n2, 229n2
Thomas, Dylan, 229n10
Thoreau, Henry David, 88, 170
"To Be Baptized" (Baldwin), 66, 70, 79–80
"To the Unknown African" (Cullen), 203
Tocqueville, Alexis Charles, 121
Tomlinson, Charles, 230n2
Toomer, Jean, 78
"Tragic Situation, A" (Trilling), 6
Trilling, Lionel, 6
Tucker, Linsay, 143, 179
Turpin, Waters Edward, 3
Twain, Mark, 2, 20, 42–43, 61–62, 81, 224n6, 228n9, 233n10
Twelve Men (Dreiser), 222n6
12 Million Black Voices: A Folk History of the Negro in the United States (Wright), 2, 4, 45–46, 84, 197, 221nn1–2, 223n1

Uncle Tom's Children (Wright), 2, 21, 27, 30–32, 36, 74, 148, 220n9, 226n10
Unfinished Quest of Richard Wright, The (Fabre), 27, 198

Valéry, Paul, 47
"Vorticism" (Pound), 92, 163–65, 184, 189, 224n8, 229n8

Walden (Thoreau), 170
Waley, Arthur, 231n9, 232n9
Walker, Alice, viii, 9, 11, 44, 170–79
Walker, Margaret, vii, 21, 164, 229n10
Ward, Clara, 198
Washington, Booker T., 51
Waste Land, The (Eliot), 8
Watkins, Mel, 230n6

"Weary Blues, The" (Hughes), 4, 197
Weary Blues, The (Hughes), 197
Wells, H. G., 219n4
Werner, Craig, 196, 198–200, 232n5
West, Cornel, 193
West, James L. W. III, 220n8
"When Lilacs Last in the Dooryard
    Bloom'd" (Whitman), 202
"When We Sang Good-Bye" (Sanchez),
    188
Whitman, Walt, 8, 143, 146, 170, 172,
    175–76, 181–82, 193–94, 202–3,
    212, 221n10, 227n6, 228n6,
    229n10, 230n3, 232n10, 232n6
Whitney, Harry, 132–33
Williams, John A., 75, 78, 223n3
Williams, William Carlos, 170, 230n2
"Wilting Jonquil, A" (Wright), 169
Wintz, Cary D., 83
Wright, Ella, 13
Wright, Ellen, 219n3
Wright, Julia, 13
Wright, Richard, vii, viii, 1–15, 19–39,
    41–48, 52–56, 60, 62, 67, 73–76, 78,

83, 85, 88–89, 101–50, 153–72,
    174–76, 180, 182, 184–86, 192, 194,
    196–98, 200–201, 203, 213,
    219nn2–3, 5–7, 220nn7, 9–11,
    220n1, 221nn1–2, 4, 222n5, 223nn1,
    3, 223nn1, 3, 224n5, 225n1, 225nn1,
    3, 226nn8, 11, 227nn1, 5, 228nn8,
    10–11, 228nn1–2, 229n10,
    230nn4–5, 7, 231n9, 231nn2, 6
"Wright, the Protest Novel, and
    Baldwin's Faith" (Kim), 223n1

X, Malcolm, 70–71

Yeats, W. B., vii–viii, 9, 47, 198,
    229n10
"You Ask Me to Run" (Sanchez), 189
"You Too Slippery" (Sanchez), 188
Youmans, Rich, 205–6

Zeami, 231n9
Zen and American Transcendentalism,
    230n1
Zola, Emile, 2, 108